DAMSON SKIES AND DRAGONFLIES

A JOURNEY THROUGH THE SEASONS IN THE FRENCH COUNTRYSIDE

LINDY VIANDIER

LIFE AT LES LIBELLULES (BOOK ONE)

A bower quiet for us, and a sleep
Full of sweet dreams, and health, and quiet breathing.
Therefore, on every morrow, are we wreathing
A flowery band to bind us to the earth,
Spite of despondence, of the inhuman dearth...
'Endymion', John Keats

CONTENTS

FOREWORD

*M*y heart sank as we surveyed the dilapidation at the back of the house. The doors were rotting, the stone staircase crumbling, and sheets of plastic hung where windows should be. "Is it too much?" I mouthed to my husband when the estate agent's back was turned. I was talking about the work involved, not the asking price. He gave me a knowing look, pursed his lips in his French way and shook his head. He was going to do a deal.

The truth was, too much work or not, the instant we saw the 300-year-old fairy-tale cottage with its red-tiled roof and quaint *pigeonnier*, it was love at first sight. Les Libellules had spun her magic web around us, and we were her willing captives.

As we had lived in a rented apartment near Paris for the past nine years, we yearned for a life closer to nature, where we could have a little plot of land so that my husband could plant his seedling trees, and I could realise my dream of creating recipes with herbs and vegetables grown in our own garden.

What I didn't anticipate as I awakened to the wonders of nature and the realities of country life, was that I was about to change just as much as the sadly neglected house, learning to live without life's luxuries and finding pleasure in the simple things.

So get yourself a cup of tea, a mug of coffee, or even a glass of French wine. Find yourself a quiet, comfy corner and join me as I set out on a journey through the seasons, discovering what secrets Les Libellules and the seemingly sleepy hamlet have to reveal, sharing my recipes with you along the way. My journey begins not at the start of the calendar year but at the end of summer when we acquired the long-awaited keys.

PART I
THE DRAGONFLY SUMMER

AUGUST AND SEPTEMBER 2017

Glory be to God for dappled things—for skies of couple-colour as a brinded
cow.
'Pied Beauty', Gerard Manley Hopkins

DAMSON SKIES AND DRAGONFLIES

*I*t's ironic that I'm reading a book in which one of the characters has writer's block, having suffered this malady myself for many years. It's both ironic and frustrating that my creative juices are now flowing like ants from a crack in the wall as I've precious little time to write. I'm eliciting cold stares and exclamations of *'Tu n'as rien à faire'* (You haven't anything to do) from my husband; hereafter to be named Mr (as in monsieur not mister) V. The ashes remain in the grate and the dishes in the sink as I scribble furiously in one of his 'journal of works' notebooks at an old gate-leg table. Alas it's too late; the torch of my imagination has been lit. So come with me on a little journey into what is, as yet, an unknown story...

* * *

The house is in the heart of wine country on the Côte-d'Or (the Golden Coast), so called because in autumn the vineyards turn from green to amber, transforming the landscape into a sea of gold. The grape harvest is fast approaching, and the local paper is full of advertisements seeking *vendangeurs* to pick grapes. If I were younger I would apply, but now the only grapes that I'll be picking are the lovely black beauties hanging from a trellis covering the garage wall.

The garden, which is at the front of the house, faces south-southwest, so it has sun almost all day, apart from a little welcome shade from the scorching August heat provided by a single tree in the late afternoon. In the evening we are treated to spectacular sunsets when sitting on our patio after dinner. The nearby screen of poplars is transformed into a dark silhouette set against a flaming backdrop of bright brassy yellow, blending into shades of dusky salmon and deep vermillion, before the sky turns midnight blue then ink black, and the realm of the stars reigns. The constellations are particularly bright here and appear closer to the earth somehow. I feel like I could stretch up and take the Plough in my hand.

This area is famous locally for its spectacular meteor showers and shooting stars that reportedly occur this time of year; but I've yet to witness this, probably because we're so tired after a long day working on the house that we eat, take a shower, and go straight to bed.

⁂

The light here is exceptional, and is fuelling an obsession of mine more compelling than being a closet writer: photography. There are three distinctive lights. The first is clear, bright and pure which intensifies all the colours, particularly the myriad shades of green. The second bathes everything in a mellow honey glow, as the glow you get on an early evening in late summer. Here it occurs in the early morning also, often accompanied by a thin veil of mist clinging to the fields until the warm Burgundy sun burns it off. In the evening this golden light transforms the milk-white Charolais cows in the field opposite to a buttery cream.

The third light I call *la lumière des raisins* (the light of grapes). This appears when dramatic storm clouds hang low, sweeping the horizon in colours ranging from dove grey to muted lavender and bruised damson, then finally, the deep angry purple of grapes. I think I love this light best of all, especially when seen in contrast against the fields of pale yellow corn.

It puts me in mind of the beautiful painting by Cézanne, 'Le Pigeonnier', that is boxed up securely in the bedroom that I call the rose room, waiting to take up its position in the living room, ten years or so down the line when we've completed all the work.

Le Pigeonnier is the first name that we gave to the house as we have quite an impressive one. When I first saw a photo of the dumpy round tower crowned by a red-tiled roof on the estate agent's website, I immediately thought of Rapunzel, one of my all-time favourite stories. As a child I used to beg my mother to buy a house with a tower so that I could live out my fantasy of tossing my hair out of the window. So you see, it was a case of love at first sight, or what is known in France as *un coup de coeur*, and no matter what horrors were revealed on inspection, particularly at the back where the agent had skilfully avoided taking photos, there was never any doubt. Our destinies were meant to be bound together.

A *pigeonnier*, for those of you who don't know, and this included me, is where families kept pigeons in a circular loft. All around the walls there are little clay chambers big enough to house a single bird, which I, in my ignorance, thought were for storing wine. (Or was that wishful thinking?)

In times of hardship the birds would provide nourishment (I hate to think of this), and the wealthier the family, the more pigeons they kept. Our predecessors must have been quite well off as there are an impressive number of little pigeonholes up there (one day I'll count them and let you know how many). I've also heard that before the revolution, you were only allowed to have a *pigeonnier* if you were a member of the aristocracy, so not only were our predecessors wealthy, they were noble as well. I can't help thinking about what fate befell them during the revolution and whether they survived or were sent to the guillotine for the crime of being 'well born'.

As I have a pigeon phobia, I wasn't keen on that name, so we switched to Le Colombier (The Dovecot) which had more of a poetic ring, but that didn't quite gel. We also toyed with the idea of Le Relais de Chasse (The Hunting Lodge), as the house was once a halt for the hunt, providing food and refreshments for both men and horses.

There is a manmade pond at the side of the house, which is known as an *abreuvoir* (watering hole), that horses and cattle once drank from. This is what attracts the abundance of dragonflies, hence giving the house her final name: Les Libellules (The Dragonflies). The pond is gorged with reeds and duckweed but remains a magical place, and it is here that captures the ever-changing light best of all. In the early morning, when the rising sun breaks through the screen of tall birch trees to the east, it casts a dappled effect on the water. By lunchtime, the half of the water now shaded by the trees is pea green; the other half is rivalling the dragonflies with a shimmering shade of apple. By evening, the entire area is a deep lime colour as the sun descends in the west. But best of all is when a golden shaft pierces through a gap in the leaves and illuminates a tiny circle on the otherwise sombre surface. I am mesmerized by its beauty, and could while away the hours watching it constantly change.

I've just been out with my camera trying to photograph a dragonfly, but I need a much better lens with a faster speed. Even so, I've managed to capture a blur of blue, green and yellow and furiously fluttering orange wings, like an iridescent fairy, ethereal and unobtainable.

I have a theory. I'm getting very good at developing theories. I think that long ago, dragonflies were mistaken for fairies and entered into folklore; this theory serves to reinforce the fairy-tale quality of the Rapunzel tower.

ALLIES AND INVADERS

*T*he sheer plethora of life here has completely thrown me. The garden is alive, though at first it appeared to be barren stony ground, with tufts of yellow sun-scorched grass. Everything is larger than life. There are snails the size of finches, rust-brown slugs as long as a lizard, enormous butterflies in every colour imaginable, ranging from bright cornflower blue to vibrant orange, red and yellow. Plus sinister, jet-black moths that like to come into the house. The ground is crawling with large, fluorescent-green beetles and things that look like a cross between oversized earwigs and ladybirds, red with black spots and pincers. There are prehistoric-looking millipedes, caterpillars, crickets, grasshoppers, tiny green lizards with yellow spots, small grass snakes and more varieties of spiders than I ever knew existed, including some the size of the palm of my hand.

I've started to believe that mosquitoes smelt my fear, and that's why I've been a target for them all my life. My neurosis resulted previously in me wearing protective bangles on both wrists and ankles, smothering myself in foul-smelling repellent, and burning lemon-scented candles, as well as planting an abundance of geraniums outside the bedroom window at our Paris apartment, and sleeping under a net with a plug-in deterrent at the side of the bed. I also had a can of hairspray at hand to paralyse their wings (I read this somewhere) should they break through these defences. All of which didn't work. Despite my efforts, I still woke up with angry red mounds everywhere from the tip of my nose to in between my toes; they obviously liked a challenge.

Week one at Les Libellules saw pretty much the same scenario, minus the net as there is nowhere to hang one up, even putting a small hook in the ceiling resulted in a hole the size of a large orange; yet another point of access for things that crawl and fly. By week two however, I was nonchalantly flicking them from my bare arms and swatting them with my bare hands. In fact they'd become almost welcome along with house flies as one of the few species that I was familiar with.

I have two unexpected allies in my war against the insects, Pussy Willow, the previous 'fly gourmet' cat, not being one of them, as flies have become as mundane to her as mosquitoes have to me. One of these allies is the namesake of the house: the dragonflies. We have two varieties of dragonfly. Small, sprightly, neon turquoise and red naiads that stay close to the water, darting just above the surface to feed on small flies and mosquitoes; and a squadron of ethereal emperor dragonflies. These aren't anything like the dainty species that I've occasionally seen in the UK. They are majestic colossi, and very curious it seems, hovering close to me as I stand still while observing them; maybe they take me for an insect farm or a sort of human convenience store. It is these spectacular creatures, with their vibrant green and yellow bodies, electric-blue tails and orange, gossamer wings that fan as fast as a humming bird's, who patrol up and down the passage behind the house, consuming everything in their flight path. They also sweep across the murky water, which I suspect is a breeding ground for biting, stinging things that fly.

My other ally is even more surprising, especially if you know me well, or even a little, as you'll know that I have an irrational fear of things with wings. Top of the list next to pigeons, are bats, usually even the name of which makes me shudder, but here I've developed a surprising affection for them. They are small, round pipistrelles, roughly the size and shape of a furry 'quidditch' ball, and travel at about the same velocity. These too act as minesweepers, patrolling the same strip of land by night that the dragonflies do by day. I've read that a single bat can eat around 600 mosquitoes per night.

Swallows however have always been my friends; I love these little fork-tailed allies. The telephone wires are laden with them; a sign that they are amassing before flying south, signalling the end of summer. It saddens me to see them go as much as it fills me with joy to hear their whoops and squeals when they arrive in late April/early May, heralding once more the onset of spring. Plus, they eat mosquitoes.

✳ ✳ ✳

I've just walked into the living room and been greeted by a scene from a Hammer Horror version of *Charlotte's Web*. Hundreds of tiny, newly hatched flies have entered through gaps in the wall around the window and are descending the lace curtains like miniature paratroopers dropping from the sky. They are gathering in an inch-thick, swarming black mass on the windowsill and tumbling onto the floor like counters in the TV show *Tipping Point*.

I call Mr V who says it's the heat that's caused them to hatch in the walls, the thought of which makes me squirm. But vacuum cleaner in hand, I proceed to suck them up, first from the floor, then the windowsill. I wrap a scarf around my head as I shake the curtains to dislodge the masses still dangling there and repeat the floor and windowsill routine. Next, I turn my attention to the top of the window, which appears to be their point of access, sucking them up as they emerge through the gap.

Mr V is now outside mixing cement that he's slapping on the wall in a haphazard fashion, filling in all the crevices from where they're emerging and climbing in through the window.

Finally, I attack the last few stragglers with my latest weapon—*Bloq' Insectes*—which is supposed to repel the little blighters, then I take down the curtains and boil alive any remaining invaders entangled in the lace and clean the window.

✳ ✳ ✳

I would like to report that this is the last insect horror story, but I've just gone outside to close the shutters against the blazing midday sun. When I unhooked them from the wall, scores of a more mature variety of the invader flies were sheltering from the heat on the back of the shutters and against the wall behind. It's time to get out the big guns. I soak them liberally with Bloq' Insectes, which sends them scurrying back into the cracks they came from. I have a feeling that I may have won the battle, but that the war is far from over...

What I've learnt today: Unhook with trepidation shutters that have been pinned against a wall, as a whole array of park life could be waiting on the other side.

CITADEL BUFFE

This morning I was out with my camera, catching the early morning mist, and I caught more than I'd bargained for. Our neighbours in the house behind Les Libellules are from the liberal city of Amsterdam, so I don't know why I was surprised to see one of them dragging the bin onto the road at 7 a.m., dressed in only a pair of minute slip-on underpants. I tried to keep my eyes on his face while saying '*bonjour*', but they were involuntarily drawn to his Netherland regions, and now I can't look him in the eye but don't know where else to look.

This isn't the only surprise that our neighbours have provided. During the night, a transit van covered in giant images of Bob Marley and swirly psychedelic patterns has appeared and parked itself between their house and ours. Not exactly what you expect to see in the heart of the French countryside. The occupant, a dreadlocked, accordion-playing Rastafarian wearing a hat in the colours of the Ethiopian flag, is sitting outside on a three-legged stool playing sea shanty-type tunes and drinking beer from a bottle. (It's now around 10 in the morning, and I haven't yet got over the shock of seeing Mr Universe putting out the rubbish.) He lifts his bottle to me in a good-humoured manner. I smile and nod and tell him he plays very well. He is Lars, the cousin of another Dutch neighbour, visiting from Rotterdam. He is a gardener by trade, and as we still don't have a lawnmower, our 'grass' is like a prairie. He promptly offers to bring his cousin's turbo lawnmower across and 'tidy things up'; a gross understatement. Four hours and €40 later, the place is transformed.

This evening we're all sitting together outside on some old crates, drinking beer from bottles and listening to Lars play his accordion until the stars come out and the beer has gone.

*   *   *

Other neighbours include Pappy Cardigan, a lovely gentleman who has a spare set of keys and keeps an eye on Les Libellules when we're not here. I gave him this name as, despite working at the local town hall, owning two or three houses of his own and at least three cars, he wears an old cardigan full of holes that reminds me of my grandfather, who would regularly fall asleep with his pipe clamped between his teeth and smouldering strands of tobacco burning holes in his clothes. Pappy Cardigan has just brought me a bag of courgettes[1] and marrows in assorted colours, shapes and sizes from his garden. He has also offered Mr V the loan of his roof ladders as he saw him dangerously sprawled across the tiles like Spider-Man without the suction pads. We're starting our renovation work from the top down, so that means cleaning and inspecting the rather steep roof and replacing any broken tiles.

Another friendly and very welcome gentleman caller is Monsieur Mouton, so called as he has a small flock of *moutons* (sheep) in a nearby field. As I've lived most of my life in North Wales surrounded by sheep, this is a rare treat for me in a land where they are very thin on the ground. Driving in the countryside when I first moved to France, I noticed that something wasn't quite right. Then I realised: the fields were completely devoid of sheep, whereas in Wales you can hardly see the grass for the wool.

Monsieur Mouton also grows vegetables, and if he catches sight of Mr V or me as he's driving past, he stops and drops off boxes packed full of green beans and dense, ruby-red tomatoes shaped like fat cigars. They taste like heaven when drizzled with a generous glug of olive oil, sprinkled with some freshly torn basil leaves, and served with some warm, crusty bread to mop up the excess juice.

Then there is the postmistress in her little yellow van, delivering mail, groceries and even medicine to those in need, always with a toot, a wave and a *bonjour*. Mr V almost trips over his own feet in the stampede to wave back (Think young Michelle Pfeiffer rather than a female version of Postman Pat). It is customary in this part of France that the postman, or postwoman in our case, knocks on the door of all elderly or infirm people on their round who live alone to check that they're OK and to see if they need anything. They also spend at least one fifteen-minute visit a week with them to have a little chat and maybe a cup of coffee. I think this is a wonderful safety net and lifeline for many who would otherwise be isolated, and a fine example of social care.

Another mobile visitor is an elderly nun who hurtles around at great speed like a boy racer, whizzing past our garden in a blur of grey (car and habit) as she administers Catholic charity to members of her flock. We've yet to become acquainted with other neighbours as it is now August, and most of the regular inhabitants are more than likely on the Côte d'Azur.

✳ ✳ ✳

We've bought a large, wooden garden table. Typically, the moment that we finish assembling it, the heavens open for the first time in weeks and the scorching temperature plummets to positively chilly. I'm determined to eat at the table, so we drag it indoors. Now here we are, taking an apéritif of tiny plum tomatoes known as *olivettes*, stuffed with tuna and capers, and cubes of feta cheese sprinkled with olive oil and cayenne pepper, drinking Aperol spritz at a garden table in front of a log fire. This is actually the first time that we've lit the fire, and never having had a real fire before I'm finding it all rather wonderful, even if it is at odds with the sunshine-flavoured paella that I've made.

15

We plan to install a wood burner eventually as it would be both more efficient, and a lot cleaner and safer than the Grimm's fairy-tale structure that we have at the moment. But this evening, reading by the glow of the firelight, sipping a glass of Burgundy wine and pausing to watch the flames flicker in the grate, I have a primitive sense of being at one with the elements, and feel the weight of the history of this lovely old house resting on my shoulders. So I decide to scrap the wood burner idea and stick with Brothers Grimm.

This morning, however, when greeted by a mountain of ash, a filthy floor and a sooty-smelling living room and cat, I change my mind, but I won't be in a hurry; I'll savour these moments while they last.

✳   ✳   ✳

We've finally eaten our first al fresco meal *chez nous* in almost ten years, at the garden table which is now sitting incongruously on the postage stamp-sized patio. As we live in a third-floor apartment in Paris with neither garden nor balcony, my dream of eating outdoors has never been realised and I relished the occasion. The table has extendable wings on each side and can seat up to twelve people, but if we do this, six of them would be sitting in the grass. The meal was nothing like the Mediterranean-style dinner that we'd planned, but a simple 'make something out of what was at hand' lunch. As both of us wanted a garden rather than house view, we sat side by side like schoolchildren at a desk. Mr V was on fly duty guarding the food, as I put on my almost ever-present photojournalist hat and photographed the meagre feast for the scrap book.

I have a confession. I'm here now at that very table. Stretched across it is my decoy: heavy lined curtains that Mr V has dutifully washed in the local laundrette. He's requested that I reattach the wooden rings that he'd cut off in case they got broken in the machine. On top of the curtains is my French exercise book. You can tell that it is French as it's filled with little squares, not ruled lines like an English one. It has a brand name on the front—'Conquerant' (Conqueror)—

16

which makes me chuckle as my husband is a Norman. I've just been discovered scribbling instead of sewing. He sneaked around the side of the house and took, if past results are anything to go by, a very unflattering photo of me wearing his little brown straw hat. I'm pretending not to notice. I continue scribbling for a few moments then swap my pen for a sewing needle and try to look as industrious at sewing as I was at writing.

*   *   *

Our home (yes, it's beginning to feel like that) is also starting to feel like the set of a certain musical theatre production. In addition to our cat, Pussy Willow, who we've brought with us from Paris, we have four regular, feline callers, one of whom is Flaubertine (formally known as Flaubert as I thought she was a male), a grey and white female around eight months old, with rose-pink paws and fern-green eyes which are rather sly. She is quick-witted and quick-footed and coos like a pigeon to seduce and cajole. She is pretty and she knows it and thinks herself a cut above the other farm cats, she even challenges Pussy Willow for her position supreme indoors. But Willow is having none of it and guards the door like a sphinx, emitting a deep, throaty growl, a sound I've never heard her make before. Then there are Mungo Jerry and Rumpleteazer, two identical tabby siblings aged around four months, but I can't get close enough to them to see if they are two Mungo Jerrys or two Rumpleteazers. I've never seen one without the other, and they particularly like the walled terrace in front of what will be the utility room. When I come outside they slope off in unison like the Siamese cats in the Disney film *Lady and the Tramp*, pausing every now and then to cast backward glances cheek to cheek.

There is a fourth: a ragamuffin female, scrawny and bedraggled with a defiant, belligerent air. Her coat is a dull, dusty orange and grey, and she often has cobwebs clinging to her head and ears. (I can relate to that.) Her eyes are the same colour as Flaubertine's, but with none of the guile, just the look of an outsider: resentful and guarded. She's definitely not going to win any beauty contests.

The other cats seem to shun her, and I found her difficult to warm to also, until last night, when she watched us from a safe distance while we ate salmon on the patio. Mr V doesn't like fish skin and had left some on his plate, so I threw it to her. It was only a small piece, but she gobbled it up hungrily and then began to purr so loudly that we could hear her from where we were sitting. This upset me, as it was obvious that this unfortunate little animal was so starved of both food and affection that she was grateful for even the most meagre scraps. All we had left of the meal was some bread and cheese. We gave her a little, and this was also received with extreme gratitude, so much so that she approached the table but didn't jump up and mew loudly like Flaubertine demanding titbits. Instead she stayed purring beneath my chair, happy just to be close to us whether we had food or not. I then offered her the only other thing that I could find in the house: a piece of madeleine cake. She liked this so much that I gave her the whole cake and also her new name: Madeleine, 'Maddy' for short.

✳ ✳ ✳

Mr V has rechristened Les Libellules 'Citadel Buffe'. It seems that word (or meow) has got out that we're running an all-day buffet, and we are under siege from the cats, who, we've discovered, come from the farm behind the house. But as the farmer and his family are on holiday (farmers take holidays? This is August and this is France...) the cats are left to their own devices. In Flaubertine's case this means stealing the prawns that were defrosting on my worktop, and in Maddy's case means attaching herself to my leg and rubbing her head on my foot while I'm trying to walk. Mungo Jerry and Rumpleteazer have taken up residence at a safe distance on the wall by the gate, and all four are there looking up at the bedroom window when I open the curtains each morning, waiting for me to perform the shutter-opening ritual.

We have three *portes fenêtres* (French doors) with double wooden shutters at the front of the house, and two windows with wooden shutters to the side. Flaubertine and Maddy take advantage of the open doors and make a dive for any half-eaten food left in Pussy Willow's bowls in the kitchen. I would have thought there would be adequate mice and other small creatures for them to feast on, but they all look very thin. As it's so hot and dry, I'm leaving fresh water twice a day in the shade for them, along with a communal bowl of Casino supermarket crunchies that pampered Pussy Willow refuses to eat, but to be honest they're not that fussed on them either.

What I've learnt today: Don't feed a stray cat, or it will tell all its mates, and you'll end up like Louis XIV with an audience at mealtimes.

───────────────────────────

1. Zucchini.

I'VE HAD AN IDEA

I have an idea. This has now become my catchphrase as I'm full of them lately. Mr V has come to dread me using it, but this one doesn't involve him, so he's safe. I haven't mentioned this until now, but along with writing and photography, I love to cook. The French find this quite novel. 'An Englishwoman who can cook'. *Zut alors*!, as they believe the stereotype that we all live off jelly and fish and chips. Just as we believe they live off frogs legs, cheese and baguettes (actually the cheese and baguettes bit is true).

As various neighbours keep arriving with a glut of produce from their *potagers*, and we are planning a vegetable garden of our own, I thought I might include a few simple recipes of dishes that I've prepared using fresh farm or garden produce. These will indeed be very simple as I don't have a kitchen, rather a collection of appliances.

When we moved in two weeks ago, all that was in the kitchen space was a sink and drainer hovering in the centre of the room, not up against a wall and with no cupboard underneath. There was also an alcove where a cooker used to be, covered in a good centimetre of brown, slimy grease. This has been scraped, scrubbed and steam-cleaned by yours truly, and now a rickety trolley on wheels sits there with oils and vinegars on the lower shelf, and an absorbent cloth for draining glasses on the top.

Mr V has knocked together a little workstation behind the sink from an old piece of worktop which has four very unstable wooden legs that Pussy Willow uses as scratching posts. Standing incongruously next to this is a brand-new, silver fridge freezer, blocking a door that we'll eventually permanently brick up. On the opposite side of the room, I've assembled a useful unit with two drawers for cutlery and kitchen utensils, and two shelves, one with essentials like tea, coffee, cups and tea pots, the other with fresh fruit and vegetables in wooden wine boxes. On top of this sits a two-ring electric hotplate, a kettle and toaster. I also have a slow cooker, electric grill, bread machine and yogurt maker, but I can only use these one at a time, partially because of lack of space, but primarily because the temporary electricity supply that Mr V has rigged up isn't powerful enough to support more than two appliances simultaneously. As I discovered when I tried to use the kettle and hotplate at the same time as making bread and fused the entire downstairs.

The latest addition to my 'field kitchen' is my pride and joy: an all-singing, all-dancing washing machine; well, maybe not dancing, but it does play a little tune that sounds like the ice-cream van and 'knocks' at the door to let me know when the cycle has ended. It also weighs the clothes before deciding how much water and power to use, so this pleases economy- and ecology-minded Mr V also.

Tins and jars and packets of dry food are stored on bookshelves in the living room. Pots and pans and electrical gadgets not in use are stored in a former haven for spiders in what will be my study-cum-sitting room, but now it's just full of boxes whose contents have a long wait ahead before rooms are ready to welcome them.

So maybe this is a good time to share my culinary skills. I shall begin with last night's dish of *haricots verts* (green beans) and tomatoes, courtesy of Pappy Cardigan.

GREEN BEANS PROVENÇALE

Ingredients

2 handfuls of green beans per person
1 small shallot, finely chopped
1 large clove garlic, finely chopped
1 tbsp olive oil
2 large, fresh tomatoes, roughly chopped
Salt and pepper to season
turmeric (optional)
1 tbsp white wine vinegar (I use *vinaigre* de Chardonnay as it has a
mild sweet flavour)
1 tbsp lemon juice

Method

Top and tail the beans and roughly cut in two.

Gently heat the oil in a deep pan such as a skillet and sauté the onion
and garlic until soft, taking care not to brown.

Add the tomatoes and cook for a further 2-3 minutes.

Add the beans and continue to cook for a further 3 minutes, stirring
occasionally.

Season with salt, pepper and turmeric (optional, but adds colour and flavour).

Add the white wine vinegar and lemon juice and let it sizzle for a few seconds then add enough warm water to just cover the beans.

Gently simmer for around one and a half hours until the beans are tender and the liquid almost all absorbed. (Top up with water while cooking if necessary.)

This is delicious served with chicken, pork or fish. Bon appétit!

FANTASTIC BEASTS AND WHERE TO
EAT THEM

*P*ussy Willow has taken to eating butterflies. I find this particularly abhorrent, and she knows it as she looks sheepishly at me from under the privet hedge where she is lying in wait, and hides her prey with a guilty paw if I look at her. Her guilty paw has also been at work on the newly laid cement next to the door at the top of the stone exterior staircase, which Mr V has had to make from scratch since none of its corners have anything remotely resembling a right angle. The left-hand side is a full two centimetres higher than the right at the top and a whopping four centimetres lower at the bottom. The door frame is so low that even I, who am only 5 feet 2½ inches (I haven't a clue what I am in centimetres), have to duck to get through it. This resulted in Mr V spending five precious days sawing and planing until he had the perfect fit. The problem then was that the floor on the landing, which has been concreted, isn't level, so although the door fitted perfectly when closed, it would only open about half a metre, meaning the floor had to be chiselled away also—hence the fresh cement. I have of course taken before and after shots, plus the signature paw impression.

I have to stop to tell you. A dragonfly has just flown in through the front door and is inspecting the living room. (I told you they were curious creatures.) My heart is in my mouth for two reasons: the first, I'm afraid it will fly up the chimney, and the second, that Pussy Willow will exercise her newly acquired hunting skills, but I think the size of it has dissuaded her. Its colours are even more vibrant in the relatively dark room compared to in the glare outside, and due to the confined space, it is hovering in the same position right in front of me. Frustratingly, for once my camera isn't to hand to capture the moment, but sometimes it's better to capture the moment in memory and observe with the heart, not through a lens.

Pussy Willow has also progressed (or regressed) from eating butterflies to trapping small lizards and bringing them into my makeshift kitchen to torment. Those that don't survive the ordeal she hides beneath a sheet of cardboard serving as a mat to put soil-caked garden shoes on. One of these hapless beasties that did manage to escape found its way into one of my deck shoes and only just wriggled out of the way in time before I squashed it with my bare foot. I found the headless corpse of another less fortunate soul still moving across the floor.

These little creatures are like mini Houdinis, appearing and disappearing up and down plugholes and in and out of cracks in the walls. I've found one in the bath, one in the kitchen sink and another sunning itself on a worktop. Being a city dweller most of my life I was unprepared for the abundance of creepy-crawly wildlife in the country, and even more unprepared for how up close and personal it gets.

What I've learnt today: Always check inside shoes, boots and slippers before putting them on or you're likely to be sharing them with a lizard.

There's an army of giant snails that muster in the garden every morning, so we have to tread gingerly when going out for fear of crunching them underfoot. Snails are a delicacy in France in general, but nowhere more so than here in Burgundy. The fridges and freezers at the local supermarkets are packed with plastic bags bulging with them, and also of fat rolls of bright green parsley butter to stuff them with. On our first visit to the house we enquired if there was somewhere local where we could have lunch and were directed to a bistro/pizzeria in a nearby village. This sounded hopeful as I'm not a big fan of French country cuisine, having been faced with stuffed bone marrow, stuffed birds' stomachs and spongy cow's tongue in the past. So a pizza would be right up my street.

The bistro looked harmless enough on the outside with its gaily painted red sign saying 'pizza'. Inside also led me into a false sense of security with red and white chequered tablecloths and Italian music playing in the background. Then I saw the *plat du jour* (dish of the day), though I got the feeling that this was really the dish of every day: *tête de veau entier* (whole calf's head). I threatened Mr V that if he ordered this I was walking out. I asked for the pizza menu and was told that there was only one option.

'Margherita?' I enquired hopefully.

'*Non, madame. Aux escargots et au persil*,' came the reply. Snail and parsley pizza! Now I do quite like snails in parsley butter, and I adore pizza, but the prospect of the two together wasn't working for me. So I asked the waitress if there was a vegetarian option. This caused her to look confused as she mentally flicked through the menu then, voilà, she had it.

'*Moules, madame. Moules-frites*.'

So I ordered the 'vegetarian' mussels and chips and Mr V *steak-frites*.

A little later a party of eight very old and very frail-looking French diners came in and each and every one was presented with a huge pot containing what I can only guess was *tête de veau*. There was a series of oohs and aahs as the lids came off and the group surveyed their gastronomical delights. One old gentleman looked so frail that I was amazed he could lift a fork never mind the lid off the cast iron pot. I would have thought a nice soft-boiled egg would have been more palatable to him, but he started tucking in with gusto. At this point I got up on the pretext of going to powder my nose and hissed at Mr V to move into my place while I was away so that when I returned I didn't have to watch the spectacle, which was quite frankly putting me off my mussels.

＊ ＊ ＊

The local market is also a lot more carnivorous than the one at my Paris suburb, where colourful stalls of fruit and vegetables rule supreme and any meat on sale is already dead.

But here there are rabbits and hares and chickens, and edible birds all in big wooden cages. The buffer zone of the supermarket packaging or even the butcher's shop window is stripped away, leaving the bare reality of where our rabbit in mustard sauce and coq au vin really come from. This morning, in the centre of the market square stood an enormous, arrogant, obviously not heading for the dinner table, cockerel, with ankles thicker than my wrists. He had the uncanny ability of standing statue still then moving at the precise moment that I released the shutter each time I tried to photograph him, resulting in every shot being a blur of red and brown plumage that could be titled 'Coq by Picasso'. He truly was a monster of a fowl, and I pitied the poor hens that were to be serviced by him.

While I'm on the subject of markets, one of the first things that I had to adjust to when I moved to France was buying food at them. Very picturesque and romantic, and all very well if you're just mooching around having fun on holiday, but faced with this as a real shopping option caused me to break out in a sweat and come home empty-handed (or with an empty, beat-up, old shopping trolley; if you're going to do this, you must look the part).

This was due to several reasons:

My lack of French, so I was confined to pointing as I didn't know the names for most of the produce, and even if I did, my accent was so off-piste that I might well have been talking Chinese.

My utter lack of understanding of metric weights and measures.

My Brit tendency to queue.

Before moving to Paris, I lived in the northern city of Lille for five months with my French friend Annie. Realising my shopping phobia, she began leaving me lists of things to buy from the small un-Parisian, queue-forming food market, but for me, even this was daunting. However, I plucked up courage and ventured forth, basket in hand. The little exercise was going swimmingly, and I was getting the hang of asking for apples and potatoes, when she threw eggs into the equation. Now I knew that one egg was *un oeuf* (pronounced almost as 'enough'), but Annie had asked for twelve. Wracking my brains as I got nearer to the front of the queue, I couldn't for the life of me think of the plural for eggs. So I asked the man for '*un oeuf, douze fois*' (one egg, twelve times). This caused uproar amongst the other shoppers, but I proudly went home with not twelve but thirteen eggs and the new-found vocabulary '*douze oeufs*' (pronounced almost as 'doooz...uh').

What I've learnt today: There's always a way around the language barrier.

A LITTLE PATCH OF EARTH

$\mathcal{I}$'ve just completed my first full day working in the garden, in fact any garden, ever! It's now 5:30 p.m., and I began before 9 with only a short break for lunch, not even pausing for my daily coffee fix. My arms and legs are scratched and bitten, and I'm turning a golden caramel colour despite regular top-ups of factor 30 sun cream. I'm aching all over but feel exhilarated at the same time. I've waited so long to have my own little patch of earth, somewhere I can plant fruit trees and berry bushes to make jam, and grow herbs, salad and vegetables to eat fresh from the soil. I've longed to be able to hang out washing and watch it billowing in the breeze, and to have bed sheets that smell of fresh air. I've dreamt of drinking a coffee and reading a book in the shade, and of eating dinner outdoors, then watching the sunset with a glass of wine and music playing softly in the background. Simple pleasures that many take for granted, but having been denied them for around ten years, it's these small things that are having the biggest impact on our lives.

When I lived in a large, detached house with a fair-sized garden (and a gardener) I never knew how lucky I was. When I moved to an apartment near Paris I would look longingly from my window at a small house with a tiny, triangular patio, just large enough to put a clothes airer, a small bistro table and two chairs, and have a few plants in pots. I feel so blessed to have been granted not only a garden but the grace to recognise how precious this is. Ironically almost all of my other home comforts have been taken away. We have no telephone land line, internet or television, and the mobile phone reception is hit and miss. So our only reliable contact with the outside world is via a local radio station playing 100% French music and regional news on the hour. We don't have a bed but sleep on an inflatable mattress; there are concrete floors in the bedrooms, and the only 'carpet' that we have is the cardboard packaging that the flat-pack furniture came in. We have no upstairs bathroom facilities and a very temperamental toilet downstairs, and if we want a fire, then we have to make one with wood. Despite all this, I am continually telling myself how lucky we are to have found this wondrous place.

✳ → ✳

The heat today is oppressive. The air is thick with it. I feel it clogging up my nostrils and weighing down my limbs. The faint buzzing of insects amplifies the silence of the afternoon. Pussy Willow is collapsed on the roof of the car; she has what my grandmother would call 'The Papsy Lals'. She has them so much that even the noise of the Kärcher as Mr V power-cleans the exterior steps doesn't rouse her, when usually she runs for cover at the mere sight of it. The shimmering afternoon sun is now so intense that the 'invader' cats have joined Pussy Willow in camp Papsy Lals. They've all called a truce and are lounging in the shade within tail swishing distance of each other. I even splashed some drops of water on Flaubertine to see if she was still alive. Instead of her customary scurrying back to her own patch she merely flicked her ear and gave me a certain look.

As it is so hot, the rhythm of our days has changed. We're rising between 6 and 7 in the morning, instead of between 7 and 8. Elevenses is now at 9:30, and we eat a light lunch at midday instead of a heavier one between 1 and 2. Dinner has been brought forward to around 7, giving us time to eat then continue working in the garden until the sun goes down.

Like the work in the house, we've hardly made a dent in the garden, but have made a start. This evening I cut away the rampant Virginia creeper that was blocking access to the path leading from the terrace to the *abreuvoir*, and strangling a lovely bush that itself has gone wild. While I'm grappling with the creeper, which isn't going without a fight, I uncover an enormous snail with a gorgeous, ochre-coloured shell. I place it on some moss on the stone wall and run for my camera. Mr V says I should put a euro beside the snail to illustrate its size, but by the time I return to the wall with a coin the snail has sloped off.

Mr V is hacking away at the hard, stony ground beneath the unidentifiable tree that Lars the Dutch Rasta gardener tells me is in fact a bush. I would like to plant spring bulbs there, but Mr V doesn't seem to think the soil is good enough; still, I'm going to put a few in and see what happens and put the rest in a pot.

*   *   *

The sounds of the buzzing and chirping of insects have been accompanied by other sounds not commonly heard in Paris: the gentle mooing of cows in the field opposite, the bleating of sheep and neighing of horses in the fields behind the woods at the back, the distant bark of a dog, and another sound that I'm unfamiliar with, the piercing screech of a bird of prey. It's an eerie, chilling sound that's carried on the breeze from high up in the sky where two of them are circling, one making wide figures of eight at high altitude, the other, smaller circles at a lower level. I wonder if they're a pair with young to feed and are working as a team, or just hunting together. I think Mungo Jerry and Rumpleteazer would be easy pickings for them, but Pussy Willow would prove much more difficult to lift off the ground.

The sounds inside the house are alien to me also: the dripping of taps, the creaking of doors and rafters, and the patter of soot falling down the chimney. It's as if the house herself is communicating with me, and I find these noises rather comforting; as if she is saying that she's happy I'm there.

* * *

I have some terrible news to report. Last night I was woken by another sound which I thought was cats fighting. But this morning I've discovered the awful truth. Maddy has been attacked, probably by a fox, and she's horribly injured. She has a huge, gaping wound in her abdomen, another wound on her back leg, plus minor injuries to her eye and nose.

The farmer who she belongs to is still on holiday. I've given her sanctuary in my kitchen with a clean piece of cardboard to lie on, where the sunlight can reach her wound, but she isn't in the full glare and heat of the sun outside, nor is she lying on dirty soil. I'm giving her regular, small, high-protein meals of chicken and tuna, and some of Pussy Willow's cat food, and encouraging her to drink plenty of water, which she is doing. She seems to understand me, or at least understand that I'm trying to help her. What's breaking my heart is that she's constantly purring, content with so little even through her injuries. I know cats sometimes do this to comfort themselves and to self-heal, but the purring intensifies when I caress her rough little head or speak to her, so I think it's genuine happiness. She is such a special little soul, and I'm learning to love her. I've been singing 'Baby Mine' from *Bambi* to her while I'm cooking or washing the dishes. She loves this and purrs even louder, curls into a little ball and goes into an unguarded deep sleep, which I'm glad of as she needs undisturbed rest.

For the night we've made a bed from a cushion covered with a cotton pillowcase in a low-sided wooden crate that she can easily get in and out of and put this in a place of safety in one of the outbuildings. We're trying to strike a balance between helping her and not interfering too much with her regular life, as we're only here until the beginning of September. Then it will just be every other weekend, and we don't want her to become dependent on us and alienate herself from the group even more. I would like to take her back with us and take her to our vet, but we can hardly just catnap somebody else's cat. Plus we plan to leave Pussy Willow in the Paris apartment with an automatic food dispenser for two nights when we come for the weekend, and although she's tolerating Maddy in the kitchen, she is attacking her if she ventures into her domain in the living room. Maddy doesn't seem to know how to fight back (or maybe she's just too weak), so this isn't an option. I hope and pray that she pulls through.

What I've learnt today: Nothing except the gift of life itself is our God-given right, but I'm resilient and adaptable and can learn to live without many things. The one true gift is being able to appreciate what you have.

THE MUSIC BOX

The heat continues to mount, and it's now officially a heatwave. We have 38 degrees in the shade at the back of the house; I don't want to know what it is at the front in full sun. Pussy Willow is lying on her side on the cool floor tiles in the living room, and I'm languishing on the sofa. Mr V has just braved the heat to visit a *vide grenier* (literally 'empty attic') which is a bit like a car boot sale that happens in most towns at around the same time, usually twice a year. The roads are sealed off, and people set up their stalls along either side. The quality of these sales varies according to the neighbourhood, some selling antiques and heirlooms, others old clothes, plastic toys and baby equipment. We've had some very good china tableware and crystal from around Paris. Mr V predicted that this sale would be mainly farm utensils, but he was hopeful of picking up some bargain tools for the house or garden. I normally love going to these sales but was so drained by the heat that I did something I very rarely do and fell asleep in the afternoon.

The French don't have quite the same business acumen as the Brits do and tend to overcharge for things, and are reluctant to negotiate on price. That is until it gets to around 5 o'clock, and it suddenly dawns on them that they're going to take home what they came with, and the idea of the exercise is to get rid of unwanted stuff. So late afternoon is the best time to bag a bargain. I once bought a jacket still with its €49 label attached. The woman had been asking €30; it was 6 o'clock, and she was packing up. I stopped to look at it, and she offered it to me for €20. I said no, €5, expecting her to say €15, and I would have willingly paid that, but she agreed to €5. They just don't know how to play the game. I went home feeling rather guilty that I hadn't offered €10.

As it turns out, it was a profitable excursion for Mr V. He's returned with three large, coach-style, outdoor lanterns which need just a couple of panes of glass replacing, €15 for the lot (they retail for around €45 each). He also picked up a gorgeous little Tiffany reproduction table lamp in perfect condition, and an antique music box just like one his grandmother used to have. It has a hand-painted tile with a picture of a couple in 19th-century attire, set in an ornately carved wooden frame. The movement needs replacing, but I love it, and it was an absolute steal at €5. I have a bit of a music box fetish and collect those little wind-up ones that they sell in the souvenir shops in Montmartre and around Notre-Dame. One of the first gifts that Mr V gave to me was a small, glass music box that plays 'La Vie en Rose'. He also had a beautiful personalised one made for me from the music-box makers Lutèce at Paris that plays 'Edelweiss', so you can see how thrilled I am to receive this, even if it doesn't work at the moment.

The man also threw in a pan stand with the same style of elaborate wooden frame and a hand-painted tile depicting spring. The tile is cracked, but I don't mind; this permits me to use it for the purpose it was made for. I don't like perfection anyway. I think it's grossly overrated. Voltaire said 'Perfect is the enemy of good'.

Speaking of imperfection, I like Les Libellules in her present state, and although I welcome all mod cons and a bit of luxury, a little part of me will be sad to see her change. We intend to keep things as close as possible to the original and even keep elements of some features.

The house has the most amazing wallpaper that covers every wall, all the ceilings that aren't beamed, and even the interestingly shaped panelled doors. It is these doors that we plan to keep; one in the living room and one in what I call the garden room (my eventual study) to preserve an element of the past.

I also intend to frame some of the paper, if I can remove a big enough section intact, and hang it on the walls of the original rooms. I've chosen the colours for the living room and garden room to complement this, so in effect the house is guiding me, not me imposing my ideas on her. The living room paper is in a bold, late Victorian style, and I even saw it gracing the walls of a rather grand house in a period drama on TV a couple of weeks ago. It has scrolls and floral arrangements in shades of blue, green and rose; as a friend pointed out, the very shades that I've chosen for the paint for the blue and rose bedrooms and the garden room. I wonder if I was subconsciously influenced by this paper which, although I initially shuddered at the sight of, has grown on me. My personal favourite is the paper in the garden room which looks to be early Victorian. It has an oriental feel with delicate blossoms and small birds in muted mauve, blue and green. The other rooms aren't so charming. The kitchen is orange and yellow '60s psychedelia, and the bathroom is a 1970s horror of chocolate-brown and pink flowers. We obviously won't be keeping these.

* * *

It is three in the morning. I'm in the bathroom, and I can stand it no longer. The wallpaper has to go and go now. It doesn't put up much of a fight. The first strip comes off almost intact. Some of the others leave jagged remnants clinging to the top of the wall. What lies underneath is a dirty-looking, chalky, white plaster but in my opinion highly preferable to what was there before. Satisfied with my night-time decorating session I go back to bed.

* * *

This morning a confused Mr V has just asked where the wallpaper has gone.

INSECT SOUP

*T*he house is crumbling. Everywhere I brush against a wall, more of it cascades onto the floor. We stopped removing the faded, musty wallpaper as the plaster was coming away with it, and washing woodwork not only removes the dirt and the paint, but the wood and half the wall as well.

I, by contrast, am blooming: my skin is glowing; my arms and legs have toned up, and despite now eating two four-course meals a day (please note, French portion sizes are generally smaller than in the English speaking world), I've lost 2.5 kilogrammes in two weeks. I have though taken to wearing some odd combinations of clothes, selecting items by indoor/outdoor temperature and how clean/dirty the job that I'm doing is. To be honest I'm wearing a lot of dirty clothes, but clean, fresh dirt, if you know what I mean.

Taking a shower confirms that the dragonflies are right in viewing me as a link in their food chain. Enough protein in the form of spiders, flies, woodlice (plus, I suspect, fleas from Flaubertine, or should I say 'Flea-bit-ine') and goodness knows what else, to feed a small, hungry nation drop from my hair and body, and I'm left standing in a sort of insect soup. This isn't the only unsavoury shower/plumbing fact I have to share. (All those of a sensitive nature, stop reading now!)

We have a flow problem, or a backflow problem, to be more precise. It doesn't take much imagination to guess what happens if you flush the toilet too vigorously as the toilet, bath and wash basin appear to share a communal waste pipe, meaning when you flush the loo, the contents can make a little detour on their way out. To combat this we have to keep all the plugholes firmly closed and the one in the bath weighed down with a two-litre bottle of water. What the estate agents don't tell you...

Here's a question: how can it be possible, in a country where electric showers don't exist as it is dangerous to have water and electricity in the same place, to have an electric toilet? I use it with extreme trepidation. It mashes everything up and sends it I'm not sure where. Having had mod cons all my life, I don't like thinking about such things, but we're limited as to what we put down (and there's even a warning about the use of toilet brushes). So it's a bit like Greece, but this is forever, not just for two weeks in August.

Another disadvantage is if there's a power cut, the toilet doesn't empty. And it isn't only power cuts that can cause a problem. I accidently dislodged the plug while mopping the floor and didn't notice. I flushed the toilet; it filled up, but the water stayed at the top. Stupidly I flushed it again, and this time the water and contents came all over the top onto the recently mopped bathroom floor.

What I've learnt today: Always check your loo is plugged in before flushing...

THE SCENT OF HAPPINESS

$\mathcal{M}$r V has just walked into the kitchen and pronounced, '*Ahhh, ça c'est l'odeur de bonheur*', that's the scent of happiness. I'm making jam from a basket of big, juicy blackberries that our Dutch neighbours brought over last night along with an invite for apéritifs at their house. The jam does smell rather good, and I think more floral than when I've made blackberry jam from berries picked close to Paris. We have our own blackberry bushes, but the path where they are growing is so overgrown that we can't reach them; so we must wait until next year before sampling our own jam.

Making jam isn't complicated, and you don't really need a recipe, but I'll give you mine at the end of the chapter, just in case you aren't sure.

❋　❋　❋

The apéritif turned into a three-hour wine tasting without the spit buckets, and a tour of their house and workshops. Their home is a rambling, three-storey former *auberge* (Inn), and we think there was once a connection between it and Les Libellules; one provided board and lodging, and the other stabling and refreshments for the horses and possibly the coachmen. The road on which the houses are situated used to be the main route for the stagecoach from Paris to Lyon. By all accounts it was famous, or should I say infamous, for attracting bands of vagabonds and brigands who lay in wait and held up the coach to relieve the occupants of their money and their jewels.

Our neighbours' house has one of the wonderful, bright, polychrome-tiled roofs that are peculiar to Burgundy, with intricate, geometric diamond designs in yellow, orange, red, green and black. We climbed the steep, winding wooden stairs to the attic, where we could see the muted pattern on the back of the tiles. I was awestruck thinking of the craftsmen hundreds of years ago being up there creating this beautiful, functional work of art which is still in almost perfect condition. The views from the third floor are spectacular, looking out onto a patchwork of fields broken only by small copses of trees and the roofs and spires of distant villages. On the second floor we encountered a huge, bright green grasshopper about 13-14 centimetres long; there must be something in the soil here that produces such giant species of everything.

Back in the kitchen the four of us are sitting around the large table where an extensive array of bottles have been placed and five glasses. I remark on this, thinking that we are expecting another person, and they explain that it's their custom always to put an extra glass on the table to welcome an unexpected guest; a custom that I like the idea of very much. The extra guest can take his pick from red, white or rosé wine, whiskey, port, rum or gin.

I choose a glass of rosé with ice, as we are drinking on empty stomachs. Mr V opts for red, and our neighbours go for the white, so we have three bottles open on the table. This reminds me of a romantic canal cruise in Amsterdam that I went on with a friend some years ago; it was a miracle we found our way back to the hotel.

Food arrives: slices of salami, cubes of Dutch cheese pitted with cumin seeds, cherry tomatoes, cornichons[1], olives, and small, spicy sardines from a tin, plus the inevitable baguette. Ella Fitzgerald is oozing from another room (PIF radio on the internet, explains our host); if only *we* had the internet. After we've drained our respective bottles, I'm feeling more chilled than I have the right to be, given all that we should be doing. But hey, this is kickback time, and we're gaining some useful tips on where to go for building supplies and what's the best kind of insulation, as it's been known for the temperature to drop as low as -30 C in this region. Plus all work and no play makes one very dull. So I sink into Steely Dan's 'Do it Again' and go Dutch.

---

1. Gherkins.

BLACKBERRY JAM

Ingredients

1 kg (2 lb) blackberries, freshly picked if you can
500 g (1 lb) sugar
2 tbsp fresh lemon juice

Method

Wash the blackberries and put in a large, heavy-bottomed pan with
the sugar and stir constantly while bringing to the boil.

Reduce heat, add the lemon juice and simmer uncovered for around
20 minutes until mixture begins to cling to a wooden spoon as it's
lifted from the pan.

Sterilise 6 jam jars in boiling water and fill with the jam while still hot,
then seal the lids tightly and put in a cool place to store. (The 'buttons'
on the top of the lids should invert, indicating the jars are airtight.)
The jam will keep for around a year if unopened, but in my house it
lasts about two months.

A ROSE BY ANY OTHER NAME

$\mathcal{M}$y French is reasonable; I'm not fluent by a long chalk (though friends and family think I am), but I get by in shops and markets and on public transport. I can exchange pleasantries with neighbours, hold my own in an argument with Mr V, and even make the odd witty remark at dinner parties, albeit with a *petit accent anglais,* that men seem to find *charmante*, telling me that I sound just like Jane Birkin (pronounced more like Jhan Beer Can). But I'm now faced with a whole dictionary of new words, and I can barely understand anything that my husband is saying. He's always asking me to bring a spanner, mole grips, monkey wrench, etc. in French, and I can hardly identify them in English.

Then there is pitchfork, pickaxe, spade, hedge trimmers, lawnmower, mop, bucket, dust pan and various attachments for a vacuum cleaner that up till now have just been 'thingies', all highlighting gaping holes in my vocabulary. He speaks of roof tiles, various electrical and plumbing components, and I'm lost in a mire of French.

This came to an ugly head the day the boiler sprang a leak, and Mr V called hastily for a *serpillière*. I didn't have a clue what this was, but I knew I had to find it urgently, and there was no time to play the usual game of charades when he tries to describe something to me. I heard the prefix 'ser', as I knew that *serrer* is the French verb 'to tighten', I scrambled about searching for a tool to tighten whatever needed tightening to stop the mini fountain in the boiler room. Voilà! I had it. A spanner. Not just any spanner, the biggest spanner I'd ever seen in my life; that was bound to do the trick. I rushed into the boiler room, proudly presenting it to Mr V. Who promptly knocked it out of my hand and pushed me aside abruptly, muttering some other colourful words and phrases to extend my French vocabulary and returned with a floor cloth. A floor cloth! How on earth could I ever have worked that one out? The joys of a dual-lingo relationship.

A faded business card was stuck with discoloured Sellotape to the top of the boiler with the number of a heating engineer. Mr V called the number, which was miraculously still in use, but it went straight to answer phone. I must point out that this was all taking place on the second Friday in August. Anyone who knows anything about France knows that it is effectively closed during August while everyone takes off to the beaches or the mountains for their annual summer holidays, returning only for the mass back to work and school at the beginning of September known as *'la rentrée'*.

Mr V left a sketchy message saying who he was and that we'd just moved into the house with the *pigeonnier*, and our ancient boiler had sprung a leak. I thought that we had about as much chance of seeing a tradesman in the middle of August (and the weekend to boot) as seeing Santa Claus's sleigh, but one can dream.

The next morning, I was taking a leisurely cup of tea when a grubby white van screeched up outside, and its driver approached our door. The boiler man had turned up, just like that, totally unannounced on a Saturday morning—in August! There was none of the cheek-sucking, air-blowing, head-shaking pessimism usually associated with plumbers and suchlike. He rolled up his sleeves, got out his toolbox, fiddled about with a pressure valve and shook our hands. Mr V asked him if he preferred cash to a cheque, and he replied that he'd done next to nothing, and there was no charge.

We were expecting a super-hiked-up call-out fee for him coming at the weekend and during the holidays. He then discussed our plans for replacing the boiler and moving its location, and our intention to create a second bathroom on the upper floor. He gave us some advice and said when we were ready to begin the work to give him a call. He knew the house and had done all the most recent plumbing. Now that's what I call good customer relations. Who said you can't get good customer service in France?

What I've learnt today: Always have a bilingual dictionary at hand for emergencies.

JACK AND JILL OF ALL TRADES

*I*t's suddenly gone very dark in the living room, which is strange as the sun is cracking the flags outside, the reason being an enormous tractor has just pulled up outside the window. It's Pappy Cardigan delivering the promised ladders. I was expecting a car with a roof rack, or maybe a small van, but outside is a shiny red leviathan driven by a strapping young farmhand (think Gaston from *Beauty and the Beast*) wearing extremely short shorts and a chequered shirt with the sleeves rolled up, exhibiting his bulging, bronzed biceps. He jumps down with ease from his lofty cabin three metres off the ground and waits for Pappy Cardigan who trundles up a few minutes later in his Peugeot partner. He then proceeds to demonstrate the various ropes and pulleys required to extend the ladder. The whole contraption doesn't look safe to me and I would prefer to call a roofer, but minutes later Mr V is straddling the apex like a cowboy at a rodeo while Pussy Willow and I sit side by side on a wall, looking up nervously.

To say that I'm impressed with my husband's ability to tackle almost anything is an understatement. Granted, all this 'do it yourself' stems from a need to save money, as there's so much to do we wouldn't get very far if we had to pay for professionals. So to date he's custom-made an exterior door and fitted it with a super-secure locking system, put two windows into outbuildings (to practise for when he tackles the bathroom), provided power to said outbuildings (which entails a precarious-looking cable swinging across the courtyard from the *pigeonnier*) and taken out a bidet. OK, he smashed up the bidet in frustration at the plumbing, but he capped the remaining pipes off nicely. And now he's a roofer. He's cleaned the moss from all the tiny roof tiles, bringing them back to a rosy terracotta, and replaced the twenty or so broken ones.

I for my part have become a dab hand at putting together flat-pack furniture. I'm particularly proud of the garden bench that I secretly made then took a photo of the finished article sunning itself on the terrace to show to an astounded Mr V. I've also put together a metal-framed fabric wardrobe, a sofa bed, and the afore mentioned kitchen trolley and garden table. I needed help with the sofa bed and table as they were rather heavy.

All this work, and he is working exceptionally hard, is giving Mr V an appetite. So I'm now providing Dutch breakfast of hard-boiled eggs and slices of ham and cheese accompanied by French breakfast of toasted baguette with jam. Elevenses (he's finally embraced the concept) of coffee and crêpes, followed by a four-course lunch around one o'clock, tea and cakes between four and five, and finally apéritif and a four-course dinner around eight. All with no real kitchen to speak of, and, more importantly, no dishwasher, so I would describe myself as chief cook and bottle washer. Do I mind? Not one bit.

RED FLAGS IN THE VINEYARDS

*A*lthough it isn't yet the end of August the trees have begun to subtly change colour, and the vines in the vineyards have a smattering of deep red leaves amongst the green, like little flags signalling that they're almost ready to give up their precious harvest. The late evenings are beginning to turn noticeably (and thankfully) cooler, and the mornings are accompanied by a magical mist that cloaks the field opposite, making the cows appear like little white sailboats floating in from the fog.

I'm standing in the dew-laden nettles taking photos with Flaubertine and Maddy at my feet, or under them to be more precise. It's a mystical experience. Ghost trees emerge and take on their solid forms as the mist unfurls itself backwards, and I naturally have it all on camera. Although she still can't run and jump as Flaubertine can, Maddy is thankfully making progress. Her breathing is less laboured; she is less tired, and her wound has gone from blood red to rose pink, though it's still gaping open, and there is still visible slough in the centre (The nurse in me is dying to clean it with some sterile water, but she wouldn't let me near).

Pussy Willow doesn't like nettles, and walks through long grass like a dressage horse, lifting her legs high in the air, much in the same manner that I've seen other cats negotiate snow, so she stays on the step. She's happy that I'm pointing my lens in a direction other than at her.

*   *   *

When I get back I'm surprised to find Mr V waiting not for his breakfast, but waiting for me in what I can only describe as an animated manner (for him, who I've never really seen get excited about anything).

'Come and see this,' he says, leading me through the house and out of the back door.

The strip of land between the house and the outbuildings is overgrown with weeds and covered in stones. We had planned to pave it, but while waiting for me to come in from my misty-morning photo shoot, he'd dug up a small patch to see what, if anything, was underneath. There he uncovered a strip of the original cobbles. So now there's no question of paving. We're going to excavate the whole area and return it to its former glory when long-gone horses trod those very stones on their way to be watered and stabled. I can imagine it all like a scene from *The Three Musketeers*: Porthos and Aramis fencing on the cobbles, D'Artagnan leaping down to join them from the stone staircase, sword in hand; the mysterious Milady de Winter hovering by the *abreuvoir*. Now, where is Athos...?

What I've learnt today: You were lied to in the Girl Guides, and you can't always find dock leaves growing near nettles.

IF WALLS COULD TALK

*A*nother of our friendly neighbours has just stopped by. He appears to be in his 60's and is dressed in a red baseball cap, tartan shirt, to-the-knee shorts and Converse trainers, looking more like a Canadian tourist then a farmer. I've seen him passing on a small tractor, (people ride up and down on small tractors or sit on grass cutters here as opposed to mobility scooters as they do in the UK) and also speeding by on a bicycle. He lives in a gorgeous old manor house with a stone archway leading to an inner courtyard under which is a cart loaded with hay. It all looks like something from a Constable painting. I've had my camera pointed at that also, and won a photography competition with the photo.

He tells us he has some old photographs of the house and the surrounding area that he'd like to show me, as he remarked that I'm never without my camera in my hand and thinks it would be interesting to compare my photos with those taken in the past. This appeals to me greatly, and I would like to write a history of the hamlet someday. He also tells us that Les Libellules dates from before the revolution, so maybe she really did exist in the time of the musketeers. We are still awaiting the land registry documents to come from Dijon to discover exactly when she was built; but now know that she's survived a revolution and two world wars. If walls could talk, what tales would these 40-centimetre-thick stones tell?

I run my hands over them, and they speak to me in the whispered voices of the past. I feel the heartbeat of Les Libellules as you feel the sap pulsing through a tree when you press your ear to its bark. She's known love and laughter, anguish and pain, betrayal, birth and death, and revolution and war.

Speaking of wars, we are very close to the former border with what was Vichy France, the name for the part of France that wasn't directly under German occupation during the first part of the Second World War (up until 1942). So named because the seat of power was at Vichy in the Massif Central, under the government of the chancellor and later president, Maréchal Pétain. Being so close to the border, there was a lot of Resistance activity in this area, particularly smuggling agents and airmen into the 'free zone'. There's a trail that begins close to here—*Le Chemin de la Résistance* (The Trail of the Resistance)—that takes in 21 sites marking places where acts of extreme bravery or barbary took place.

The village of Dun-les-Places is the martyred Burgundy village that suffered the greatest during the Second World War, enduring three days of horror when about 3,000 German soldiers occupied the village, massacring a significant number of the population before looting and burning it down. The villages of Montsauche and Planchez were also destroyed, and the farm at La Verrerie burnt to the ground in retaliation for German troops suffering heavy losses there in an ambush involving Resistance fighters and British SAS paratroopers. There is also a museum—*Le Musée de Chemin de la Résistance en Morvan*—and a visitors' centre.

The French Resistance movement came into being in the Morvan in 1941. Initially it was loosely organised groups of men and women known as *les maquisards* because they hid out in the *maquis* (shrubland). By 1944 there were up to 10,000 maquisards, and it is they alone who liberated the region. If you get the chance see the very funny French film *La Grande Vadrouille* (available subtitled in English) about a group of English airmen shot down over France, then you'll be treated to scenes shot both in the Burgundy countryside and in and around the Hôtel-Dieu at Beaune.

THE DAY THE RAINS CAME

*I*t's the first of September, and the weather has changed suddenly from stifling heat to having a nip in the air in the morning and evening. There's been overnight rain, ushering forth a posy of early morning snails (I counted seventeen when I opened the garden room door). The wind has got up also, sending leaves fluttering to the ground like golden snowflakes. Mr V has been reinforcing the three entrances at the front of the house as there were large gaps under all the doors (gateways for lizards and spiders). He'd just smoothed the last piece of cement when the first rumblings of thunder began. The sky turned the yellow of tailor's chalk, then coral, then purple and now deep grey, and the heavens have opened. Within literally minutes the side road has turned into a mini river, and a canoe would be more useful than a car.

Flashes of lightning are illuminating the living room, and Maddy and Flaubertine are cleaving to the meagre shelter of the step like bookends. I open the door to close the shutters to keep out the rain, and both cats run in. There's a smell of wet fur and something else, I fear. I think that Maddy's wound has begun to go septic. The good news is I hear that the farmer and his family are due back tomorrow, so hopefully they'll take her to a vet, or at least give her some antibiotics. She seems well in herself and is still performing her rolling-on-my-feet trick. She stays at the living room door and regards Pussy Willow who is sitting on a cushion on the sofa listening to her favourite music. I can see longing and confusion all over Maddy's little face. Why is she not that cat, the one on the sofa?

I put a cushion on one of the dining chairs and move it a safe distance away from Pussy Willow. Maddy struggles to jump up, and I don't want to lift her for fear of hurting her, but she manages it and sleeps out the storm to the sound of her namesake, Madeleine Peyroux. Flaubertine stays in the kitchen in the hope of being given, or stealing, food. This is her sole motive for seeking us out, while with Maddy it's the human contact that she craves.

Sadly, this is our last night here until the end of the month. We return to Paris in the morning. I pack my things with a heavy heart. Les Libellules has become so loved by us in such a short time. I feel like I'm part of the fabric of the house. I know that I'm now part of her history as much as she is of mine. We are bound together for a brief moment in time.

PART II
MORNING MISTS AND
FIELDS OF FROST

OCTOBER AND NOVEMBER 2017

Season of mists and mellow fruitfulness,
Close bosom-friend of the maturing sun.
'To Autumn', John Keats

LIFE IS A LONG SONG

*W*e're having an Indian summer. It's the first of October, the sun is strong and mellow, but the evenings are arriving earlier and bringing with them the cool night air. We've put an extra cover on the bed and are lighting the fire after dinner, even if it's warm enough to eat outside while the sun is still up.

It has been three weeks since we were last here, and I've missed the house greatly. I woke this morning with a sense of wonderment that she is ours. But then I stopped and thought of all the people who have lived here before us, all waking in this very room and thinking that they own her too. None of us do, or did, of course. We'll come and go, make our changes, leave our mark until the next custodians arrive and try to make her their own, but she's stood the test of time and will continue to do so. There's a responsibility that comes with being the guardian of such an interesting old house: not to make your voice so loud that it drowns out the sound of the others. We're all just passing through.

I've found some old photographs that belonged to the previous residents. Charming images mounted on crinkly-edged fine embossed card, protected with a sheet of opaque paper. A pretty bride and a proud groom in 1950s attire, smiling from a matt black and white portrait. There was a second photo of a traditional wedding group, at the front of which is a row of scowling, cross-legged children. I presume that the happy couple were the people who owned the house before us, and the children, probably those who'd inherited it. I found it sad that the lady's family, however distant, had no interest in these photos. But then again maybe it's more fitting that they remain here as her legacy, the forever smiling bride.

Photos aren't my only find. The former occupant ran a little primary school from the house, and I came across a box of stubby red pencils, each one chewed at the base by no doubt deciduous teeth. I wonder about the little hands that gripped and scribbled with these pencils, and the little mouths that sucked and gnawed on them as they concentrated on their letters and numbers. Where are they now? Older than me, I suppose, their lessons long forgotten.

Can you guess what I'm supposed to be doing? Yes, I'm (not) sewing more rings on the heavy curtain that will soon be needed behind the living room door. I've been caught red-handed once again and say sheepishly to my husband that the curtains are my inspiration. He laughs and says, 'I see that.' He's happy that I've found a fountain of words after a nine-year drought.

✻ ✻ ✻

We've just welcomed and said goodbye to our first house guests. They weren't strictly 'house' guests as they stayed outside in their camper van, which was a lot better equipped than our house. In the absence of Pussy Willow, Maddy has promoted herself to 'top cat'. She led the way from room to room as we showed our friends around the house, like a little feline estate agent, displaying obvious pride in her new-found status. She really is a remarkable little animal, more like a dog than a cat. She follows me around, often as far as the recycle bins at the edge of the hamlet. She has also taken to coming on an after-dinner evening stroll with Mr V and me, walking between us looking from one to the other as we speak, as if she's part of the conversation. Far from being the outcast amongst the other cats, she is now the envy of all, and she knows it. She is moving better, can jump onto the wall and run after us for short distances. I'm encouraging this to try to build up her muscles and make her stronger. Mr V is worried, however, as she doesn't bury her business like a normal cat, and he says she isn't covering her scent and is therefore more vulnerable to predators. She isn't stupid, but he's right: there's something decidedly un-catlike about her.

* → *

Meals were a bit tricky while our friends were here as Ceri is vegan, so not only does she not eat meat or fish but doesn't eat cheese or eggs either. Never fear, I still had a crate load of courgettes and tomatoes to use, so I decided to make a ratatouille. Classic recipes use aubergine[1], but as I'm allergic to them, I used a jar of artichoke hearts instead, and the result was excellent. Here's my version.

---

1. Eggplant.

RATATOUILLE

Serves 2 as a main course or 4 as a side dish

Ingredients

6 large, ripe tomatoes
1 green, 1 orange and 1 yellow courgette, cut into chunks
1 green, 1 red and 1 orange pepper, cut into chunks the same size as
the courgettes
1 small, red onion, roughly chopped
1 large clove garlic, finely chopped
200 g (7 oz) jar artichoke hearts in olive oil, drained
2 tbsp olive oil
1 tbsp tomato puree (I use one with added vegetables)
1 tsp herbs de Provence
1 tsp sugar
1 tbsp red wine vinegar
400 g (14 oz) tin chopped tomatoes
Salt and freshly ground black pepper to season
Fresh basil leaves

Method

Score the fresh tomatoes in a cross at their base and cover with
boiling water in a basin for around a minute. Drain and cover with
cold water and leave to cool.

Peel off the skin once cooled.

Gently heat the oil in a large, heavy-based saucepan.

Soften the courgettes and peppers for about 10 minutes, taking care not to brown.

Add the onion and garlic and cook for a further 5 minutes, taking care not to brown.

Add the tomato puree, herbs de Provence, sugar and red wine vinegar.

Roughly chop the tomatoes and add these along with the artichoke hearts.

Add the can of chopped tomatoes and a can of warm water.

Season with salt and black pepper to taste.

Cover and simmer over a low heat for around 40 minutes until the sauce has thickened.

Sprinkle with the freshly torn basil leaves and serve immediately.

I served this with some warm, crusty baguette and a little parmesan cheese. The men had it as a side dish with a pan-fried pork steak, and we girls had it as a main.

EAGLE ROUTE

*T*he Indian summer persists. We're driving down from Paris through virtually deserted roads flanked by trees in their early autumn splendour, with tints of russet, gold and chestnut brown. The sky is bright blue, but the telltale sun has a silvery glow as it pierces patches of mist and fog that cling to the low ground.

The halfway point of our journey is marked by a dune-shaped hill rising from the otherwise flat landscape that I have christened the 'hill of happiness', and my heart always quickens at its sight. Today however, I'm filled with both excitement and trepidation. I've not been to Les Libelulles for three weeks, and I fear that little Maddy may no longer be with us. Mr V reported that the smell from her wound had become worse when he came alone a fortnight ago…

You can all relax. Maddy is alive. It took her all of ten minutes to realise that we were back. Her wound is less offensive, and although she is painfully thin, she is as affectionate as ever. I'm feeding her up again on cat food and her new favourite delicacy: my homemade quiche Lorraine. Pussy Willow is home alone once more with the automatic cat feeder, and a friend will call in on her this evening (we're only away Saturday morning until Sunday evening). I hate leaving her, but she equally hates the almost three-hour car journey to get here, so for short visits it's better that she stays in Paris. Maddy has now taken up Pussy Willow's 'guard cat' position at the back door, ensuring that Flaubertine doesn't gain access into the inner sanctuary.

＊　＊　＊

The Côte-d'Or is truly living up to its name. We're en route to Dijon for building supplies to insulate and board the loft. Pappy Cardigan has kindly lent us his trailer, which we've just fitted with our number plate. We're passing through terraced hillsides drenched in vineyards, shimmering in the beautiful autumn sunlight. It truly is a breathtaking sight, and I let out a spontaneous 'Oh my!' when they come into view.

These fields of gold haven't been the only sight that has made me gasp this morning. We've just passed through *la Route des Aigles* (Eagle Route), so named by me: a long, tree-lined lane following in the footsteps of an ancient Roman road. We drove past four birds of prey (not actual eagles) sitting sentry on the posts between the now almost bare hedgerows. Still as statues, the only movement their feathers ruffling slightly in the breeze. Their eyes, sharp as diamonds, scanning the freshly turned fields for signs of small rodents whose safe haven of crops has been gathered in. I'm no expert, but Mr V and I deduce by their size that the birds are probably falcons. A little further along, the pillar-box physique of a huge owl is balanced on an impossibly fragile-looking branch. He's probably sleeping, as he'll be hunting tonight by the light of the harvest moon, I imagine.

Trips to the retail park have never been so scenic. We drive through picture-postcard villages that look like they've stepped right out of a calendar, with duck ponds and haywains, and churches with tall, pointy steeples adorned with the traditional yellow, brown and orange zigzag patterns of Burgundian tiles. Then we pass *Les roches de Baume*, imposing limestone rocks that wouldn't look out of place in a Western movie. We trace the flow of the Burgundy Canal with its locks and bridges, and small barges moored at its banks, and finally climb winding, forested roads to a plain of vast farmland, before descending into more vineyards. It certainly beats the M56 to Manchester. For all serious shopping other than bread, cheese, wine and groceries, we have to make the 90-minute round trip to Dijon, famous for its mustard and *pain d'épices*, a type of ginger loaf that's a speciality of the region. I've heard that Dijon is a beautiful historic town with medieval streets, gothic churches and the majestic palace of the former Dukes of Burgundy; but I wouldn't know as I've not got past Castorama and IKEA.

※　☀　☀

The people in Dijon are like a different race: small in stature and solidly built, not fat, but with a lot more meat on them than I'm used to seeing in Paris; thick set, with broad, flat, sallow faces, and dark eyes and hair. Usually being the shortest (and in Paris the heaviest) of the bunch, I'm finding myself one of the tallest and slimmest while strolling around Castorama. No longer a hobbit, I'm now Galadriel, head and shoulders above the rest of the women. The Burgundians in general have this squat physical tendency, but here in Dijon it's more pronounced. Their voices are quite distinctive also. The men in particular have deep, rich, coffee-brown tones, which make them very attractive to listen to, if not to look at. Mr V, being Norman, therefore from Norseman (Viking) stock, stands out like a beech tree amongst mulberry bushes, and quite a lot of people stare at us as we glide down the aisles of tongue and groove and polystyrene. It's as if we're wearing our Paris number plates on our backs. The fact that I got a bit excited about going to town and 'dressed up', putting on lipstick and a proper coat, not an anorak like everyone else, and Mr V is wearing a smart black Stetson-style hat, instead of a flat cap, is fuelling this conviction (the hat making him look even taller).

Although we've come predominantly for construction materials, I can't resist looking at the kitchens, bathrooms and floor and wall tiles, and take note of things that will probably be obsolete by the time we're ready to buy them. I content myself with a door stop and some 'magic', green, Velcro-type tape that, according to the in-store video, does everything from wrap up your electrical cables to stop you slipping in the snow. Then it's off to IKEA for some coloured candles, and Swedish meatballs for lunch. The delights of Dijon once more will have to wait for another day.

EVERY PICTURE TELLS A STORY

*I*t's still unseasonably warm during the day, and I'm at the garden table, which we've moved from the patio to the terrace overlooking what will one day be our kitchen garden. I've just spied someone wearing a *gilet jaune,* a yellow 'be seen on the road' waistcoat, cycling past the house; only they haven't cycled past. They've stopped and dismounted and are calling *'Bonjour, madame,'* from the gate. I look up and see a small, stocky person with cropped, dark hair and dark eyes. I hesitate, as I'm not sure whether to reply *Bonjour madame* or *monsieur.* I take a chance on *madame,* and thankfully it's the right choice.

She's the neighbour from the house behind, whose land is separated from ours by a copse of trees that no one seems to know the ownership of. She's obviously come for a nose around, so I invite her inside. She's astonished at what we've achieved so far. Although we haven't started any visible renovation work, just the fact that the house has been cleared and cleaned has made an enormous difference. (Pappy Cardigan organised the clearing on behalf of the sellers; the cleaning was down to my mammoth efforts.) Apparently, the lady who lived here before us was a hoarder on a vast scale and kept absolutely everything from newspapers and yogurt pots[1], to broken plant pots and bins full of used medical ampoules, all inside the house. To enter any of the rooms it was necessary to walk side on like a crab and weave your way between boxes, bin bags, stacks of magazines and all the advertising bumf that most people put straight in the bin without even looking at.

Our neighbour, who I shall call Martine, was born in the hamlet, which was once indeed a village. She tells me that there used to be a bakery, post office, general store, café, bar, small hotel and even a train station. I've already told you that the house had served as a village primary school and, in the days of stagecoaches, a halt for the mail coach from Paris to Lyon, and a *relais de chasse* (Hunting Lodge). Martine tells me that the husband of the house ran an unofficial bar in what I plan to be my utility room, with tables and chairs spilling out onto the terrace. Local men would gather there to drink, smoke, play cards and generally escape their wives while partaking of the *eau de vie* (literally water of life), a moonshine liqueur that ironically shortened his life as he allegedly died of the drink in his late 40s. Not only were Martine and her husband both born here but her parents and grandparents also, so she has a wealth of knowledge of the history of the place; but maybe not all of it, as you're about to find out…

Spurred on by her evident enthusiasm in sharing all this information with me, I go to find the photos of the happy couple at their wedding, before their lives took a sadder turn. I show the first photo to Martine, explaining that I would like to put it in a frame and display it somewhere as part of the history of the house, and that I thought it was a shame that none of the relatives had cared enough to have kept such a lovely photo. She looks at it and does that thing that French people do with their mouths as they shrug their shoulders when they don't have an answer.

'But that isn't 'er,' she says. 'I don't know who this couple is, and this photo was taken far from here, south of Lyon; see, there is a stamp from the photographer.'

'That's strange,' I say. 'Maybe it was the wedding of one of the cousins whose children inherited the house. I have a second photograph of the entire wedding party with a group of children in it.'

I show her the second photo, and she scans the group, her eyes finally coming to rest on a woman at the back.

'That is 'er,' she says. 'And that,' pointing to the man that was standing with her, 'is my 'usband.'

This has obviously come as a shock. There are none of the accompanying explanations, such as 'Oh yes, they were a couple before we married' or 'I remember now. I was ill and couldn't attend this wedding'. Plus, this 'couple' were in their late 40s/early 50s. I would hazard a guess that this photo was taken after the lady of the house's dearly departed succumbed to the drink.

Fortunately, Mr V walks in on the scenario, and being his most charming self, whisks Martine away in a flurry of French to show her the progress he's made on the outbuildings, thus getting us out of a very embarrassing situation.

Needless to say she hasn't been back.

What I've learnt today: Some things are best left in the past.

---

1. Containers.

SHADES OF AUTUMN

*T*he Indian summer is a trompe-l'œil. The tall, green birch trees at the back of the house have been transformed into a shimmering, golden yellow. The morning mists are now full-on fog as Halloween approaches. The watery sun of the fading year filters through, casting an eerie light that gives the little hamlet a *Sleepy Hollow* effect. I half expect to see a headless horseman galloping down the lane. The sounds of autumn abound also: the tinkling of brittle leaves when the freshening breeze passes through them; the satisfying crunch of those that have already fallen to form a deep carpet underfoot, and the gentle thud of shiny, saddle-coloured conkers landing amongst them.

The 'feather tree' is ablaze. (I have no idea what it's really called, but its foliage is like delicate feathers.) Its dark green of summer has turned first citrus and now tangerine. It puts me in mind of a much-loved book, *The Flame Trees of Thika*. The crimson screen of Virginia creeper has withered away, and the poplars are bare skeletons of their former majestic selves, now forming a lacy screen through which the spectacular sunset can be seen in all its glory. Nature is truly magnificent. Who needs TV and the internet?

The supply of local produce from various neighbours continues, but now I'm receiving windfall apples, plums, pears, butternut squash and carrots, begging me to make more soups, chutneys, jams and compotes. Another sign that winter is approaching is the change in the passing traffic, from tractors laden with hay to wagons loaded with logs to keep the home fires burning throughout the coming season. We have our own impressive log store; impressive both in size and the way in which Mr V has stacked them, truly a work of art, judging by which I think he's done this before.

What I've learnt today: Logs for firewood are sold in steres, a stere being one cubic metre.

＊　＊　＊

The shortening days are emphasised by the shortening time between the ritual of opening and closing of the shutters. The other major change is the constantly fluctuating temperature throughout the day, mirrored by my constant change of clothes. I begin the morning in a thick, woolly, polo neck[1] with a camisole underneath and sleeveless gilet on top, jeans and thick socks and boots. The gilet is the first to go, and by the time I'm taking my morning coffee on the terrace, I've swapped the jumper for a long-sleeved T-shirt. Come the afternoon and I'm in a short-sleeved T-shirt, cropped pants and canvas deck shoes. Then the whole process begins again in reverse around afternoon tea. At this moment, I'm outside in shorts and tank top, painting patched-up shutters from the back of the house. Mr V has taken them off their hinges and stood them against a south-facing wall, hence the heat. Meanwhile he is wearing a heavy boiler suit with jeans and sweater underneath as he replaces guttering to a north-facing wall; it's like a different country back there.

Having finished the gutters, Mr V has turned his attention back to the loft. He wants to work until the battery goes in his cordless screwdriver, so dinner has to be something that can be ready with ten minutes' notice. Our eating habits have once again changed. Out with fresh tomatoes and cucumber and in with soups and curries made from seasonal root vegetables. This evening, however, I've opted for cottage pie as this can be heated through and browned while he's tidying his tools and taking a shower. The only problem is I'm short on most of the regular ingredients. But as I have my recently donated butternut squash, carrots, a couple of sweet potatoes and some of the green beans that I'd previously frozen, I padded out the potato topping with the sweet potatoes and roasted some cubes of butternut squash to add to the mince, diced carrots and sliced green beans, then popped it all into my newly acquired mini oven. The result was delicious and far more interesting than my usual dish. If you want to have a go, here's the recipe.

---

1. Turtleneck.

ALTERNATIVE AUTUMN COTTAGE PIE

Serves 2 generously

Ingredients

1 small/medium squash, cut into 1 cm (½ in) cubes
1 tbsp olive oil
200 g (7 oz) minced beef (veggie option—200 g (7 oz) green lentils). I
like to mix 100 g (3.5 oz) of each
2 large/4 small carrots, diced
1 medium shallot, finely chopped
440 ml (¾ pt) beef stock (I used an Oxo cube. For veggie option use
some Marmite or a vegetarian stock cube.)
2 small/medium potatoes, cut into medium chunks
2 small/medium sweet potatoes, cut into large chunks
2 handfuls green beans, sliced into quarters
Salt and pepper to season
Knob of butter

Method

Roast the squash in a little olive oil in a moderate oven for around 30
minutes until tender and beginning to brown slightly.

Dry-fry the mince in a heavy-based saucepan for 5 minutes. (If using
lentils, add after the carrots and shallot.)

Add the carrots and shallot and season lightly.

Add the hot stock and simmer for 20 minutes.

Boil the potatoes and sweet potatoes together in salted water until just tender.

Add the green beans to the mince and simmer for a further 10 minutes then stir in the roasted squash.

Taste to see if more seasoning is required then pour into an ovenproof dish.

Mash the potato and sweet potato together with a little butter and some black pepper.

Top the mince mixture with the potato and bake in a medium oven for around 20 minutes until the top begins to brown and crisp.

As we eat small portions here, I always have one left over for lunch the next day.

MAKING COMPOST

I have a new-found fascination and respect for nature. Autumn is upon us, and as I've said, things are winding down for winter. Even the feather/flame tree has lost its lustre overnight and is now a patchwork of muted orange and dusty brown with tiny remaining accents of green. Not everything is giving itself up to autumn so easily though. The solitary, spindly rosebush in the centre of the garden is still defiantly producing buds even as she withers.

The ground is alive, and now that the relentless sun has stopped scorching the earth. A carpet of green, thick foliage is pushing up everywhere. In one small rectangle of land, I count seventeen different species: delicate ferns, luxuriant moss, pretty little pansies, dandelions, buttercups and a host of others I can't identify. The stone walls are also alive with moss and grass and minute purple flowers protruding from every crack and crevice. We've something else protruding from the soil in a little box in a dark corner of the garden room. I've had my mini harvest of chestnut mushrooms grown in a box. It was such a thrill to see them pushing up out of the compost, and they were delicious fried in some salty butter with poached eggs for breakfast.

Speaking of compost, with all these fruit and vegetable peelings we've decided to start a compost heap. Apparently this is a lot more scientific than just throwing all your garden and cooking waste willy-nilly onto a pile; we even have an extensive booklet provided by the Environment and Energy Management Agency to guide us through the process. I won't bore you with the entire 23 pages devoted to 'How to make your own compost, reduce cooking waste and fertilise your garden organically'. But for townies like me, here's a simplified version:

- First you need to choose your site not too near where you plan outdoor eating; one that's fairly level and has good drainage to facilitate the worms getting in and doing their job of breaking down the waste.
- Either make or buy a sturdy compost bin that won't rot, and one that you can add waste to the top and take compost from the bottom.
- Good things to put in are healthy plant prunings and grass cuttings, fruit and vegetable peel and waste, eggshells and tea bags. Fallen leaves and old egg boxes can also be put in to provide fibre.
- Avoid putting weeds in as they could take root, and absolutely no dog or cat muck. The trick is getting the right balance between green (wet) and brown (dry) waste and regularly turning the compost to aerate it (putting some scrunched-up cardboard from time to time helps add air pockets).
- The compost is ready for use when you have a black/brown, soil-like layer at the bottom of the bin.

A SERIES OF UNFORTUNATE EVENTS

I'm having a bad day, if it's possible to have a bad day here. Maybe a series of unfortunate events is a better way to describe it. Firstly, the rings that I painstakingly sewed onto the heavy curtains a couple of weeks ago must all painstakingly come off as Mr V has found the original metal hooks that came from those particular curtains in an old cat food box (where else?). These rings belong on another set of curtains that he can't remember where he put. Secondly, I opened the door of an over-packed cupboard, and a box of pretzels for the apéritif spilt out all over the floor and dutifully smashed.

Then, while taking down the kitchen scales from the top shelf of the same cupboard (stupid place to put them, I know), the balance wasn't adequately screwed down and fell off, hitting me and causing a bruise like a bindi in the centre of my forehead. Next, I proceeded with the scales to the kitchen to weigh flour to make bread. There is obviously a problem with the balance, as despite me screwing it securely (or so I thought), the whole lot tipped over onto the floor, and all over my black sweater and jeans, that are now white.

Maddy, who was in the kitchen with me, came charging over to see if anything edible had fallen and went skidding in the flour. So now *she's* covered in it also (you couldn't make this up) and is leaving floury pawprints everywhere. Then to top it all, I selected the wrong programme on the bread machine, so when it was cooked, the bread was like a house brick and inedible.

'*C'est la vie*,' says Mr V. That's life.

To stay with the cooking theme, I'm pleased to say that I made a fruit compote with some of Pappy Cardigan's apples, plums and pears, without any of the above drama. I stewed four plums, two pears and a large, misshapen apple (all roughly chopped) with a handful of raisins, a sachet of vanilla sugar, a little cinnamon, a glug of red wine and enough water just to cover the fruit, until it reached a jam-like consistency. I served this with warm, homemade cardamom custard. I usually bash the cardamom pods with a steak hammer to release the seeds, but as I don't have one here, I came up with the idea of crushing them in a garlic press, and this is how I'll always do it from now on. The marriage of the lightly sweetened, tangy fruit and the slightly spicy, fragrant custard is sublime. I saved a little of the compote to serve with porridge for breakfast. I think in retrospect that I should have made a huge panful and stored it in preserve jars, but as we've already eaten the remaining fruit, this is one for next time. I'll give you the recipes for both compote and custard at the end of this chapter.

Mr V isn't thrilled at the prospect of porridge; he's eyeing it suspiciously and saying that this is what "orses eat', but I've convinced him that it isn't only perfectly edible but delicious. I've given it to him with the compote and a little warm milk, and he seems to enjoy it, but now he's looking for his baguette.

What I've learnt today: The iconic French baguette was invented in the 1920s after a law was passed prohibiting workers to begin work before 4 a.m. In order to have the bread baked in time for breakfast bakers began making long, thin loaves that cooked faster. The word baguette means wand, because of its shape. Therefore, in French, Harry Potter has une baguette magique.

FRUIT COMPOTE AND CARDAMOM CUSTARD

Serves 4

Compote

Ingredients

4 plums, roughly chopped
2 pears, roughly chopped
1 large apple, roughly chopped
Handful of raisins
Sachet of vanilla sugar
Cinnamon to taste
100 ml (a generous 3 fl oz) red wine
Water

Method

Gently stew the plums, pears, apple, raisins, vanilla sugar, cinnamon, red wine and enough water just to cover the fruit, until it reaches a jam-like consistency.

Cardamom Custard

Ingredients

300 ml (½ pint) full fat milk
6 cardamom pods, crushed
25g (1 oz) vanilla castor sugar
1 dsp[1] cornflour[2]
2 free range egg yolks

Method

Gently warm the milk in a pan with the cardamom pods.

Mix the sugar and cornflour in a large basin, then add the egg yolks, mixing well to avoid lumps.

When the milk reaches boiling point, quickly remove from heat and pour over the egg mixture, whisking vigorously.

Wipe the milk pan to remove any burnt milk stuck to the bottom, then return the custard to the pan and gently reheat, stirring constantly.

At this stage you can remove the cardamom pods, but I like to leave them in.

———————————————

1. Dessertspoon.
2. Cornstarch.

DECK THE HALLS

W e've had our first mail in our little green letterbox. Not mail exactly, but something other than publicity from various shops. The first was an envelope from the town hall. It contained a letter from the mayor, welcoming us into his commune, and a house number plaque with cream-coloured numbers on a claret-coloured tile. Part of me thinks this is a nice gesture; the other part is a little bit irked by being told what sort of plaque I should display. I was thinking of buying some Mediterranean number tiles, but they would have been totally out of place, so maybe Monsieur le Mayor is right. The second letter (more of a note really) is inviting us to a meeting in a neighbour's barn, to discuss what everyone is going to do to contribute to the Christmas decorations for the hamlet. And informing us that workshops are going to be held every Saturday afternoon throughout November and December in the *salle des fêtes* (village hall). We've also learnt that on every Friday evening during Advent the whole community traditionally gathers for a get-together.

So, off we trot to the meeting. But this isn't to discuss stringing up a few garlands and decorating a tree. This is like an executive board meeting in a barn. There's a secretary taking minutes to distribute to those unable to attend, and a treasurer taking donations from those who, like us, aren't physically contributing. This is *la France profonde* (deep rural France) at its deepest. There's to be a large *sapin de Noël* (Christmas tree) of course. But there are also wooden *sapins de Noël* to be made and displayed on the trunks of the trees lining the street. Plus, a wooden chalet the size of a double sentry box, containing 24 individually styled candles, one of which is to be lit each evening during the period of Advent, then all 24 to remain lit every evening until the New Year.

And to top it all, a scale model of Monsieur Mouton's farm, outside of which the Christmas tree and chalet will stand. Someone has just offered to make a miniature model of the farm, chalet and tree to place alongside a crib and nativity scene that another has agreed to make. I'm impressed and, I must admit, a little bit scared. This is serious business; people have notepads and pencils, hands are flying up asking questions about what size the wooden trees should be, is there any particular colour scheme, and how will the candles be protected from the wind and rain. It's decided that the candles should be long-burning varieties of those that you can buy in glass jars and containers, and two or three of the ladies said they'll paint and decorate the containers individually at the weekly workshops. Others suggest they make holly wreaths to hang on every front door or gate —no mean task.

We dutifully drop €20 into the bucket by the door, and I make a mental note to watch *Blue Peter*[1] Christmas specials on YouTube before next year.

* * *

Other news to report is that Maddy's abdomen is healing nicely, but she smells again from the wound on her leg. I'm continuing with the four meals a day, abundance of water and a little milk regime, and she's at this moment on the sofa on a cat cushion that belonged to Pussy Willow when she was a kitten. I've covered it in a heavy, floral cushion cover as she pads with her sharp, little claws and would rip it to shreds otherwise.

The next time we come will be the autumn half term holiday, so we'll have Pussy Willow with us, and she won't be allowed such privileges.

---

1. A British children's television programme, now the longest-running children's TV show in the world.

THE BONUS HOUR

*I*t's the last weekend of October, and we've just arrived with Pussy Willow. The spicy aroma of wood fires tinged with a base note of horse manure stings my nostrils. Local shops have notices in their windows advertising *fumier de cheval* (horse manure) for sale like they advertise prams and nursery items in Paris, and every chimney has a plume of ash-grey smoke spiralling into the sky. The clocks 'fall' back tonight, giving even fewer hours of daylight to make the house watertight and draughtproof before winter has us in its grip.

I don't believe in time. Those of you who know me well will know I always do things at the last minute and never know what day it is. I think that time is subjective and irrelevant and was invented by man. So, no surprise that here at Les Libellules we're not putting our clocks back. In fact, we hardly ever look at them anyway. We rise when we've had enough sleep, sleep when we're tired, eat when we're hungry and stop work and close the shutters when it gets dark. We have no trains to catch, meetings to attend or even TV programmes to watch. The only reference that we make to time is when I give Mr V a ten-minute warning that we're about to eat, but even this is a figurative reference, as it's measured by how much estimated cooking time is left, not what it says on the clock.

We shall have to put our watches back of course when we return to Paris in ten days. But we prefer to choose ourselves when we do this and take our 'bonus' hour (as this is how we look at it) when we most need it.

✳ ✳ ✳

It's 4:30 in the morning (or 3:30 if you insist). I'm at the open window in the rose room, with front row seats for the most spectacular sight. I've already told you that this area is famous with stargazers, and I've toyed with the idea of making part of the *pigeonnier* into a mini observatory, an idea that I'd now like to see come to fruition. There are thousands of stars sparkling like sequins on the inky velvet canvas of the night sky. I can easily make out numerous constellations but am no expert so would need a book to identify them. The air is crisp and cold, and although it's the middle of the night, I feel so awake and alive. I have a deep-rooted sense of happiness, and feel at one with the universe. Pussy Willow has been sleeping in her basket on the landing, she pushes the door open and comes to stand on her hind legs beside me, her front paws resting on the windowsill, staring up at the sky; she understands these things. My only frustration is that I don't have my best camera with me to capture the spectacle.

The clear night skies have produced our first frost. The field opposite looks like it's been dusted with icing sugar and is glistening in the early morning sun. The contrast with the golden autumn colours is stunning, and once again I curse myself for not bringing my Pentax with me. I'm nevertheless out in the crispy grass with my little bridge camera. The cows in the field are very obliging and practically pose now when they see me. Well two of them do; the other prefers to show me her derrière. I've christened the cows 'The Three Degrees'; notice I said three. There were five, and I try not to think where the other two might have gone. Mr V says that maybe they've gone skiing, which conjures up amusing images for me, as I'm sure it does you, but the truth is, the closer I'm living to animals, the more vegetarian meals I'm making. How can I accept a joint from one of Monsieur Mouton's sheep when I talk to them?

Despite the early morning frost, summer hasn't exactly given up the ghost. The day has transformed into one with cobalt-blue sky. It is officially sixteen degrees, though much warmer as three pairs of Mr V's heavy work jeans have dried on the line in less than two hours. I'm wearing a salmon-coloured, long-sleeved T-shirt and black jeans and have just walked to the recycling bins on the edge of the hamlet. A pleasant walk that takes me past fields of docile grazing sheep and to the war memorial at the crossroads where there are lovely views across open farmland to the hills in the distance. The autumn breeze has blown away the carpet of conkers and leaves and left gravel to crunch satisfyingly beneath my feet.

On my return, I have the entire hamlet stretched out in front of me, the gently curving, unmade road with its honey-stone houses and hydrangeas still in faded bloom. If you took away the handful of cars parked at the side of the road, you could be looking at a scene from another century.

As I approach Les Libellules I have a hairy moment. Both Pussy Willow and Maddy are waiting for me on either side of the corner of the garden wall. I have a good view of them, as they do of me; but they can't see each other. Unaware and off guard they begin to run towards me—and the corner—therefore also towards their rival for my affection. They come to a screeching halt as they meet face to face. I freeze, fearing the worst, but they both flatten their ears, bare their teeth, hiss and promptly flee in opposite directions.

It's the 1st of November, *Toussaint* (All Saints' Day), a public holiday in France. We don't have the frenzy of Halloween here as they do in the UK and USA. Rather than the shops being filled with plastic pumpkins and witches' hats, the pavements outside florists and general stores are crammed with chrysanthemums in yellow, orange, gold, purple and white. These are also in abundance in the local markets and outside the cemeteries, which are in turn packed with families laying the plants at the graves of loved ones and ancestors.

But the trend of dressing up and going from door to door for treats is beginning to catch on; the trick part thankfully isn't—as yet. Children tend to greet you with a smile and say, *'Bonjour, madame/monsieur,'* rather than pelt your door with a box full of eggs if you don't answer. A little troupe of three- to thirteen-year-olds accompanied by two adults came calling last night. Nine of them in total, all the children of the hamlet in fact, this way people were only disturbed once during the evening. The majority were dressed as cats with a couple of the older girls dressed as non-scary witches. Still, our Dutch neighbour was taken totally by surprise because this hasn't caught on at all in Holland, and the only thing that he had to offer them was cheese. I fared only marginally better with tangerines and some biscuits. We've both made a mental note to make sure we have a tub of Haribos next year.

✳ ✳ ✳

Mr V and I are outside on our tatty little terrace drinking our morning coffee with a cat growling beneath each chair. Pussy Willow and Maddy are having a stand-off (or sit-off). It's such a treat to be out in the sunshine, regarding the jungle of long grass and molehills in front of us, dreaming up plans of where to plant the fruit trees and bushes, and beds of vegetables and herbs. There's so much to do, we don't know where to start, but I'm not striving for 'French country home style'. I already have more than I ever imagined possible right here in this small outdoor space. I have somewhere to sit and have a coffee and read a book, somewhere I can put washing to dry, and somewhere to have plants such as basil, mint, tomatoes, geraniums and lavender in pots; with all this and so much more, I feel truly blessed.

I dislike that concept of the house ever being 'finished' and am relishing the simplicity of life at the moment. I like the fact that I don't have a kitchen as such, so no need to continually wipe down worktops, constantly brush up crumbs or keep things in order. I like the fact that we've limited intrusion from the outside world and are liberated from the non-stop news and social media feeds that subtract from life as much as they add. I take pleasure in small things and appreciate all with a heightened awareness: the crackle of logs in the fire, the soft light filtering through the antique lace curtains, the aroma of freshly brewed coffee and recently baked bread, the smell of wood smoke pervading the air, and the sense that I am at last complete.

What I've learnt today: It isn't the bright, dancing flame but the smouldering, red embers that give heat from a fire. Maybe this is an analogy for love as it isn't the first flush of excitement that sustains but the deeper, mutual respect, acceptance and tolerance, all of which are needed in bucket loads when taking on a project like this.

ONE MAN'S TRASH IS ANOTHER MAN'S TREASURE

We've just returned from an enjoyable afternoon with some very good friends, one of whom is blind. I refrained from taking my scrapbook of photos charting the modest progress so far at Les Libellules as I didn't want her to feel excluded. (When she reads this she'll tell me I was being ridiculous; she has a programme that scans text and speaks the words.) But it's made me realise that I've not included much actual description of the house. So, this is for her benefit and indeed for all readers to furnish your minds with pictures.

Les Libellules nestles on the edge of a small hamlet that consists of one road that curves like a longbow from the main road and back again. She is small and low and set back a little, dwarfed by the buildings either side, making her hidden from view until you're almost on top of her. She is an extremely pretty house even in her present state, with many square-panelled French doors with chocolate-brown shutters that I intend to paint in the same claret red as the number plaque. The roof is made from terracotta tiles, and the greyish render is crumbling, revealing large patches of her stone walls. There's a *pigeonnier* that looks like a small turret with a round pointed roof that is begging for a weathercock to be placed upon it.

To the front there's a fair-sized garden, which we'll eventually divide into a *potager*, a plantation for fruit and vegetables, and extend the patio unto an area for eating and entertaining. At the rear there's a large outbuilding separated into two; one part is used as a garage, and the other, having secure inner rooms, is used as a wood store and tool shed. To the back the land is bordered by tall silver birch trees and to the side by the *abreuvoir*.

Inside, downstairs we have a living room with a large, open fireplace and imposing chimney breast with tall windows either side looking out onto a romantic ruin, which our neighbours have left standing to provide a private enclosure to their back garden. The living room leads into an average-sized kitchen with a partition wall forming what was a downstairs bedroom that we intend to take down to make a kitchen/dining room. This in turn leads to what I refer to as the garden room, an odd-shaped space which is partially below the *pigeonnier*. It's here that I would like to create a quiet sitting room and my study. There's a downstairs bathroom and a later-built (we think), single-storey extension housing an enormous fuel tank the size of a young elephant. This will eventually be a utility area once the elephant is no longer in the room.

Upstairs there are two moderate-sized double bedrooms, a landing large enough to put a second bathroom, plus the entrance to the *pigeonnier* with its 500 or more pigeon holes full of dust, cobwebs and rubble waiting for me to clean in spring. There's an ancient, bolted door that leads from the *pigeonnier* onto a small Juliet balcony with metal railings, big enough for two people to stand on (or two people and a cat), which gives views over the gentle rolling hills and farmland beyond, and the spire of the church poking out from the terracotta roofs in the next village.

Inside the living room resembles Steptoe's yard with an eclectic mix of furniture including a 30-year-old nursery cupboard, which I'm particularly fond of, that stores towels and toiletries. There are two carver chairs from a care establishment where my cousin works, a small, gate-legged table that belonged to the father of a friend, an IKEA sofa bed, and a packing case full of breakables covered with a piece of cloth and serving as a side table. Sitting on a wooden trolley with wheels is a small combined television and DVD player that only plays DVDs as we have no TV aerial. In the centre of the room is an oversized coffee table that I use as a desk which looks like it came from a Moroccan restaurant, and probably did, as Mr V found it on the street with *les encombrants*.

I need to digress once more to explain *les encombrants* to those unfamiliar with them. In Paris, and I should imagine other large towns in France, on every third Sunday in the month from around 6 p.m. onwards, locals leave a variety of unwanted articles at designated collection points on the street. It is customary for people to go out and see if anything is there that interests them, and what's left the bin men take the next morning. I was horrified when I first moved to France at the idea of scavenging through other people's rubbish, but there's no stigma in this, and it's quite normal and accepted. The French as a nation are much more conscious of waste than the Brits. The concept of repair and reuse, rather than throw away and buy another, is much more prevalent in their society. This is a way of reducing waste and cutting down on manufacturing and unnecessary expenditure. We've had some marvellous finds including a brand-new, double electric hotplate still in its box that I'm using now; an also brand-new bread machine, just missing the instruction booklet that Mr V subsequently found on the net, an elegant, barley-twist-legged trolley on castors, a cat basket and a hideous vase that turned out to be the French equivalent to Troika and worth a few pennies.

This scavenging instinct has now spread to the local tip, and we seem to come back with as much as we take. Mr V is in his element climbing into skips, salvaging roof tiles, guttering, pieces of kitchen worktop, bits of wood and plastic tubing and even two metal wine racks that hold 100 bottles apiece that he's taken all the rust off with a wire brush and dutifully painted in special black metal paint. They are now in the *cave* (cellar) with the beginnings of our wine collection. Please note: this was the first thing that he did when we got the keys; talk about getting your priorities right.

The man at the tip, David (pronounced Dah-veed), a sort of

younger, bronzer version of David Essex with bad teeth, has taken a bit of a shine to me. He keeps things to one side that he thinks I might find of interest, such as a gorgeous, gilt framed, bevelled-edged mirror and some pictures, which in themselves weren't interesting, but their frames could come in useful. He's also told me that he has a nice carved cabinet that he picked up at a house clearance. He runs a little business on the side, selling things for people for a small profit for himself, so he's a handy bloke to know.

This culture of upcycling goes much deeper in our little community. Neighbours stop on their way to the tip with their loaded trailers to see if anyone can find anything useful before disposing of the contents, and it isn't unusual to see a little group rummaging through what someone else considers junk. This way I've found another single hot plate in perfect working order, an African-print tablecloth perfect for outside, and a mop and bucket, which I was in dire need of as I couldn't find a traditional mop bucket with a wringer anywhere.

To return to the tour of the house. The kitchen, as I've mentioned, is little more than a collection of appliances and an assortment of working surfaces fashioned out of bits of old worktop, some of which indeed came from David's skips, but I manage to feed Mr V his four-course meal twice a day. I think you've already got a pretty good picture of the bathroom facilities. And even without its immense size taking up a good quarter of the space, the smell from the elephant sized fuel tank prevents us from using the utility room for anything more than to store the garden table and chairs. I think I'll be on my fourth book before I can describe anything more salubrious.

ALL MOUTH AND NO TROUSERS

*P*ussy Willow and Maddy seem to have called a truce and are both in the same room. Pussy Willow is on the sofa and Maddy on my dining chair. She's doing that contented cat padding thing again on my elephant cushion. What she would have really liked was to be up on the sofa alongside Pussy Willow, but Willow was having none of that and gave a throaty growl when Maddy showed signs of trying to jump up. Still, this is a great improvement. Pussy Willow won't tolerate Flaubertine in the least and actively attacks her now if she approaches a door or window. Maddy has also begun to hiss if Flaubertine gets too close, as though Pussy Willow is tolerating her individually; if she comes with Flaubertine in tow, she gets attacked also.

Pussy Willow's new-found bravado doesn't extend to humans however. She's all mouth and no trousers and is pretty much scared of her own shadow. I was patrolling the garden with her earlier, when a tall, elderly gentleman appeared dressed in 'town-people' clothes, as opposed to looking like a farmer or building site labourer like the rest of us. I smiled, waved and returned his *bonjour*. Pussy Willow by contrast instantly crouched down in the long grass, terrified. I have to claim a degree of responsibility for this. When she was a kitten, to prevent her from darting out of the apartment whenever the door was opened, I invented 'the cat catcher', a man who comes with his sack to collect the naughty cats and dump them in the river. (I know, I know; this isn't nice, and cats can't understand, can they?) Well it seemed to work. It worked so well that when my extremely tall stepson arrived dressed in black with his backpack slung over his shoulder, she hid under the bed during his entire visit. As I write, she has realised that I'm no longer on 'playground duty' and has come looking for me to escort her outside again.

This fear of strangers manifested itself again when we had a visit from a young woman who came to discuss our *abreuvoir*, which has been officially classed as a *mare*, an area of wetland that attracts wildlife. This astonished me as usually Pussy Willow is very fond of young female visitors who don't resemble the cat catcher, but she shot off as soon as the young woman appeared at the French doors. I had no idea where she'd gone until later in the afternoon I found her hiding on the deep marble window ledge behind the curtain in the bathroom.

I must explain why the bathroom curtain is permanently drawn. We're not overlooked at the back of the house, and I was in the habit of going to the toilet in full view of the large window, which is very old and many panelled, not a modern variety with frosted glass. This is the only source of natural light in the room, and if the curtain is closed it's very dark. I've mentioned that we have frequent neighbours stopping by, bearing gifts or just coming for a progress report. What I've not mentioned is that Mr V has the same 'tour guide' tendencies as Maddy. It was on such an occasion when yet another passing farmer stopped in the hope of being offered an apéritif (as also often happens). Mr V decided to show him the window that he'd just fitted in one of the outbuildings directly opposite the toilet. I prayed that they wouldn't turn around, but my husband was already starting to say that the next window he planned to replace was the one that I was sitting behind minding my own business. Needless to say, I didn't join them for a Pastis on the terrace.

*   *   *

Now to get back to the purpose of the said young woman's visit. Our *mare* is overgrown with duckweed, and as the water is stagnant, it is filthy dirty. We were surprised that it attracted dragonflies, who generally favour clean water, so we planned to drain it and clear the surrounding area in spring then plant lilies to aerate the water and add some carp to eat the mosquito larvae. The young woman, whose name we learn is Lisa, from the Burgundy Wetlands Networks, part of the Autun Society of Natural History, was driving past, and noticed that we had a small *mare* so left a note in our mailbox asking could she come and discuss with us how best to look after it. Thankfully she stopped us in time, as our plans would have been devastating for the very biodiversity that we were hoping to encourage.

Emptying the *mare* in spring would have destroyed all the larvae harbouring there, including my beloved dragonflies. Plus introducing fish would have further threatened not only larvae, but any frog, toad or newt eggs (these all feast upon dragonfly larvae also, but not on such a grand scale as carp). These *mares* are the natural habitat of many threatened species, providing a unique environment for both aquatic and terrestrial plants, insects and amphibians. They are mostly not natural wet areas, but man made, so if not cleaned and maintained, they will fill in over time, leaving the species that have made them their home nowhere to go. We've now become members of the Society for the Protection of *Mares* in Burgundy.

What I've learnt today: Don't sit on a toilet with the curtains open.

HOW TO CREATE A WILDLIFE-FRIENDLY POND

- Your pond should be in a sunny position and protected from the wind.
- It should have a minimum surface area of 8 metres square, and be a minimum of 1.2 metres to a maximum of 2 metres deep, but not uniformly, as ideally it should have terraced sides to allow animals to climb out easily. The depth in the centre will help prevent it from totally freezing during winter and drying out in summer.
- After you've dug your area, bank down the ground before covering with a layer of sand, then cover the sand with a sheet of polystyrene and finally another deeper layer of sand, followed by large pebbles.
- Don't put soil in the pond.
- It's better to fill the pond with uncontaminated rainwater collected in a water butt; tap water can be used but sometimes contains chlorine and lime, which can alter the delicate chemical balance.
- Don't put fish into the pond as these aren't natural inhabitants, and they'll eat insect larvae and amphibian

eggs. (If you want fish, construct a separate, ornamental fish pond.)

- Likewise, don't use any pesticides or chemicals to clean the water. It's recommended that no pesticides or treatments are used within 5 metres of a pond, lake or well (including treatment of gutters and drainpipes, reservoir tanks, etc.).
- Discourage people, especially children, from throwing food (bread, etc.) into the pond to feed the wildlife; this will rot and decay and contaminate the water.
- Remember amphibians are protected in most European countries, so it's illegal to collect frogspawn from the wild, even if you intend to populate your pond. You must have patience and wait for them to find you.

Plants should be planted in four levels:

1. Plants on dry land at the water's edge, with abundance of foliage providing shelter and shade.
2. Plants with their roots in the water, such as reeds with long stems that larvae hatched in the water can climb up.
3. Plants on the surface, such as lilies, providing shelter and shade beneath the water, but they spread very quickly and must be controlled otherwise the pond won't be able to obtain oxygen through its surface, and they'll choke out other plants.
4. Plants totally submerged for underwater feeding.

DON'T PANIC!

It's a well-known fact that I suffer with claustrophobia in the extreme. This isn't totally unfounded, as I've been stuck in more places than anyone else I know. It's as if life is trying to desensitise me, only it's not working, as I'm becoming more and more neurotic. This all began when I was about five and was stuck in my grandparents' outside toilet. I combatted this fear until I moved to Paris—a city where over 7,000 people are reported to be stuck in lifts a year.

The second incident was in a hotel toilet in a very old part of the city. It had one of those cogs that picks up the thread on a bar, which in turn slides to open and close the door. This cog had been around so long that it was now more of a smooth disk with absolutely no teeth to engage with the bar, hence someone had to come with a screwdriver to get me out.

I fell victim to another old worn lock in a toilet in the Tuileries Gardens, and this time it was Mr V who came to my rescue with a screwdriver. (He always has a small screwdriver and torch in his jacket pocket; he's lived in Paris long enough to know how things don't always work as one would expect.)

The fourth incident was in a lift, again in an old building. It was the type that the inner concertina-style door must fully open before releasing the catch on the outer one. The inner door didn't fully open, becoming jammed about ten centimetres from the frame. I spent a very panicky five minutes or so travelling between the ground and sixth floor with the door partially opening each time the lift stopped, until a man was waiting on the ground floor and wrenched the door, releasing me from my cage. We have one such contraption in our 1920s apartment building at Paris which I never use now after my suitcase containing my passport and tickets got stuck between the second and third floors when I was on my way to the airport, and I almost missed my plane.

I can now add Les Libellules to my list of toilet tales. I knew that the handle on the door was dodgy so always left it slightly ajar (warning Mr V not to bring any unsuspecting neighbour for an interior tour), but a gust of wind slammed it shut, and it jammed. I couldn't escape through the window as it has security bars only wide enough for Pussy Willow just about to squeeze through, plus Mr V was drilling and banging in the loft so couldn't hear me screaming and banging downstairs. In the end I pulled on the handle so hard that I ripped open the base of my thumb, but I succeeded in freeing myself. Needless to say, I insisted that Mr V remove the handle altogether, so now you must block the door with the laundry basket to prevent it from swinging open while you're on the toilet or in the shower.

I'm not alone in being trapped at Les Libellules. Mr V himself has been trapped in his toolshed, and, he has only just admitted, was trapped in the loft after the ladder fell while he was there alone one weekend. As the ceiling is over three metres high he had to phone Pappy Cardigan, who has a key, to come and replace the ladder. But worst of all was Pussy Willow's experience...

I'd completed the nightly closing of the shutters, and we settled down for an apéritif before dinner. Now, I must tell you that Pussy Willow's nickname is aperocat as she likes to sit between us on the sofa and join in. This particular evening she was unusually absent, which was very strange, as we had her favourite—foie gras. I called her, but she didn't respond. What was even stranger was the fact that we were having duck for dinner, by far her preferred meat. I went upstairs and looked in the bedrooms to see if she was there, and went into the *pigeonnier*, even though it is kept closed. I looked in the kitchen and the dining-room-cum-dump, behind the bathroom curtain, inside boxes in the garden room, and in the utility room, but there was no sign of her. Thinking she must have slipped out while I was closing the shutters, I went outside to call her and heard a muted cry in response. And that's when I found her, over an hour after we noticed that she was missing, trapped in the narrow space between the closed shutter and the garden room door, standing on hind legs, her panic-stricken eyes and ears just visible through the glass panels which start a third of the way up the door.

Sadly she'd missed the foie gras but happily was in time for a plate of duck.

What Pussy Willow has learnt today: Don't sneak out of a door once the shutters are closed on the other side, or you could find yourself trapped between the two.

HAPPY FAMILIES

*O*ur first real guests have come to stay at Les Libellules: my youngest daughter, Natasia and her husband Tim. They'd already seen the house briefly in summer when they came with us on an accompanied visit. That time there was still a lot of rubbish and rubble to be cleared, and the place had an abandoned air, so they can see a big difference now.

My daughter is a cat person; my son-in-law is a cat magnet. We have no idea why, but cats just gravitate towards him. Pussy Willow spends her time on his shoulder like a fat, overgrown parrot when they visit us in Paris. Maddy has also fallen for his charms. She's attached herself to his shoe like a pom-pom on a slipper, and he's having to slide his foot across the floor to walk. My daughter is trying her best to entice Maddy onto her knee, but Maddy's chosen her champion for the weekend, and no one else is getting a look-in.

It's so lovely to have family staying here. I long for the day when the house will be ready enough to have both my daughters and their husbands at the same time to all share a meal on the patio, as I've dreamt of so many times over the past ten years living in a small apartment. I would also love to have a couple of grandchildren playing in the garden; but for now I'll have to content myself with cats.

※   ☀   ☀

We've been walking in the hills that look down on the hamlet and could make out Les Libellules tucked in amongst the huddle of houses with her distinctive, red-roofed *pigeonnier* and curly smoke rising from her chimney. Maddy walked with us part of the way, weaving around our legs from one to another, undecided who to walk beside: her trusted friends or these exciting newcomers who have been lavishing her with affection. I'm happy to report that she's looking, and smelling, much better. Her wound is healing nicely, and she's put on some much-needed weight. Her coat is smoother, and she's generally in a much better condition. Mr V says that she'll be pretty when she's grown, and I can see that she's beginning to blossom. My daughter and son-in-law are both enchanted by her, and the attraction is obviously mutual. On our return she was waiting for us at the limits of her comfort zone with a rather sulky little expression on her face at having been left behind. She was more than compensated by strokes, cuddles and cat treats from my daughter.

※   ☀   ☀

We're visiting the nearby town of Saulieu, the capital of the Morvan district, which is home to the beautiful Morvan National Park. Saulieu is an interesting little town in itself. It has a lively Saturday morning market, which in summer has a wine bar in the centre where locals meet up and stand at high round tables knocking back bottles of chilled rosé at 10 o'clock in the morning. There's also a van where people stand around sampling wines in a try-before-you-buy manner. From what I've witnessed, there seems to be more trying than buying.

The goods on sale are varied, with stalls selling glorious, fresh seasonal fruit and vegetables, pungent cheeses and local honey, and people selling eggs direct from the boot of their cars. There's a stall packed with brightly coloured rustic baskets and another selling North African handicrafts, ethnic leather sandals and beaded bracelets. There are flowers and plants and live chickens and birds. Plus, another stall of bric-à-brac that has a vast selection of porcelain doorknobs that I adore and have a tin full of them waiting for furniture to put them on.

But as it isn't market day, we head for Café Parisien in the square in the town centre to have a coffee and people watch. Café Parisien dates from 1832 and is officially classified as a Historic Café of Europe and quoted in the Inventory of Historical Buildings of Europe. Despite the temperature being quite chilly, it is fine and dry, so we sit outside, looking out across the cobbled square to the basilica and fountain of Saint-Andoche. There are a group of expat Americans at the next table, who I've seen here regularly, but I've not met any Brits as yet. Apart from the Americans, all the other customers are French and are quietly smoking, and reading their newspapers while drinking their coffee, red wine or Cognac.

The café has long been a meeting place for musicians and artists and was frequented by both the sculptor François Pompon and two-Michelin-star chef Bernard Loiseau, for whom the town is also famous. Exhibitions and concerts are still hosted in the back rooms that were once used to play billiards and cards.

As well as the striking Romanesque Basilica of Saint-Andoche there's the Museum of Pompon on the life of the sculptor who hailed from Saulieu. There's a life-size bronze replica of one of his most famous animal sculptures—*Le Taureau* (The Bull)—standing in the town. A collection of huge resin animals by the acclaimed French artist Richard Orlinski is also dotted around. These include a giant red gorilla at the top of the steps at the entrance to the market, fighting polar bears at the fountain, and most bizarre of all, a bright red crocodile in the medieval courtyard behind the basilica, sharing the space with a classical, limbless torso of Christ.

After our coffees we meander through the small back streets and pass a shop with its very own bizarre statue: a huge male mannequin over two metres tall, wearing a lumberjack jacket and a pair of cheap denim jeans. This wouldn't be so odd if the shop were also selling outsized men's wear. Instead it's displaying ladies winceyette nighties, lacy underslips, nylon housecoats and dummy legs sporting American-tan-coloured stockings. The entire shop window is like a scene from the 1950s. I can't resist the temptation to pose for a photo, causing other shoppers to look at me as if I'm mad.

There's another shop from another world, selling what I first thought were walking canes, but on closer inspection I saw they were long-handled shoehorns with fabulous handles such as a mock ivory horse's head, and the head of a parrot very similar to that on the handle of Mary Poppins's umbrella. I don't know anyone who uses a regular shoehorn anymore (although they do pop up with regularity in Christmas crackers), let alone a long-handled one. I'm so tempted to buy a couple to display on a wall somewhere.

A little further down the road we entered into another mini time zone: an ancient patisserie with a jolly lady of West Indian origin serving the most amazing cakes and pastries at a third of the cost that I would pay for the same thing in Paris. (I know, every patisserie in France serves amazing cakes and pastries, but I've sampled a lot, and this is one of the best.) There are juicy whole figs stuffed with vanilla custard and wrapped in almond paste flavoured with pistachio nuts, *mille-feuilles*, layers of flakey pastry filled with custard or cream, that I dread someone wanting as, along with other words containing multiple vowels; I have great difficulty in pronouncing. There are easier to pronounce classic 'opera' cakes, like a sophisticated tiramisu, and sumptuous tarts with wafer-thin pastry loaded with various seasonal fruits.

If you looking for more than a cake to eat, Café Parisien serves simple, regional meals, but if you want to really push the boat out, then there's the two-star Bernard Loiseau restaurant and spa which has welcomed many celebrity diners, including Prince Rainier, Orson Wells, Charlie Chaplin and the Aga Khan to name but a few. But be warned—menus range from a €75 lunch to an eye watering €330 dinner. Meanwhile back at Les Libellules we're having a five-star raclette—stars awarded for company and ambience.

For those not familiar with raclette, it's the name of the Swiss cheese which is best suited for melting. A raclette grill takes its name from the cheese and is a hotplate and grill combined that griddles meat (notably ham) on the hotplate and melts raclette cheese under the grill. It is traditionally served with finger-sized cornichons and small boiled or steamed potatoes in their skins, which you pour the melted cheese over. I usually also cook slices of lean steak and serve with a bowl of green salad, but as my daughter doesn't eat meat, we've cooked strips of haloumi cheese and large prawns on the griddle also.

A raclette is a really fun thing to do. There's a good atmosphere around the table as everyone cooks their own food; another plus is that people can eat as much or as little as they like. Traditionally in the Alps it's served with white wine, but as we're in Burgundy, we opt for a light red. The fire is blazing and the wine and conversation flowing and, on the insistence of my daughter, Maddy is allowed to stay while we eat and is rewarded for good behaviour (i.e. not jumping on the table) with a little plate of ham and steak.

After the meal we gather around the coffee table in front of a log fire and play a game of Frog Families (happy families with frogs) that my daughter bought as a joke for Mr V for his birthday.

A perfect way to end a perfect stay.

PART III
THE WINTER OF FIRE
AND ICE

DECEMBER 2017 AND JANUARY 2018

No boughs have withered because of the wintry wind;
The boughs have withered because I've told them my dreams.
'The Withering of the Boughs', W.B. Yeats

MULLED WINE AND 'GINCE' PIES

e're driving back to Les Libellules through a winter wonderland. The trees lining the road are decked out in their finery of snow; no longer green, gold, russet or brown, but pure dazzling white. The sun, huge and low in the sky, has a silvery hue, tricking me into thinking that she was the moon. The roads are miraculously snow-free. I say miraculously as year after year in the UK this scenario is met by traffic chaos. We pass through a tunnel of alabaster branches that bend low to greet us, weighed down by their wintery burden, and emerge into a Christmas card vista of frosted fields, sparkling in the light of what is now undeniably the sun. The milky sky has melted into blue, the scene is breathtaking, but all is not well at Les Libellules, notably the absence of Maddy as we get out of the car. Normally she's in the garage before the engine is switched off. Flaubertine arrived after we'd been here about ten minutes, so the meow is out that we're in residence. I don't like the way that Flaubertine has planted herself on the back step as she never does when Maddy is around. Mr V says Maddy has found another house (as he says the cows have gone skiing), but I fear the worst.

Also, the tool store is flooded. Any light objects are floating around in over 30 centimetres of water, like ducks on a murky pond, and Mr V's prized lawnmower is partially submerged. There must have been exceptionally heavy rain as the *mare* and two ditches on a neighbour's land at the back are full to overflowing, and the trickle of a stream that runs behind the copse of trees at the rear of the house is now a small, fast-flowing river. To top it all it looks like we have mice; a box of dry cat food that was on the kitchen floor has been chewed through by some nimble, little teeth. I'm imagining these are field mice akin to those who don bonnets and sing in *A Muppet's Christmas Carol*, so I'm not going to 'bah humbug' about them at the moment.

The hamlet, by contrast, is looking very festive. The decoration workshops have obviously been a success, so much so that we've attracted a film crew from TF1 (France's equivalent to BBC1), so the model of Monsieur Mouton's farm and the giant candle Advent calendar are going to be on TV. It's just a shame that we can't see it.

※ ※ ※

We're at the Advent get-together in the barn where the meeting was held. Between 20 to 30 neighbours are already crammed together around two enormous vats of both red and white *vin chaud* (mulled wine), and more are arriving with plates of apero nibbles and mini desserts. I for my part have made some 'gince' pies (mince pies liberally laced with gin) as an English novelty, and also brought foie gras and a warm baguette as a safer bet.

Monsieur Mouton looks like what my father called a Teddy Boy when I was growing up, with slicked-back hair, black leather jacket and his ample derrière squeezed into a pair of tight jeans with ten-centimetre turnups. His muddy wellies are replaced by totally unsuitable, black winklepickers, and his usually whiskered face is clean shaven and scrubbed to a shine to rival his shoes. The entire effect is a little disturbing. Mr V says that it's for my benefit, and as he holds up his third gince pie and beams at me from the other side of the room, I think Mr V could be right.

Martine is here also, her cropped hair hidden beneath a black hat that looks like an upturned plant pot covered in large, red, crocheted flowers. She's wearing bright red lipstick; her face is flushed and her eyes sparkling with the effects of the wine. I get the feeling that she's avoiding me after the wedding photo revelation. I in turn am occupied by a tiny retired carpenter who Mr V has thrust in my direction to sweeten him up before he asks him for help fitting much-needed double-glazed windows in the bedrooms. He reeks of something much stronger than wine, and I can't understand a word he's saying as he's slurring his speech. He's grinning at me, so I grin back and nod in agreement when I think it's called for. Mr V says his breath smells of home-made *eau de vie*. I think it smells like methylated spirits. I hope nobody lights a match.

I'm presented to so many people that I've no chance of remembering all their names, and even the faces are becoming bleary as my plastic cup of steaming wine seems to be permanently full. Everyone is eager to know how we are settling, and even more eager to hear that we love it here, as they clearly all do. One lady, Solène, is particularly welcoming, and I get the impression that she's a bit of a matriarch, sort of the Queen Mother of the hamlet, respected by all. Mr V is smiling and nodding at me approvingly, so I'm obviously doing a good PR job, and my French seems to be flowing as effortlessly as the wine. I read somewhere that alcohol aids language production, so I'm putting this down to research...

✳ ⚊ ✳

The evening has been a great success. My gince pies have gone down a treat. The neighbours are very friendly and welcoming; it was kisses all round and many neighbours have asked me to *tutoyer* them (call them by the '*tu*' form of the word 'you', usually reserved for family and close friends instead of the more formal '*vous*'). Towards the end of the evening, there was no room at the inn, and people were standing outside drinking *vin chaud* in the snow. There were babies in prams, assorted-aged children sneakily taking the bonbons from the table, couples, singles, pensioners and even a few cats (but sadly no Maddy). It's so lovely to feel part of this unique little community, and it's magical walking arm in arm with Mr V, warmed by the wine and the welcoming ambience, through the softly falling snow, past the little chalet of half-lit Advent candles to our fireside.

PUT A LITTLE BIRD HOUSE IN
YOUR SOUL

e've woken to another winter wonderland scene, but these snowflakes are far less amicable than the ones that floated down upon us last night, dissolving like gentle kisses on our cheeks. They stab and sting my eyes like tiny, frozen arrows, and explode on my lips and tongue. There's a stillness all around, and the sound from the nearby road is muffled like it's passing through cotton wool. Mr V's bird houses are a hive of activity with gorgeous blue and yellow tits hopping in and out and swinging from the balls of grain and fat. Apart from setting up the essential wine racks, another of Mr V's priority jobs was making these little, wooden feeding stations. We'd seen a variety of small garden birds pecking in the soil during autumn. As the winters here are harsh and the ground too hard with frost for little beaks to penetrate, we were concerned for our feathered friends.

We were also concerned that as we've been providing an all-day buffet for the cats they'd see the birds as being on the menu, so we had to come up with a cunning plan to kitty-proof them. I'd seen a programme on TV about an amazing lady who had turned her garden into a virtual bird sanctuary. I don't have such grand designs, but many of her ideas were ingenious, such as fastening small, plastic sieves full of birdseed to trees. These are just strong enough to take the weight of the smallest birds, and they provide good drainage for the seeds if it rains. Another idea was filling a cheap rubber balloon whisk with a fat ball. Fat is much needed during the winter months as our little resident robin can lose up to 10% of his body weight in a single night, just trying to keep warm. Mr V's houses are indeed houses: one bright yellow with a green wooden roof, the other, cream with a red tile roof.

Now the problem of how to deter the cats. It had been suggested to put nails in the tree trunks to prevent the cats from climbing up, but we're very conscious of the sensitive nature of trees and felt that this would harm them, so we've attached the bird houses by a metal band around the trunks, secured with a clip. It was logical then to find a wider strip of sheet metal to form a slippery reflective band to stop the cats scaling the heights to the restaurant in the sky. In reality I think that any self-respecting bird would fly off at the mere sight of a cat in the garden. That being said, Pussy Willow is pretty slick for her size and almost had a finch feeding from seeds on the branches of a bush in summer. It was only my quick action with a salad bowl of tomatoes that alerted the bird and shocked the cat, with tomatoes raining down on her. Passata was on the menu that evening.

If you want to attract different varieties of birds you need to provide a selection of seeds and nuts, but a universal favourite is the insides of sunflower seeds (the husks are too hard and take too much valuable effort to remove). If you'd like to make your own fat balls then here's the recipe that the lady on TV gave, which I've tried, and it goes down a treat.

FAT BALLS FOR WILD BIRDS

Ingredients

(Equal amounts of each)
Apple, chopped
Sunflower seeds, hulled
Sugar-free muesli
Wild birdseed
Lard

Method

Hull the sunflower seeds by crushing them with a rolling pin and removing their hard shells.

Mix the ingredients together.

Roll into balls the size of golf balls and set in the fridge overnight.

You can make little sacks to hang them in from the netting in which you can buy fruit and vegetables.

NOT QUITE THE WEEKLY SHOP

e've just returned from food shopping at the local Aldi with a large, carved antique cabinet and a piano! Not special offers of the week, I hasten to add. We had a chance meeting by the freezers with David from the tip, and Mr V casually mentioned we wanted a piano. I in turn had casually mentioned the day before that I would like to learn to play. (I also casually mentioned that I would like to go to New York, but as yet there's no evidence of any plane tickets being booked.)

'Ah, I don't get many of those,' was the response. 'But as it happens, I did a house clearance last week and I have a small upright that needs a little tuning but is in excellent general condition.'

Ten minutes later we're hurtling at speed around icy bends with our New Year's supply of wine clanging about in the boot, following David in his little, silver Citroën, who is driving like a maniac, as if it's his intention to shake us off his tail rather than lead the way.

We finally come to a halt outside an isolated bungalow half buried in snow. I can't decide if it's surrounded by the most enchanting or most disturbing garden I've ever seen. To the back and sides of the bungalow there are six or seven wooden chalets of different styles and sizes, one of which David explained was a house for his ten cats, who are also of assorted sizes, shapes and colours, and not entirely tame. Some of the chalets are little more than elaborate garden sheds, others with balconies and lace curtains at the windows.

The whole scene in the snow is like a magical Christmas village, complete with numerous garden gnomes depicting the seven dwarfs lining the paths that weave between the chalets, all of which have been made from pieces of wood, glass and broken windows and doors that David has salvaged from the skips. He clearly has a talent, but what is bizarre is that this guy is in his mid-30s and lives with his toothless mother who Mr V said looked exactly like the witch from *Snow White*.

I confess to being more than a little apprehensive entering the bungalow. Inside is like Ali Baba's cave. Every room is lined with wardrobes in styles ranging from elaborately carved 19th-century mahogany; elegantly panelled Art Deco rosewood; 1960s rustic pine, and flimsy, white, flat-pack circa 2000. These wardrobes were in turn crammed with all manner of collectibles. Miniature, dye-cast vehicles in plastic cases, model railways complete with model villages, Polly Pocket houses in the form of giant teacups, 'master disk' CDs the size of LP records, plus a machine to play them, Star Wars figures, giant plastic M&Ms on legs, cuddly toys, electronic games and gadgets, perfume bottles and countless other things that I would bore you with if I went on, but you get the picture. All these things were presented with pride and obviously treasured, and I didn't know whether to be sad for this guy's existence or envious of it. He was so much wrapped up in this strange Neverland that I can't imagine the worries of the world penetrating these walls.

He showed me the cabinet he'd told me about some weeks earlier, and it is truly Gothic, with elaborate, carved panels on the doors and large brass locks and hinges, and just the right height and width to display my wooden elephant candle holder and Moroccan lamp when we have a room to put them in. The piano is in a similar coloured wood and also not too high or wide, so we bought the two. We must be completely bonkers purchasing a piano no one can play to put in a room with a concrete floor full of packing boxes, but this is the driest place and the unlikeliest of thoroughfares for building traffic at the moment. I see it as a symbol of the future and imagine, if not me sitting sedately playing the theme tune to *Game of Thrones*, then a gaggle of giggling grandchildren bashing out 'Chopsticks'.

* * *

We are now firmly in the season of soups and raclettes. The market stalls are full of fat, toadstool-shaped *cèpes* (porcini mushrooms) which put our little mushroom crop in the shade, and girolles that look more like they've come out of the sea than the earth. There's also an abundance of chestnuts. Neighbours are bringing me bagful after bagful, and I haven't got a clue what to do with them. Previous encounters have so far been limited to the chestnuts sprucing up frozen sprouts for Christmas dinner, or buying them roasted, and quite often burnt to a crisp, in little paper cones from the street vendors in Paris.

But fear not, France has come to the rescue and is doing the same for chestnuts in December as it did for figs in September. Every time I put on the TV in Paris someone is showing you how to roast, boil and puree chestnuts, or adding them to soups, stuffing, casseroles or pâté, and creaming them with sugar to make desserts such as the famous Mont Blanc[1]. Likewise, every supermarket is including recipes for chestnuts in their special offers brochures alongside sales of fresh, frozen, tinned and jarred varieties.

In the end it was Mr V who roasted and peeled them all, and I made a lovely, warming chestnut and pumpkin soup.

---

1. Meringue base filled with sweetened chestnut purée, topped with whipped cream.

PUMPKIN AND CHESTNUT SOUP

Serves 2 as a lunch or 4 as a starter

Ingredients

1 small/medium pumpkin, cut into small cubes
1 tbsp olive oil
1 tbsp butter
100 g (4 oz) roasted chestnuts, very finely chopped
1 small shallot, very finely chopped
1 tbsp cornflour
1 ltr (34 fl oz) vegetable stock, warmed
Salt and pepper to season
Fresh cream to decorate (optional)
Fresh thyme to decorate (optional)

Method

Spread the pumpkin on a shallow roasting tray, drizzle with the oil
and roast in a moderate oven for around 30 minutes, until just tender
and beginning to caramelise.

When the pumpkin is ready, melt the butter in a saucepan and sauté
the chestnuts and shallot over a gentle heat for 5 minutes, taking care
not to brown.

Add the roasted pumpkin, then add the cornflour and coat all the vegetables.

Stir in the warm stock and bring to the boil, stirring continually to avoid lumps. (If this happens just continue stirring with a balloon whisk until they disappear.)

Reduce heat, cover and simmer for around 20 minutes until reduced and thickened slightly.

Taste and season accordingly.

Allow to cool a little then blend to a smooth texture.

Reheat and serve with a swirl of cream and a little thyme.

Just what you need on a cold winter's evening.

ANYONE FOR JELLY?

*I*t's the week before Christmas. The days are short and cold and damp with none of the romance of the snow. There's an unspoken sadness hanging in the air as heavy as the smoke from the open fire as there's still no sign of Maddy. I periodically go to all the windows and doors in the hope that she's waiting for one of them to open, but I know the little genie comes in like a mouse, swift and unseen until she's rubbing her furry head on our feet. I'm taking a little heart in the fact that Flaubertine hasn't come a-calling either this morning and that Maddy looked plump and clean and well the last time we saw her, so maybe someone has given them permanent sanctuary, or they're snug as bugs in a barn somewhere with a well-stocked larder of field mice. Still, I miss the little ragamuffin beneath my feet.

Talking of field mice, I've just met one of our co-inhabitants. Mr V was chasing a small, chocolate-brown creature through the rooms with a wooden mousetrap in his hand. Did he imagine that it would stop and obligingly put its head in the trap à la Louis XVI? I don't like the idea of dispatching them, but neither do I want to open a rodent rescue centre, and Pussy Willow is too well fed to be interested. I think they are Parisian mice as they've somehow got into a locked larder cupboard and scoffed a packet of couscous.

I've had it from a very reliable source that chickens eat mice. I ask myself how people come across such knowledge. Are they born 'country folk', or are they learning by numbers like me? I would like to keep chickens, but as we're not permanently resident at the moment, it isn't practical as we'd need to be sure they were safe from evil foxes. Mr V says they smell, and somewhere in the vestiges of my brain I have a memory of a neighbour when I was a little girl putting chicken droppings (being polite) on his roses, and it did rather pong. I tell Mr V that it is good fertiliser for the vegetable garden when we eventually have one, but he isn't buying it. If I'm having this much opposition to chickens, I don't know how I'm going to fare negotiating a donkey.

Speaking of chickens and donkeys, we've just had a visit from Pappy Cardigan and his wife, Noëlle, who I learn has both, along with ducks, geese, rabbits and a goat. She's invited me to come and meet them all in spring, and I'm more than a tad excited at the prospect. Noëlle is larger than life and exudes warmth, love and motherliness. It was our first meeting, but she swept in and gathered me into an embrace before planting a real kiss on either cheek. (In Paris we merely kiss the air.)

The word had obviously been spreading like wildfire about our plans and progress at Les Libellules and had even reached the ears of the 90-year-old sister-in-law of the former lady of the house who lives in a village about twenty minutes' drive away. Noëlle tells me that the old lady is delighted that we have the house and that she was worried that someone was going to come in and modernise everything and not preserve anything from the past. I for my turn have asked Noëlle if she thought that the lady would like to come to visit when the weather is warmer. Apparently, she would like this very much and had already expressed a longing to see the place again.

I've been keeping two scrapbooks of photos, one charting progress and disasters, the other a selection of scenes capturing the essence of the house, garden and countryside throughout the seasons, a sort of pictorial accompaniment to this memoir. I thought that maybe it would be nice if Noëlle could take me to see the lady and show her these books, something she again agreed upon. It struck me that if this lady were the sister-in-law of the former occupant, then she would be the sister of her husband. Therefore, there's every chance that we are now living in her childhood family home. Once again, the sense that we are merely temporary custodians, and of the need for us to respect the house and her history, is emphasised.

Then Noëlle revealed another little snippet of history that added a further piece to the jigsaw. Apparently the copse of trees at the back was a popular meeting place for lovers in the past, and as it borders both our and Martine's land, this gives a little more credence to the idea that there was some sort of liaison between the occupants of the two houses.

We go from room to room with me telling Noëlle of our plans. Periodically she spontaneously hugs me and tells me that everyone in the commune, which includes a group of two hamlets and three villages, is pleased that Leah's House, as Les Libellules is known locally, has been bought by a couple who are going to breathe life into her again. It seems that there's a real affection in the community for our poor, neglected, little lady.

Pappy Cardigan is delighted that his wife and I have hit it off, and they were evidently in no rush to leave. Two hours later and we were sitting around the table drinking tea and eating slices of my homemade Christmas cake that Pappy Cardigan was as suspicious of as Mr V was of the porridge. They were both astounded when I told them that in the UK we often eat it with a slice of crumbly, Cheshire cheese. The conversation strayed into the strange culinary habits of *les Anglais,* such as eating *les haricots* on toast, putting vinegar on chips and eating jelly. There's a hard-held belief amongst the French that we're a nation of jelly eaters. I've tried to tell them that the last time I ate it was at a fifth birthday party, but they aren't convinced.

A VERY HAPPY UN-CHRISTMAS
TO YOU

*W*e're not spending Christmas at Les Libellules this year but going to Wales to visit my mother. We'll take her to my daughter, Natasia's house where we'll have a traditional British celebration with a huge dinner on Christmas Day, where everyone eats far too much and can barely move then collapses on the sofa to watch the Queen's speech on TV.

Things are done a little bit differently in France; something that I didn't realise when I first moved here. It is on Christmas Eve, known as the *Réveillon de Noël*, that French families have their Christmas meal, exchanging gifts at midnight, or if they're practising Catholics, after attending Midnight Mass. The meal usually consists of an extended choice of apéritifs/starters including oysters, coquilles Saint-Jacques (scallops in a white wine and cream sauce traditionally served in a large scallop shell), smoked salmon and foie gras.

In the lead-up to Christmas the shops are packed with slices of smoked salmon in various marinades, and foie gras in every shape and form imaginable, often adorned with tiny red currants called *groseilles*. You can buy special, small, slim slices of bread flavoured with figs to toast and serve with foie gras, and blinis to serve with smoked salmon. This is followed by a relatively simple main course consisting of some sort of fowl or game served with chestnuts, sliced green beans and maybe potatoes. Then comes the cheese course: there will generally be at least four excellent cheeses to sample with fresh, crusty baguette. And finally the dessert, notably a *bûche de Noël,* an elaborate Yule log made from layers of ice cream, sorbet, butter cream and often fruit compote and meringue, which in addition to various types of chocolate, also comes in flavours such as forest fruits, pear with salted caramel, lemon and mandarin meringue, and praline. Don't think 'chocolate log', many of these *bûches* cost in excess of €45, and more decorative creations can cost over €100 and come in the form of Swiss chalets and giant igloos and even Christmas crackers (which is odd as they don't have Christmas crackers in France).

Christmas Day has more of a British 'Boxing Day[1]' feel to it with families going out for walks or visiting relatives (the 26th December is an ordinary working day in France). I now actually prefer the French way of doing things as it avoids the Christmas morning frenzy of opening presents and cooking and eating a marathon lunch in time for the Queen.

⁂

I committed a huge faux pas on the first *Réveillon de Noël* that I spent with my then thirteen-year-old stepson. I'd planned an extended buffet with lots of different finger food and went to the Marks and Spencer food store near St Michel in Paris to buy Chinese and Indian nibbles, plus some traditional English ones, as well as all the usual French suspects such as foie gras and little festive *verrines,* small glasses with a variety of savoury fillings. I'd also bought three festive films (*Santa Claus, Jack Frost,* and *The Muppets Christmas Carol*) in French with English subtitles, and I anticipated a successful evening.

When my stepson arrived, he was in a very excitable mood saying, '*C'est Noël. C'est Noël.*' (It's Christmas. It's Christmas.)

I kept correcting him saying, '*Non, ce n'est pas Noël. Demain c'est Noël.*' (No, it's not Christmas. Tomorrow is Christmas.) But he was poking at the presents beneath the tree, asking could he open them immediately. I told him he could open one later, after dinner, which caused a lot of (what I thought) unnecessary protest, as unknown to me the poor kid was expecting to open them all after dinner.

Worse was yet to come. We put on one of the films that he seemed to be enjoying, but he hardly touched the buffet, which puzzled me as he usually eats like a horse, and I knew he loves Chinese and Indian food. I asked him if he wasn't eating because he was unwell, to which he replied that he was fine but saving himself for the dinner. He thought €75 of buffet food was the apéritif!

When I asked Mr V why he hadn't told me any of this in advance, he replied that he presumed that it was the same in the UK as in France; as I'd presumed the opposite. Fortunately, my stepson is a very easy-going boy. When his father then explained to him that things are entirely different in the UK, and it would be fun to have a British Christmas the next day, complete with crackers and silly hats, and more food on one plate than he'd ever seen in his life, he responded with, '*Ce n'est pas grave*, Lindy,' (It's OK) and proceeded to demolish the buffet.

The dinner was a big success, and my stepson said that he preferred Christmas the British way, as sometimes it was too late for him to wait to eat in the evening, and it was definitely too late for him to play with all his presents. He loved pulling the crackers and loved it even more when he made his father reluctantly wear a paper crown.

To put the icing on the cake it snowed during the night, and we woke to a crisp winter's day with the sun shining in a clear blue sky and pristine white snow glistening on the ground. I put the turkey in the oven, and we all went out for a snowball fight in the Bois de Vincennes.

What I've learnt today: The French celebrate Christmas with a special meal and presents on the 24th December.

---

1. The day after Christmas Day and a public holiday.

OH CHRISTMAS TREE, OH
CHRISTMAS TREE

*I*t's an unseasonably warm Saturday morning on the 30th of December. We're leaving Paris for Les Libellules, driving through drizzle and spray from the surface water on the road. The countryside is hidden from view in a veil of grey without the romance and mystery of the usual, frosted morning mists. Pussy Willow is in the car, and she isn't happy. In fact she's so unhappy that she's just relieved herself on my coat on the parcel shelf; something that she has never done. She is now sitting on my knee, pushing her little wet nose under my hand in a 'protect me' manner. I dislike dragging her up and down the country against her will, but the alternative is to leave her alone in the apartment with neighbours popping up to feed her twice a day, as they've just done the last week over the Christmas period while we were with family in the UK.

We are passing through plantations of sapling conifer trees no more than 30 centimetres high. Just one week after Christmas they're already taking the places of those adorning halls and living rooms all over the country. We live in the land of the Christmas tree. The Morvan is the region where the majority of them are grown in France; even the one for the Presidential Elysée Palace comes from here. When these saplings go on sale next season, people can come with a bucket or tub, dig up a tree by its roots and leave it standing in its own soil, watering it while it has pride of place indoors over the Christmas period. Then when the festive season is over, it can be planted outside or returned to the forest, roots intact. Next year we'll have one of these little saplings as our Christmas tree, but this year we have a small, fibre-optic one on the packing case which is serving as a table next to the sofa. Mr V detests this tree as it makes a whirring sound, but I find it very therapeutic to look at the flickering, changing colours.

I come armed with a bag of Christmas decorations that were in my daughter's loft. Although the main event has now passed, I position a festive statue of St Nicholas dressed in green hat and coat on the mantel piece, along with two golden cherubs with legs made of crimson velvet which are dangling over the edge wearing what look like red Dr. Martens boots. Note that St Nicholas is wearing green, not red. Myth has it that green was the traditional colour of his robe until Coca Cola decided that red looked better on their advertising posters as it matched the logo on their bottles, hence the popular image is now of a large man in a red suit with a bushy white beard. Walt Disney did the same thing in reverse to leprechauns in the 1960s film *Darby O'Gill and the Little People*, changing their traditional, rusty brownish-red coats to green, and again the popular image changed, with almost every shop in Dublin displaying a picture of a jolly green leprechaun.

Mr V has got the television working. We now have an aerial twice the size of the television itself balanced precariously on top of an open cupboard door as this is the only position that we can pick up a signal. The door has a large basket filled with logs pressed firmly against it to prevent anyone forgetting that the aerial is there (how could you?) and shutting the door, bringing it down on their head like a giant metal stork. This means that all of Mr V's electrical tools are on full view, as he no longer trusts keeping them in the tool-shed after it was flooded. So they're now sharing the apéritif cupboard along with bottles of brandy, whiskey and port, and boxes of pretzels and shelled walnuts. I'm at this moment sitting comfortably on the sofa watching my very first programme at Les Libellules. It's a festive edition of *The Little Murders of Agatha Christie*. The fire is burning merrily, and my tiny, fibre-optic Christmas tree is undulating in the corner. The only cloud on my horizon is that there's still no sign of Maddy.

WINTER OF FIRE AND ICE

*T*he year is ending in a blaze of warm winter sunshine (15 degrees), and what a year it has been, with us realising our dream and delighting in the ownership of this enchanted place. Although there's much to do, we don our walking boots and head for the hills behind the hamlet for an end-of-year walk. The Virginia creeper that adorned the houses with an abundance of green in summer and red in autumn, now bare of its foliage, grasps at the walls like gnarled and knotted witches' fingers. And now that the snow has departed, the newly revealed fields are the same greenish yellow as the lichen that clings to the birch trees.

There has been a lot of heavy snow followed by rain in our absence, and the previously bone-dry drainage gullies at the sides of the fields babble and gurgle past us like small streams. The gullies aren't the only things that the ample rainfall has swollen. The *mare* has overflowed and seeped into the surrounding ground, turning it into a soggy marsh, and the feeble trickle of water behind the copse is now a teeming torrent.

All is quiet as we walk past closed doors, the families inside preparing for the biggest night of the French calendar. *Le Réveillon*, the term for New Year's Eve, which is celebrated in rather a different manner than in the UK. Yes, we have spectacular firework displays at the Eiffel Tower and Arc de Triomphe in Paris, but these are mainly attended by tourists and teenagers. Most French families will be celebrating at home together with a big festive meal, similar to that of *le Réveillon de Noël*.

The peace of our walk, however, is soon shattered. On the usually deserted back road we've met three vehicles racing past us in as many minutes. Another four follow, all driven by mean-looking men wearing bright orange and black animal-print, weatherproof jackets. They are *chasseurs* (hunters), explains Mr V, and a much-feared and detested species who tramp across people's land, guns blazing in hot pursuit of some poor creature, usually steaming with drink and often shooting either an innocent dog or dog walker, or one of their own party. One recent incident involved a man killing his own son, mistaking him for a wild boar.

Apparently, France is the only country in Europe where hunting is permissible every day; hence it's the country with the highest number of hunting casualties and fatalities. On average around twelve people are killed and two hundred injured each year, Sunday being the most dangerous day to be out and about. A 'hunting on Sunday' ban is in the pipeline, but whether it will ever take effect I very much doubt as French country folk are very attached to their rifles and hunting traditions.

We're now halfway from the safety of the hamlet and unsure whether to continue or turn back. We can hear guns going off in the near distance, and I feel very vulnerable walking along the country lanes half-concealed by hedgerows on a day when most people are indoors preparing their festive feasts. All dressed in black I fervently wish that I'd worn my cream quilted jacket instead of my trench coat; at least that way I could be seen. We continue going forward, talking loudly; at one stage I begin singing 'We're Busy Doing Nothing' at the top of my voice to let them hunters know that there are other humans in the vicinity. We pass a couple of them staked out in the bushes near the roadside; they look annoyed that we are making so much noise and alerting their quarry. I'm now equally as afraid of being charged at by a wild boar as it tries to escape as I am of being shot by a stray bullet.

Finally, we reach the relative safety of the road leading from the village to the hamlet and hasten towards home, breathing a huge sigh of relief when we're at last indoors and intact.

✳ ✳ ✳

As it's New Year's Eve I'm making a special effort and mopping the floors. Any of you reading this who has ever tackled a house renovation of this scale will appreciate the futility of this action and, hey presto, right on cue, Mr V has just marched through the living room in his muddy wellies. I'm a great believer in 'all things happen for a reason'. The reason that I mopped the floors was so that I could find myself stranded in the garden while they dry and witness the glorious setting of the sun as it goes down on the year like a ball of fire behind the field which is shimmering like any icy lake. I muse at how this analogy of fire and ice also reflects our personalities—me the fiery, passionate Stromboli (the volcano that Mr V calls me after), and he the sang-froid Frenchman—and how, like this beautiful winter sunset, we complement each other perfectly.

Our meal this evening is to be an apéritif of foie gras with *pain d'épices*, a main course of guinea fowl stuffed with morel mushrooms, served on a bed of crushed potato laced with black truffle, and green beans, followed by the traditional cheese and *bûche*. We had planned on having oysters but forgot to bring the oyster knife, and it's both nigh on impossible and downright dangerous to try and open them without one (actually it can be dangerous to open them with one also). Even more importantly we've forgotten to bring any champagne, and the *cave* is dry as we've quite rightly shared all our bottles of bubbly with family and friends. We do have a rather nice bottle of red Burgundy though, and I've found some coquilles Saint-Jacques in the freezer to soften the blow of being oysterless.

We've held back some presents from Christmas to open this evening. I've bought copies of *Au Plaisir de Dieu* (At God's Pleasure), a

132

book by the great, recently departed French author Jean d'Ormesson, in both French and English so that Mr V and I can read it simultaneously. I've also bought a photo block picture of Les Libellules in the snow and a National Trust diary for Mr V.

Mr V for his part has blown me away by restoring the 19th-century music box and fitting it with a beautiful, intricate movement of 'Clair de Lune' by Claude Debussy. The delicate tinkling notes sounding like icicles tumbling onto a frozen pond. My ambition now is to be able to play this on our piano one day.

The joy at spending New Year by our fireside is indescribable, only to be surpassed by a future occasion when the house can receive both my daughters and their husbands and we all celebrate together.

THE TEMPEST

The New Year has started with a frenzy. A tempest has struck the Atlantic coast of France, and we're getting the tail end, plus Pussy Willow has sharpened her hunting skills and has tracked down a mouse in the cupboard where I keep my best etched glasses for the aperitif, that I'm now trying to retrieve from underneath her without them breaking, which she isn't appreciating. Next, she turns her attention to a spider the size of a saucer and proceeds to gallop in a circuit around the house with its legs dangling and dancing from her mouth. I'm terrified that it will sting or bite her and cause her harm, but she eventually drops it, and it scurries off to join the mouse in the space beneath the cupboard. Pussy Willow then sets up camp with her head and shoulders under the cupboard, but her hindquarters, being much too large to join them, remain sticking out into the room. All this and it isn't yet 9 a.m.

✳ ✳ ✳

It's now midday. The sky is charcoal grey, and the tempest has picked up its momentum. Wind and rain are lashing the windows, but we are snug inside with a roaring fire, a joint of gammon roasting in the mini

oven, and music live from Vienna on the mini television. I'm hoping
that we'll still have enough power to finish both the roast and the
programme, but the lights are flickering, the television is crackling,
and the picture keeps breaking up into tiny squares. The storm isn't
content to stay outside, and we have a serious amount of water that's
passed both underneath and through the panelled doors in the living
room, kitchen and garden room (in fact all the doors that are made of
wood). Mr V is frantically battling against the wind to shut the
shutters while I'm juggling roasting parsnips and potatoes with
mopping up the flooded floors. (You see, I told you that it was futile of
me washing them yesterday.) This puts me in mind of *The Jumblies*, a
poem by Edward Lear:

> *The water it soon came in, it did,*
> *The water it soon came in...*
> *...Though the sky be dark, and the voyage be long,*
> *Yet we never can think we were rash or wrong.*

Just like the Jumblies, even with a storm breaching our defences on
New Year's Day, not for one instant do we question what we've done,
or wish for anything else.

※　※　※

The storm has turned into the worst that France has seen in over 30
years, with wind speeds up to 200 kilometres an hour in some parts.
The hatches are well and truly battened down, and I feel like I'm in a
fortress with all the shutters permanently closed and the house in
darkness. Plus, the bulb has gone in my little Christmas tree, so I don't
even have that to brighten up the room. To top it all I have a stinking
cold; my nose and eyes are streaming, and I can't stop sneezing.

Pussy Willow doesn't like the noise of the wind, and she's padding
on my knee, which is very sweet but also very uncomfortable as she
weighs a ton. The shutters are banging and rattling, as are the interior
doors, and icy tunnels of wind are whistling through the keyholes. I've

found some button-sized fridge magnets with miniature scenes from Claude Monet paintings on them that I purchased a while back from the gift shop in the Petit Palais in Paris. I was saving them with other bits of frippery for when we've finished the house, but they're now serving as rather posh draught excluders covering up various keyholes.

The wind is also blowing smoke back into the room, which is aggravating my already itchy eyes, and a wood burner or 'insert' is going further up the list of priorities. I'm feeling as battered as the house.

The storms are now unprecedented, and even Paris hasn't escaped, with people being injured by falling masonry. The ski stations in the Alps are all closed, and many families still there for the holidays before the children go back to school are trapped inside their chalets playing ludo and eating raclettes, while controlled explosions trigger a series of small avalanches before Mother Nature triggers larger, more dangerous ones. For our part I'm considering renaming the house Château d'Eau[1]. I finally have an opportunity to wear my William Morris corncockle-design wellies to brave the elements and take some photos. When I told Mr V to wait while I put on my wellies before going out, he heard *valise* (suitcase) and couldn't understand why I wanted to take that outside in a storm. Being French he simply refers to them as *bottes* (boots) as an article of clothing named after one that the Duke of Wellington wore at Waterloo is a bit of a sore point.

The Dutch neighbours have had enough and are packing up to return to a country better equipped for dealing with unruly water. I understand now why so many Brits who have undertaken renovation projects in rural France shut up shop for winter, and I question our sanity in leaving what appears to be a sunny UK immediately after Christmas.

What I've learnt today: Bottes *in town are leather boots, and* bottes *in the country are wellies.*

*   *   *

It's now the 6th of January, and it's rained constantly since the 1st. I feel trapped by the fact that we can't open the shutters as the rain comes pouring in through the doors, and even if we do venture to open one, I feel equally trapped by the omnipresent greyness outside. My cold has developed into some horrible lurgy that's caused me to break out in angry, red lumps on my face and given me an annoying, tickly cough that's keeping me awake at night. I can't even take to my bed during the day to try and catch up on some sleep, as a blow-up mattress on a concrete-floored bedroom, with drilling and banging going on in the loft space immediately above, isn't compatible with rest and recuperation.

We now have a third hole in the ceiling where a hammer or suchlike has fallen onto the not-yet-boarded floor, so the bed is covered in plastic sheeting to catch the grit and dust that periodically comes showering down. I would like to take a shower, but the bathroom is freezing, and as Mr V refuses to put up a plastic shower curtain, the floor gets soaked when I wash my hair. By the time I've mopped it up, I feel like I need to take another one.

*   *   *

As Pussy Willow is confined to barracks due to the weather, mouse hunting is now de rigueur. She's continually darting like an arrow off the sofa where she was seemingly asleep and thrusting as much of herself as she can under the cupboard where the mouse appears to have taken up residence. She's also taken to using the dining table as a springboard to jump on top of the nursery cupboard, and from there into a small alcove above the mouse cupboard, where her paws can reach spiders who are spinning their webs between the rafters. (I have a wire brush, with a head shaped like a giant morel mushroom, on an extremely long handle specially designed to remove cobwebs, but then you end up with spiders in your hair, so I prefer to leave them living on the ceiling.) This exercise of Pussy Willow's isn't entirely a success as it's easier for her to get on top of the cupboard than it is to come back down, this results in her launching herself directly onto the table, which has led to a broken lamp and Chianti bottle that I was using as a candlestick.

She has also developed a fascination with the *pigeonnier*, giving a whole new meaning to putting the cat amongst the pigeons. She wails at the door until I let her in, then spends hours in there doing I've no idea what, and it's too cold and dirty to hang around to find out.

As it's so cold everywhere, not only in the *pigeonnier*, I'm going to make a curry. I was very excited to find parsnips in an organic supermarket as they're a bit of a rarity in France. So I'm having a parsnip fest, roasting them with carrots, potatoes and sweet potatoes, making spicy parsnip soup, and today, adding them to all sorts of leftover vegetables to make a hearty, warming, root vegetable and chickpea curry. The result looks delicious, so here's the recipe.

---

1. Literally 'water castle', the name for the water storage towers seen in French cities.

ROOT VEGETABLE AND CHICKPEA CURRY

Serves 2

Ingredients

1 large parsnip, diced
2 medium carrots, diced
1 medium potato, diced
1 tbsp oil
1 small shallot, finely chopped
½ medium fennel bulb, finely sliced
1 tsp curry powder
1 tsp turmeric
½ tsp cumin powder
1 tsp fennel seeds
6 cardamom pods, crushed (discard husks)
440 ml (¾ pt) vegetable stock
400 g (14 oz) can of chickpeas, drained and rinsed
2 cabbage leaves, rolled into a cigar shape and finely shredded
2 tsp dried green coriander leaf
1 tbsp coconut milk (optional)
1 dsp green jalapeños, chopped (optional)
Salt and pepper to season

Method

Gently heat the oil in a large heavy-based saucepan and sauté the parsnip, carrot and potato in the oil for 6-7 minutes until beginning to caramelise a little.

Reduce the heat, add the shallot and cook for a further 2 minutes until beginning to soften.

Add the fennel and all the spices (except the coriander leaf) and cook for 2 minutes, stirring so that the spices coat the vegetables.

Add the stock and bring to the boil, then reduce to a gentle simmer.

Add the chickpeas and season to taste with salt and pepper.

Cook for around 20 minutes until the vegetables are soft, then add the shredded cabbage and cook for a further 5 minutes.

Add the coriander leaf and coconut milk if you want a milder taste and jalapeños if you want a hotter taste.

The fennel isn't essential; it's just what I had left in the fridge, but the cabbage adds colour and crunch—just don't overcook it.

(As Mr V is French and doesn't like things too hot and spicy, and I'm British and like nothing more than a fiery curry, I serve a little bowl of yogurt flavoured with coconut cream on the side for him, and one of chopped jalapeños on the side for me.)

I AM A CHRISTMAS TREE

*a*s rain has stopped play at Les Libellules we're heading back up north to the house of some very good friends, Corrine and Bernard, who live on the edge of the Champagne region. 'Lived' would be a better word, as they've sold their beautiful, quirky home and have moved to Alsace to be nearer to Corrine's elderly parents. We're devastated to see them go, as they were an easy hour and a half drive from us at Paris, and we've celebrated marriages, christenings and birthdays together there over the years. They won't be there when we arrive but have left the key with neighbours. Their new house is in town; therefore they don't have the space to store many of the things that they had in their garage and outbuildings, and have told us just to take what we want, so we have the trailer to fill with plants and garden tools and various DIY materials.

Corrine is one of my husband's oldest and dearest friends, but when we first met, our relationship was strained to say the least, and this had nothing to do with the particular brand of female rivalry that French women are famous for. Mr V and I were guests at an informal family dinner party at her home, and she didn't warm to me. How could she when I was displaying about as much personality as a dining chair? Corrine could simply not understand what, beyond sexual attraction, her amusing, charming, articulate and intelligent friend could possibly find interesting in someone so bland, blonde and foreign. This is a widely held view by Mr V himself, as on meeting a much aesthetically altered friend of mine, he said, 'The looks can attract, but if there's nothing between the ears, they can't keep a man.'

I knew how I was being viewed but was powerless to do anything about it. Bound and gagged by my inability to communicate, I couldn't display any wit or intelligence, nor express an opinion. Me, who is bursting with language and ideas and funny stories and miscellaneous facts, was in effect mute. Like *The Little Mermaid* I had traded my voice for love and was locked inside my body without the means to animate it. I was the invisible woman; my entire substance had dissolved with my voice. Language is so much more than a tool for communication and expression; it identifies us, and to be able to adopt the tongue of a host country shows our willingness to integrate. Language unites but also divides. I had to take drastic action and fast.

As I'd only ever studied (very loose use of the word) French for two years at secondary school, where I learnt to sing '*Il est Né, le Divin Enfant*' (He is Born, the Divine Child) without having a clue what I was singing about, and once stood up in front of the class and proudly announced, '*Je suis un arbre de Noël*' (I am a Christmas tree—Christmas obviously featured heavily in the lessons), I took myself off to a beginners' French class at night school.

Now, for those of you who've never attended one of these classes, there are two types of beginners who go along. The first, like me, is a minority of absolute numpties who hardly speak a word of the given language. (I have it on excellent authority that it's the same in Spanish and Italian classes.) The second is a sort of serial language-class taker who has holidayed every year in the Dordogne (or wherever) since the 1980s. They go to the classes to show off their conversational skills and insider knowledge, and make people like me feel stupid and intimidated.

My French extended beyond '*je suis un arbre de Noël*' to counting to twelve (I also knew that *quinze* was fifteen, as I stayed in a hotel with room number *quinze* in Paris when I was seventeen), plus I could rattle off about twenty nouns: *la maison* (the house), *la voiture* (the car), *le jardin* (the garden), *le chien* (the dog), *le chat* (the cat)—that I mistakenly pronounced with a 't'—*la table* (the table), *la chaise* (the chair) and other such relatively useless words. I had a sketchy grasp of the verb *être* (to be) and an even sketchier one of *avoir* (to have). The first email that Mr V sent to me in French consisted of four lines and took me 40 minutes to decipher with the aid of a French/English dictionary; the only word that I was sure of being *je* – I.

But although I evidently didn't possess natural language acquisition skills, my motivation was strong, and soon I was the only numpty left in the class, the others having dropped out under the sheer weight of humiliation. As I visited Paris more and more frequently, and with a bona fide French person, my insider knowledge began to surpass that of the smug elements in the group, until many of them left also, leaving a pleasant little core of genuine learners.

My linguistic journey had begun. Backed up by listening to *Teach Yourself French* CDs in the car, and reading the advertising posters when travelling on the Metro, I made tentative steps into simple exchanges in shops and restaurants. Although most of the time I was met by a look of total confusion, sometimes accompanied by an astonished '*Comment?*' (What?) from the recipient of my ramblings. On the odd occasion when they did understand me, I was frustrated by the fact that they mostly replied in English. This was either because the French love to practise their English, or they couldn't stand the sound of me murdering their beloved mother tongue.

Eventually I was able to read short reports in *Direct Matin*, the Parisian newssheet distributed free at Metro stations, with relative ease, and grasp the gist of what was being said on TV. If I couldn't exactly join in a conversation fully, I could at least nod and smile in the appropriate places. A major breakthrough came the day that I made a French person laugh for the first time; a snooty shop assistant in a fancy boutique on the Rue de Rennes to boot. Humour is a marvellous key for opening the door of acceptance.

My breakthrough with Corrine came at another dinner party, at our apartment by which time my French had improved quite a bit. There is now genuine sisterhood between us which I never could have envisaged.

What I've learnt today: Laughter is the common language.

GIVE US A CLUE

We've bought a bed, so soon our nights bouncing around on a giant beach ball will be over. This wasn't as simple as it sounds as in my haste to get out after being housebound for five days by the infernal storm, I forgot to note the reference number and only had the name, which I hadn't written down either but memorised, as it happens, incorrectly. Mr V, who is super-efficient, frowned on this as he writes everything down in his little notepad, which he never forgets. He's also afflicted by the universal male trait of refusing to ask for help in shops (which also extends to an inability to ask for directions). Therefore it was left to me to persuade the obliging little man called Yves in BUT furniture store to search through literally thousands of beds on their website looking for the Armitage bedroom range, but there appeared to be no bedroom furniture of this name. At this stage Mr V had walked off, telling me to find another bed; but this was 'the one', and I wasn't leaving the shop without ordering it.

The exercise had now turned into something akin to a French oral examination for me and a game of 'give us a clue' for Yves, as I exhausted my use of adjectives and powers of description.

'It's made of wood.'

This narrowed the choice down to about 900.

'It's made from oak. I think.' Now we're down to about 450.

'It looks like a bed from another century.' I couldn't specify which.

'It has panels on the headboard and footboard.' I don't even know if footboard is the correct name in English.

Miraculously we succeeded. The bed was from the Artisan range; at least I had the first two letters right!

I think that once Yves got over his initial exasperation, he found this far more interesting than the usual boring customer presenting him with the correct name and reference number. He told me that it was the first time in over twenty years that he'd had to find an item purely on description. But as anyone who's ever received directions from me will know, my mind works in pictures and images not facts and figures.

I was now on a roll and told Yves that I could also be interested in the matching wardrobe, and he suggested two *tables de nuit* (bedside tables) and a *commode*. This didn't mean that he was offering me a chair with a chamber pot in the seat (although he did point out the *tables de nuit* came in two styles, one with three drawers and the other with one drawer and a small cupboard to conceal a chamber pot). A *commode* in French means a chest of drawers and is one of many *faux amis*, words that look as if they're the same in French and English, but have entirely different meanings.

Mr V miraculously returned once the dilemma was resolved, and we decided to think about the wardrobe as we have nowhere to put it at the moment. Next came the process of choosing a *sommier*. For those of you who have never had the odd experience of buying a bed in France, French beds are merely frames; if you want something to place a mattress upon then you have to buy this separately. We were now faced with a staggering array of *sommiers*: some with wide, wooden slats that joined in the middle, others with narrower slats that also joined in the middle, neither of which appealed to me, as we've slept in this type of bed before, and they have parted company in the night on more than one occasion. So, it was a solid base to fit inside the frame that we were looking for. Did we prefer one that was raised, making the mattress higher, or one that formed a cradle for the mattress, making it flush with the frame? Then what type of fabric did we prefer: nylon wipe-clean, cotton stay-cool, quilted extra-comfort? The choice was boggling. We decided on...I honestly don't know what; it will be a surprise when it arrives.

Now for the mattress. Again, the choice of springs, foam, memory foam, and if opting for springs, how many, what depth, what fabric for the cover, and what price range, as this was staggering. The next part was more fun as Yves encouraged us to lie down and emulate our sleeping positions and 'have a good bounce up and down' on a variety of mattresses which matched our preferences. We made our choice and headed back to the computer station to place our order. All was going swimmingly, then, an extraordinary thing happened. There was an incomprehensible muffled announcement over the PA system, and everyone stopped what they were doing and began making their way to the doors. I was seconds away from buying my dream bed from what I now knew was a discontinued range, when the previously compliant Yves shut down his computer. For me the only reason to evacuate a busy shop in the middle of a large retail park at 12:30 in the afternoon was that there was a bomb scare, not in Dijon apparently. They were closing for lunch. Yes, a huge furniture store, packed with people trying out beds, testing sofas, perched on high stools looking at virtual kitchen plans on computer screens, came to a standstill, and they all just stopped what they were doing and left.

Now I applaud a culture where the small shops in my Parisian suburb close between 12:30 and 2 (actually some don't reopen until 2:45) for lunch, but surely a store as big as BUT has enough staff to stagger lunches. When I asked Mr V what we were supposed to do until two o'clock while waiting for it to reopen and continue placing our order, he looked at me as if I was mad and replied, 'Eat.' Silly me. What else?

One and a half hours later we joined the stampede of shoppers trying to be the first to get into the store to pick up where they'd abruptly left off, along with the new arrivals who were hoping to jump the queues. I was off the starting blocks and straight for the bed department where I tracked down Yves who completed the transaction as if nothing had happened. We then went to Castorama to pick up a trailer of our own, as these trips for supplies were obviously going to run for years to come.

* * *

Have I told you about Mr d'Arsy? We have a schizophrenic GPS that randomly alternates from giving us directions in a bossy female voice to a belligerent male one that I call Mr. d'Arsy (drop the 'd'). The female is generally accurate, but the male is completely off the wall. Each time we give him a command, he responds with his stock phrase of, *'Désolé, je ne comprends pas,'* (Sorry, I don't understand) in a tone that indicates he's anything but sorry that he doesn't understand. This gives Mr V and me hours of amusement asking him increasingly silly requests, but as far as wanting him to direct you to a pre-programmed address, forget it. This afternoon we had the sole pleasure of Mr d'Arsy's company, and he decided to take us the scenic route along the banks of the canal, through numerous picturesque villages and some extremely narrow winding and hilly roads. I imagine he intended to put Mr V's driving skills, and patience, to the test as he negotiated all this with a large trailer stacked high with tongue and groove in tow. The route, though precarious, was truly scenic, and I was oohing and aahing almost as much as Mr V was peppering the conversation with expletives aimed at Mr A who, throughout it all, characteristically claimed not to understand.

As for the bed, there's a seven-week waiting list for it to be delivered. I only hope that when it arrives it fits in the room.

NO GIRLS ALLOWED

*I*t's late on a frosty Friday evening when we arrive back from a week in Paris. The sky is inky black, and the stars are gathered in the centre like a celestial dot-to-dot of the face of God. The moonlight is making the ground sparkle like a crystal carpet. Throughout all the drive down, there have been signs on the autoroute warning of violent winds tomorrow. I don't much like the sound of that as recent storms across Holland and Germany have been devastating. No cats come to greet us, not even Flaubertine, but maybe it's too cold, or perhaps they've seen the weather forecast.

We're now in mid-January, and the mercury has plummeted once more. Thankfully, there's no sign of the threatened violent winds as yet, but the water from the roof has frozen mid-descent, before reaching the gutters surrounding the house, and is dangling in tiny, pointy icicles that look like leftover Christmas lights. The water has also frozen in the disposable dehumidifiers that we left in every room after downstairs was flooded the week before; as a result, the house still feels damp.

I make a fatal error and open the bedroom window to air the room. The force that I had to exert on the damp, swollen, wooden frame should have served as a warning, but I persisted, and now it's impossible to shut it again with a blizzard brewing outside. I've never experienced such extremes of weather, and as I look back over my scribbling from August and September, this is a different world. I slam and bang, but all to no avail, so I concede and call Mr V. He slams and bangs also and finally succeeds in closing the window. All this slamming and banging has caused large chunks of plaster holding the window in place to part company with the wall, and splinters of wood to part company with the window. Once more we have to reassess our priorities from constructing an upstairs bathroom and refitting the downstairs house of horrors with the back-flowing electric toilet, to fitting double (or triple) glazing in the bedrooms. But before we can tackle this, layers of concrete covering the original tiled floors have to be smashed up. I think that as soon as spring arrives, we're going to literally hit the ground running.

* * *

We're en route to yet another builder's suppliers, this time closer to home. It's snowing again, but this is no winter wonderland variety. This is total whiteout with what appear to be mini snowballs charging at the car. The cows in the fields are huddled together beneath the meagre shelter of bare trees and hedges. The countryside is clothed in a dismal fog of flakes. I yearn for spring, but at the moment it seems a very long way off.

We arrive at Brico Dépôt, the builder's suppliers. Have you ever seen the 1980s cult movie *An American Werewolf in London*? If so, then you'll remember the scene when the two young Americans walk into a pub on the Yorkshire Moors and all goes silent. Well it was just like that. A woman had just entered a male domain. *Quelle horreur*! I feel like I'm in a Victorian gentleman's club in Mayfair, only they're wearing lumberjack shirts instead of smoking jackets.

My friendly smile and *bonjour, messieurs* on entering only furthers the awkwardness of the situation, as looks dart between them, obviously unsure how to respond. (Who would be the first to break the code of silence?) One of the younger assistants says *madame* (note

150

no accompanying *bonjour*); another man nods uncomfortably at me; the rest just bury their heads in the catalogues on the counter. I flick through a few leaflets on a stand by the door, one on insulation, another on paving slabs, and retreat with a subdued *merci* and *au revoir*, leaving Mr V to scour walls of pigeonholes filled with washers, bits of copper pipe, screws and nails, and I go to sit in the freezing car.

* * *

We're back at home, I've forgotten to bring my warm, woolly, Peruvian legwarmers, and my legs are freezing. So I've ingeniously cut up an old pair of leggings and fastened them around my calves, finding another use for the magic, green Velcro tape. Hardly haute couture, but I think it could catch on as my legs have now gone from freezing to extremely cold. I think of how the chic Parisiennes dress, and here am I like a scarecrow.

It's officially warmer in the fridge than in the kitchen, and we're having to keep the butter in there to stop it freezing. The olive oil has gone solid in its bottle, and I have to put red wine and cheese next to the fire to bring them up to room temperature before serving.

So in an attempt to warm ourselves up, I turn once more to making comfort food, and you can't get more comforting than Guy's Soup, so named after a dear departed friend who made this for me in an hour of need. As I've just bought a large net of overripe Moroccan tomatoes, what better way to use them up?

GUY'S TOMATO SOUP

Serves 2 as lunch or 4 as a starter

Ingredients

6 large, ripe tomatoes
1 tbsp olive oil
1 small shallot, very finely chopped
1 clove garlic, crushed
1 medium potato, very thinly sliced
2 tsp dried basil
1 chicken or vegetable stock cube made up with 1 ltr (34 fl oz) hot water
Salt and pepper to season

Method

Score the fresh tomatoes in a cross at their base and cover with boiling water in a basin for around a minute. Drain and cover with cold water and leave to cool.

Peel off the skin once cooled.

Gently heat the oil in a large, heavy-based saucepan.

Roughly chop the tomatoes and sauté in the oil until soft.

Add the shallot and garlic and cook for a further 2 minutes over a gentle heat, taking care not to brown.

Add the potato and basil and cook for a further 2 minutes.

Stir in the stock and season with salt and pepper.

Simmer for around 30 minutes until the potato is soft and breaks up easily.

You can either blend the soup to make it smooth, or leave it chunky, which I prefer.

You can also add finely diced red pepper, carrots or celery at the potato stage, and small pasta shapes 10 minutes before the end of cooking (but if you do this you must add extra salt) to turn this soup into a minestrone, but this is Guy's original recipe.

The smell when it is cooking is amazing, and as it's so quick, simple and cheap to make, who needs to reach for a can?

ALWAYS READ THE INSTRUCTIONS!

*N*ow that we have our ceiling mobile TV aerial and can get two French channels (well, one French; ARTE is German, so I'm watching a German programme with French subtitles), we have splashed out on a bigger TV than the 21-inch TV/DVD player that came from our bedroom in Paris. This in turn has called for a bigger table to stand it on than the trolley a friend made for a school woodwork assignment many moons ago. As it's the time of the winter sales, we made a little detour to IKEA as we were leaving Paris and picked up a flat-pack: a stylish, practical unit with three deep drawers and spaces for a Digibox and DVD player. Although not in the ultimate style of the room, it could be painted and stencilled and put somewhere less traditional like the garden room at a later date.

I'm a picture person. I like my files in image view on my computer as sifting through lists sends my brain into freefall. Mr V, however, is the complete opposite. He loves sifting through orderly lists and can't abide it when I confront him with a screen full of images. That said, you can understand why he doesn't appreciate IKEA's language-free, universal, diagrammatic instructions. (I, by contrast, succeeded in making a slatted garden bench no problem.)

I told him to study the instructions before starting and to get all the bits out of their bags and identify which exactly is NBP27 and which is NBP24, even if they do look virtually the same. In addition, it was essential to ensure that various minute (read too small for the screws supplied) holes were facing the right way. But all of a sudden he's an expert in self-assembly furniture, so armed with his cordless screwdriver and little wooden mallet, he begins to proceed in the 'obvious' manner.

Marvellous. He's assembled it in less than the 40 minutes' recommended time. There's just one small snag: the drawers are facing the wall. I take the *merde* (crap) instructions and tell him that he needs to take it all apart and begin again at step one. But he doesn't want to do that. He snatches the sheet from me and says, 'Non, non, step five,' (actually *étape cinq*, but you know what I mean). This is followed by the dreaded phrase, 'It is good.' (You can add a French *bof* here. *Bof* is a frequently used French expression that can mean yes, no, maybe, I don't know, I don't care, or something else along those lines.)

Great. Admittedly without too much grumbling, he's taken it apart and reassembled it from step five, and the drawers are facing the right way around; the only problem is, they are now upside down.

Three hours and a lot of expletives later, plus returning to step one as I told him, we have functioning drawers facing the right way.

What Mr V has probably not learnt today: Always read all instructions before beginning any task.

EMPTY CHAIRS AND EMPTY TABLES

*I*t's the last week in January, and we didn't escape the promised violent winds; their evidence is lying prostrate on the floor of the forests. It saddens me greatly to see beautiful, majestic trees ripped up by their roots. It appears that about a third of them have been affected by the storms with either their branches hanging at odd angles like fractured limbs, or their roots in the air instead of in the earth. In his enlightening book *The Hidden Life of Trees*, Peter Wohlleben describes them having a social network to care for each other, and sometimes even giving nourishment to the stump of a felled tree. All ours seem to have survived except for one broken branch that will need an expert to remove as it's so high. Miraculously all the tiles are still on the roof, and even more miraculously no more water has entered the house, so the steps that Mr V built up to keep it out have worked.

There isn't a lot for me to do in the house at the moment, except for cooking and washing dishes, keeping the fire going and fetching things that Mr V has forgotten to take upstairs as he's plumbing in a much-needed radiator on the landing. (Is there no end to his talents?) Keeping the fire going is a bit of a full-time job. I've discovered that not all wood burns at the same rate. Being no expert, I've no idea which logs are going to disappear in a puff of smoke, which are going to go up in flames, which are going to snap, crackle and pop and send up sparks like a Roman Candle, and which are going to smoulder with hot embers that are often still red in the morning. So I regularly leave the room to come back twenty minutes later to a dead fire and have to try to revive it with kindling and pine cones.

As I haven't a lot to do, I'm concentrating on writing. I write in longhand. I feel the intimacy with the page, hear the scratch of the pen on the paper and watch my thoughts come to life, projected down my arm into my hand, through my fingers into the ink that makes the words magically appear. How wonderful it is to be able to create images and emotions in the minds of others. Hopefully I'm better at writing than fire-watching as it's gone out again.

* * *

Twenty-seven hours after we arrived we're packing the car to leave again, yet it feels once more like we've been here forever. Time takes on another dimension here. With each visit, however brief, we are laying down memories like seams of coal.

As we head back there are still vestiges of snow on the ground and vestiges of Christmas decorations hanging in tatters from doors and roofs, battered by the wind and rain. Wonky Christmas trees, their baubles scattered like acorns on the ground, are propped up forlornly against walls. As we pass a roadside café the owner is arranging his lime-green and mauve metal tables and chairs outside as if it was the height of summer, brushing snow from the chairs and wiping down the table tops, setting glass ashtrays in the centre. That's what I call optimism. I wonder if any customers will come to sit at them or whether they'll remain empty.

What I've learnt today: There's an art to putting logs on a fire.

PART IV
PRIMROSES BENEATH
THE SNOW

FEBRUARY AND MARCH 2018

Harshness vanished. A sudden softness
has replaced the meadows' wintry grey.
'Early Spring', Rainer Maria Rilke

YOU CAN'T MAKE AN OMELETTE
WITHOUT BREAKING EGGS

*T*he Côte-d'Or could more aptly be called the Côte-de Cuivre, as the countryside is more copper than gold. The angle of the early morning sun is casting a rose-gold glow onto the fields and trees that are lying beneath a deep eiderdown of snow. We've left a besieged Paris, which has seen the heaviest snowfall on record, where people have been skiing down the steps of the Sacre Coeur, and tobogganing on the esplanade in front of the Eiffel Tower. Along the route close to home, next year's Christmas saplings are beginning to form fledgling forests, and some are already over 60 centimetres tall. In this light they appear to be draped in silvery-white tinsel shimmering on their copper branches.

It's the first of February; the official last month of winter, and signs of spring are already emerging. Creamy-white and jewel-pink primroses that have been nestling beneath the snow reveal themselves as it shrinks back in the cold, crisp air. Yellow catkins dangle from the Alder trees, and the sheep are fat in the fields, full of lambs and the promise of the eternal cycle of rebirth. I am encouraged by the first tiny buds on my little lilac tree, which didn't look too happy after I transplanted it from its pot in autumn, making me fear that it wouldn't make it through the winter. The rosemary and mint are sprouting green leaves also, making me yearn to make large bowls of fresh salad to eat outdoors. I look forward with a growing anticipation towards spring and all the changes and challenges it will bring to Les Libellules.

Pappy Cardigan has just been to call and brought with him another offering; this time three boxes filled with twelve assorted eggs from Noëlle's hens, ducks and geese. It's easy to see which eggs come from which birds, as the goose eggs are pure white and twice the size of the honey-coloured hen's eggs, and the duck eggs are shiny, blue grey and half the size. I've never cooked a goose egg in my life, so I ring Noëlle to thank her and ask her how best to use them. She tells me that they have a richer flavour and a much bigger, fattier yolk than hen's eggs, and she recommends that I make an omelette with truffles. As I don't have any truffles to hand, I make an omelette and add some rehydrated porcini mushrooms, and a drizzle of olive oil infused with white truffle.

I take the fact that the hens, ducks and geese are laying in abundance as another sign that spring is around the corner.

⁂

We've just been shopping and as often happens here, we entered the shop in blue sky and sunshine, and exited into a snow blizzard. It is as if Aldi is a magic wardrobe leading to a Narnia-like world of eternal winter. As we drive back through thickening flakes, we congratulate ourselves on taking the decision not to put the shopping off until tomorrow. The snow is sticking fast, and with temperatures of -3 C forecast, it would be like an ice rink in the morning. We're looking forward to a hot cup of tea and a generous slice of the yogurt cake that I'd made with some of Noëlle's hens' eggs. But as I open the door to the garden room, I'm greeted by five centimetres of water. Bags of supplies that we brought from Paris and haven't yet emptied in our rush to go shopping are sopping wet. The temperamental electric toilet is having an off day.

The boiler room is under about ten centimetres of water, as is the bathroom. The steps that Mr V raised to keep the rainwater out, are now serving to keep the floodwater in, and my super rubber deck brush just pushes it around from one place to another without means of escape. Using a mop would be like trying to soak up a pint of milk with a cotton bud; an eiderdown or two are what is required. So we resort to the only things we have: a small dustpan with a long handle, and a small dustpan with a short handle, and scoop up about 100 millilitres at a time which we tip into a washing-up bowl, then empty the bowl into the bath. Four hours and much exchanging of dustpans later, as the short-handled one was a backbreaker, we are finally ready for the mop. The bath has a thick layer of mud in the bottom, which in turn we scoop out with a dustpan (this is where the short-handled one comes into its own) and throw it outside in the snow.

Time for tea and cake? Not on your life...it was time for apéritifs.

What I've learnt today: Always check that the toilet has stopped filling before leaving the building.

We eventually had our tea and cake the next day, and here's the recipe for you to try.

YOGURT CAKE

Serves 8-12 slices

Ingredients

Use an individual yogurt pot to measure everything. As long as the same pot is used for all ingredients, the recipe will work though may take longer to cook if you use a larger pot than the 150 g (5 fl oz) one I use.

1 pot of yogurt (natural or flavoured)
2 pots castor sugar (I add a sachet of vanilla sugar to mine)
½ pot melted butter
3 pots plain flour
½ sachet of dried yeast
3 medium eggs, separated

Method

Cream the egg yolks and sugar together with a wooden spoon until they become pale and fluffy.

Mix the yogurt with the melted butter, then add the egg and sugar mixture.

Add the yeast to the flour and fold into the rest of the ingredients a little at a time.

Whisk the egg whites and fold these into the mixture.

Pour into a 1 kg (2 lb) buttered loaf tin.

Bake in a preheated oven at around 200 C/gas mark 6 for about 40 minutes.

If the top starts to become too golden, cover loosely with some foil.

A lady who owns a rustic B&B near Annecy in the Alpine region of France gave me this recipe. It's one of the simplest, most foolproof cakes that I've ever made and lasts for a good five days wrapped in foil (if you can resist it that long). It's also great spread with a little jam at breakfast time (this is how I first tasted it).

I made my cake using my homemade, organic, live yogurt flavoured with some of my own jam/compote made with Sicilian clementines as they're in abundance in the markets at the moment. You can use any good quality natural yogurt and flavour it with some seasonal fruit or berries if you want to experiment with the taste.

STOP, IN THE NAME OF LOVE

*I*t was Saint Valentine's Day two days ago, and it's the Chinese New Year today. Normally we don't celebrate either, but this year is special on two counts. Firstly, because it's our first year at Les Libellules, and secondly because it's the beginning of the Year of the Dog. This is my year, and the last time it was the Year of the Dog, I met Mr V, so I have high expectations.

As I don't want to spend the evening cooking and washing pots and pans, or to risk another calf's-head restaurant experience, I've come with a freezer bag full of supplies from Picard, the French woman's secret weapon. Picard is a frozen food store extraordinaire, and the trick is to weave their dishes in amongst home-cooked ones, and only the other women at your dinner table will know (as they all do exactly the same). Like everything else, our nearest Picard is at Dijon, so I stopped at one on the outskirts of Paris on the way down. The meal is neither a traditional Saint Valentine's nor is it a Chinese banquet. Picard has a new Vietnamese range that looked delicious, so I opted for a taster-style meal with lots of different little courses, and a dessert of two pink sugar, casing hearts filled with mango ice cream and raspberry sorbet.

In retrospect, we may have been better off staying in Paris and going to a restaurant as so far the trip down has cost us around €200, and that isn't counting what I spent on the food or the wine. On top of the costs of the tolls on the autoroute and the price of petrol, we incurred another little unexpected expenditure…

The slip road after leaving the autoroute takes us onto a short stretch of dual carriageway before the road narrows into single lanes to pass through the small towns and villages en route. At the approach to this stretch of road there is a stop sign, but visibility is up to about 500 metres in each direction, so it's easy to see if the road is clear or not. If making a left turn and the road is busy, it's necessary to cross it in two stages, waiting on the central reservation until you can continue. Hence the stop sign.

On this occasion, a sunny morning with blue skies and good visibility, it was plain to see that there was no other traffic on the road, but we stopped nevertheless. Alas not long enough apparently. Although there is 'no minimum amount of time that you should stop prescribed by law, the vehicle must be seen to stop, and not merely slow down and keep rolling, and the driver must have the time to take note of, and act in a manner in accordance with, the traffic and the rules of priority'. (My translation of the *Code de la Route*, the French equivalent of *The Highway Code*.)

We pulled out onto the deserted road and continued for about 50 metres past an isolated house. A police car had been lying in wait in the concealed lane next to the house and came shooting out in hot pursuit with sirens blazing like something from *The Streets of San Francisco*. I didn't suspect for one minute that it was us they were chasing and wondered what on earth could have happened in such a backwater to elicit such a response. Mr V pulled over to the side of the road muttering, '*Merde flics,*' (in this instance meaning damn cops) and other unprintable, less than complimentary, expressions.

Instead of racing by as I expected, they stopped in front of us, and out of the patrol car came the worst possible scenario: middle-aged, paunchy, jobsworth policeman, complete with US cop-style shades and wet-behind-the-ears trainee. He first produced his badge, then his little, overused notebook, and throwing a smug sideways glance at his protégé, asked if we knew why we've been stopped. I was in the process of saying *pas du tout* (not at all), when I was drowned out by an unusually compliant Mr V admitting his guilt. To try to explain, negotiate or plead would have been futile, and to argue would have been downright stupid. This cop was on a mission, and he had an adoring audience. So we dutifully paid the colossal €90 on-the-spot fine (otherwise it would have been an eye-watering €135).

This in itself, as annoying as it was, didn't annoy me as much as the fact that huge international juggernauts hurtle down departmental roads, honking their great horns at local farmers, causing major traffic congestion in small towns along their route, particularly on fête days and market days. Plus, continuing to do so on a Sunday, flaunting France's no heavy goods at the weekend laws, except for local livestock and fresh food transportation, which Italian, German and Scandinavian haulage companies are obviously not carrying. This is in order to avoid paying the autoroute tolls therefore using France, with its central position sharing borders with eight other countries, as a virtually free thoroughfare. It is the people who live in these departments who are paying for the upkeep of these roads, that were never designed for such heavy frequent traffic. In addition, communities are being lost, as residents can no longer bear to live on the roadside with constant lorry noise that continues even through the night, and cafés and restaurants are going out of business, as eating outside on a summer evening would be like having a roadside table on the autoroute.

I feel that rather than rubbing their hands with glee each time they catch some unsuspecting driver jumping the gun on an empty road, the police would be better enforcing the weekend lorry ban and taking hefty fines from them to pay for the maintenance of the roads.

Welcome to the Year of the Dog...

What I've learnt today: Shut up and pay up if stopped by the traffic cops.

PRETTY POLLY

There are an extraordinary number of women of a certain age sporting some very peculiar hair colours, taking the concept of the blue rinse 50 shades further. I'm used to seeing boho, mature ladies in and around Paris with red, plum or even orange hair, but yesterday in the supermarket I counted five otherwise conservatively dressed (read frumpy) ladies looking like parrots with bright blue, turquoise, green and purple 'dos. No one else batted an eyelid as they strolled around with their nondescript husbands. It's I who elicit stares in my smart black trench and oxblood knee boots, and most noticeable of all, blonde hair. The one unifying factor that we shared is we're all wearing scarves. No self-respecting French person, man or woman, young or old, would venture out without a scarf of some description nonchalantly draped around their neck, unless the mercury reached at least 27 C. Over the years I've adopted this habit and become a little neurotic if I don't have one lurking in my bag, even if it's too warm to wear it.

Another tendency amongst the older female population in France in general is the wearing of extraordinarily bright tights. Colours such as vermillion (think of the Wife of Bath in her red stockings), deep purple and tangerine aren't uncommon. I find this strange in a country where the young women don't go in for highlights and hair straighteners, and definitely not caterpillar-thick eyebrows, fake tans or gel nails. They prefer a much more natural and discreet look, making overdressed tourists stand out a mile in Paris. Plus they adopt a kind of uniform of jeans and trainers in summer, and ankle boots and the obligatory black coat in winter. Once Mr V went to meet my daughter, Natasia at the airport in place of me, and I sent her a text message to say that he was waiting for her in the arrivals area wearing a black coat, to which she responded, 'Mum, they're all wearing black coats.' Maybe by the time they reach their 70s they feel the time has come to release their inner colours and *pourquoi pas*! (Why not!)

Talking of strange modes of dress, we look like characters from the classic British TV show *Last of the Summer Wine*, me dressed as the Nora Batty character with legwarmers wrinkling down my legs, two T-shirts, a sweater, a sleeveless gilet and wool poncho padding me out to twice my normal size. A woolly hat, scarf and fingerless gloves complete the look. Mr V looks like her ageing admirer Compo, in a woolly hat, actually, now I come to look at him, Mr V looks more like a giant Smurf than Compo, in a blue boiler suit with a blue beanie hat that has risen to a point on top of his head. To cap it all, my nose is a sort of purplish blue with the cold, and Mr V's is bright red to match his cheeks, like Mr Punch. Safe to say we're not the most attractive couple in the world; just as well we love each other, as I don't think anyone else would.

What I've learnt today: When buying tights in the UK I'm size medium; in Paris I'm large, and in Burgundy I'm small.

SWINGS AND ROUNDABOUTS

Our lives are shaped by our decisions and the choices that we make. It isn't possible to have your cake and eat it. The saying 'when one door closes, another one opens' is also true in the reverse. If you want something badly, then you have to make sacrifices to have it. When I met and fell in love with Mr V, I had to make a choice: either to stay in my comfortable life, in a job that I loved, surrounded by friends and family, or give everything up for a new life in a different country and culture, where I could barely speak the language.

I chose the second, and although it hasn't always been easy adjusting, especially once the honeymoon effect had worn off, I'm happy with my decision. I can't say that I made the right one, as who knows what other path may or may not have opened up for me if I'd stayed? Life is like that, so best not to ponder.

The same goes for our decision to buy Les Libellules. We'd strived for so long to have our own house, and more importantly our own land, but in order to achieve this, we now have very little money and virtually no time for anything else. The house is all-consuming, even preoccupying our thoughts, and the fact that my writing now centres around her.

Weekends used to be spent visiting châteaux or gardens, or walking in Paris, eating in our favourite crêperie and going to the cinema. But now we are…well, if you've read this far, you know the answer. We've shelved all plans for holidays or weekends away as our priorities have changed, and we would rather buy a window for a bedroom than have a week by a pool. Plus, with so much to do, our time is precious. We're not complaining; it's our choice. The châteaux will still be there, but now we have one of our own, and I feel blessed every day, even when I'm scooping up water with a small, floral dustpan.

Our saving grace has been the fact that we didn't get the keys to Les Libellules when we expected them around the end of February last year. She was being sold on behalf of five children, cousins of the previous occupant, as she had no immediate heir. Each inheritor had to be verified as legitimate, so it was the end of July before we had possession. Frustrating as this was at the time, in retrospect it was the best thing that could have happened. If we'd received the keys in early spring, we would have begun work immediately, but by mid summer was too late in the year to take on major works, so we decided just to live and enjoy and get to know the house.

This has given us time to get a real feel for what we want to achieve and what needs to be prioritised, and our plans have changed many times over the last six months as both problems and possibilities that we'd never even thought about have come to the foreground.

When we first arrived, I was obsessed with cleaning and mopping the muddy floors. Mr V found this frustrating, and he told me crossly, *'C'est un chantier ici.'* (It's a building site here.) But I now see that I was doing the very same thing that Pussy Willow did when she first arrived, going around rubbing her cheeks on every surface imaginable. I was making the place my own. Now I'm quite happy with mud on the floor but am a little apprehensive how our friends will feel about this when they arrive for a short visit at the end of the month, as we see none of the mess, only the task in hand. I think that others imagine that, as I am a writer, I embellish the facts for dramatic effect, which I can assure you I do not.

Taking on a project like this pushes you to your limits and beyond, physically, mentally and emotionally, and we've barely begun. But already I'm learning that I can live without many things that I thought were essential, and I'm living with many others that I never imagined I could (mice for example). Life is a balance of swings and roundabouts; you have to take the rough with the smooth.

Talking of swings and roundabouts, the blow-up bed has burst. I think that was partially due to me. I sat down rather heavily on my end to put on my boots, and I heard a loud pop. It looks as if I've displaced a fair amount of air, and the increased pressure on Mr V's side has caused a wall dividing two chambers to burst, making one large chamber that's now up in the air like a ski jump, forcing us both into the metre space at my end. I've not told him the reason why, but he'll know soon enough when he reads this. The good news is BUT has sent me a message saying that the bed is in stock. The bad news is it is impossible to get the telephone number of the store from the internet to arrange a delivery, and there wasn't one on the message or the receipt.

CHALK AND CHEESE

*O*ur very good friends Paree Jacques (PJ for short) and Panda have arrived at our Paris apartment from Wales in what is atrocious weather, which saw them taking four hours instead of two to get to Manchester airport in treacherous driving conditions. They had a two-hour flight delay as the plane needed to be de-iced twice before take-off. Then they were further delayed on the train from Charles de Gaulle Airport into Paris, stopping for fifteen minutes at each station en route in freezing temperatures with no heating. It was getting on for midnight when they finally arrived, so they required a lot of thawing out with hot baths and rum before we all fell into bed to be ready for an early start to Les Libellules the following morning. The UK is seeing some of its worst weather on record, with waterfalls frozen in mid-descent, and waves freezing as they break onto snow-covered beaches. Many isolated villages are cut off, so it's a miracle they made it.

I must explain our friend's name. Paree Jaques is so called as she studied the French Revolution as part of a BA in European history, and she's utterly bonkers about France, particularly Paris. She trots around in a beret and stripy top, photographing everything in sight, and immerses herself in the language, culture, food and wine. She can't get enough of fresh, crusty baguette; stinky, runny cheese, and if Charles Trennet isn't belting out 'Boum' on the hi-fi when she arrives, she gets very upset. Her husband, Panda, however, is a horse of a different colour. A Yorkshireman through and through, who shunned a glass of Bordeaux with his 'dinner', preferring a cup of milky Yorkshire tea with his 'tea'. He harbours a deep distrust of all things French, once uttering the immortal words 'cheese isn't a course' when PJ tried to persuade him away from a 'proper dinner' and serve him some 'fancy French muck'. Over the four evenings they will be staying, I've planned *confit de canard* as PJ adores duck, *boeuf Bourguignon* and a raclette, softening the cultural blow with the inclusion of a cottage pie and steamed cabbage. I also have an arsenal of eggs standing by to make emergency omelettes, which he loves, if it all gets too fancy, French and mucky for him.

On paper Mr V and Panda are a disaster. The cultured Frenchman, who, except for the fact that he doesn't wear a stripy top and beret, nor sport a handlebar moustache, is a living, breathing stereotype. He's as equally suspicious of all things un-French as Panda is of all things French, and his immortal words when I once had the audacity to try to serve him beans on toast were, *'Mais c'est un légume'* (But it's a vegetable), arguing that you wouldn't put peas on bread. It was futile to try to explain that baked beans aren't the same as peas, and toast is different from bread, and they're quite delicious and nutritious; bread in his world is for cheese. He *bons* and *bofs* his way through conversations, says yes when he means no and vice versa. I, being fluent in Gallic gestures and mannerisms, can tell by that 'Frenchie' thing he does with his mouth, as if he's trying to tackle an itch under his nose without touching it, what he means.

Then we have the Yorkshire terrier Panda who has a tattoo, smokes 'rollies', snacks on bags of crisps and Kit Kats, and listens to AC/DC, while Mr V reads Proust and Voltaire and huge, dull-looking biographies about obscure, political personalities. He snacks on foie gras and oysters, and listens to Mozart and Beethoven. And yet they get on like a house on fire. They're like two little boys playing together, both in their element to be left alone to hammer, saw and drill and mooch around DIY shops with their bilingual dictionary of building terms.

Panda has taken to answering *'oui, oui'* to everything Mr V says, and talking in that deliberate, drawn-out manner that people do when speaking to foreigners, even though Mr V's English is excellent. Mr V for his part has taken to calling Panda Pandy (his real name is Andy[1]) all of which is cracking up PJ and me. To top it all both of them are now wearing Smurf suits; Panda has arrived with a red boiler suit and domed-shaped hat, which even adds to the comedy, especially as he is a good twenty centimetres shorter than Mr V.

Some amazing transformations are beginning to happen. Panda has just had a glass of wine with his *boeuf Bourguignon* and stated, 'The food isn't *that* bad,' which I'll take as a huge compliment. He drew the line at cheese though and opted to go straight to *mousse au chocolat*.

PJ has earned herself a new nickname: Fire Starter. She's gone from being terrified of the open log fire to becoming positively possessive and territorial over it, so much so that should Mr V approach with a log, she snatches it from him, not allowing him to disturb her masterpiece. She's continually in and out, stocking up the log basket and clucking over the flames like a mother hen if they show signs of going out. I was worried that she would find it all a bit too rustic, but she's left Paree Jacques in Paris where she belongs and let Les Libellules work her magic.

Speaking of transformations, PJ and I are cleaning the *pigeonnier*. We've donned out-of -date surgeon's gloves, masks, visors and hats. (PJ works in an operating theatre, as I once did.) We look more like forensic scientists going to investigate a contaminated crime scene than the Mrs Mops that we actually are. We're armed with an extra-long cobweb brush to clean the very intricate rafters, a sort of square mop head on a long pole to reach inside the higher pigeon holes, and a dustpan and brush, plus a stiff floor brush, a couple of buckets and a large supply of bin bags. I'm hoping to find some treasure squirreled away, but so far we've only unearthed a lot of cobwebs and dead spiders, copious amounts of dust, and a couple of mice with rigor mortis. In fact, the dust is so thick that we have to keep going out onto the little Juliet balcony to breathe. To top it all, I've developed yet another cold, and my nose is dripping into the mask, making matters ten times worse.

All I find of dubious interest is a metal plaque advertising motor oil, and an old ledger with nothing very remarkable written in it. PJ has found a small, oval, cardboard box that looks like one I used to get Turkish delight in at Christmas, but it's so blackened and thick with dust that I think its origins will remain a mystery forever. Still, I put these items to one side in the rose room, while all else goes into bin bags which Mr V unceremoniously throws over the balcony. PJ has attempted to clean the box, but no amount of rubbing is removing the patina of grime, and rubbing any harder would destroy whatever was underneath anyway, so she abandons it with the rest of the junk on the landing.

*　*　*

The Smurfs have gone to Dijon to pick up the bed, so PJ and I now turn our attention to deflating the blow-up mattress in preparation for its arrival. This involves one of us kneeling on the floor like the little Dutch boy with his finger in the dyke as, having lost the attachment, this is the only way we can open the valve to allow the air to escape. The other one has the joy of rolling around like a sea lion on the bed to try to force the air towards the valve. All that seems to be happening is that we're shifting it from one place to another as the mattress rises and falls in large rubber waves. During this unflattering exercise we develop some interesting postures: the downward dog, spread eagle and reclining Buddha to name but a few, plus PJ's delicate British digestive system isn't handling all the cheese courses as well as my Franglais one, which results in her letting out about an equal amount of air as the mattress. It takes us exactly the same amount of time and a lot more effort to extract all the air and roll up the mattress as it did the Smurfs to get to Dijon, pick up the bed and drive back, but we're decidedly hotter and sweatier.

One hour, two screwdrivers and four people later, in the space where the hideous, ski-jump, inflatable contraption once resided, is a gorgeous, oak-framed bed. I get a little carried away and crack open the rather luxurious new bedding that I was saving until the room was decorated, as it would be sacrilege to put anything else on that deep, densely sprung mattress. For the first time in seven months, I'm looking forward to bedtime. It can't come soon enough, as my dripping nose has progressed into me burning up and aching all over. I've never been happier to slink between satiny sheets and sleep.

*　⁂　*

This morning I awake to a knock on the bedroom door. I've indeed slept long and well. Mr V is nowhere to be seen, and PJ comes in with a much-appreciated cup of tea. She places it on a folded-up paper tissue on the bedside table and leaves. Five minutes later Mr V appears, bearing a tray of more tea and toast, something that would have been impossible to negotiate on the blow-up bed. The sleep has done me good. I'm still full of cold, but the fever has subsided. I take the cup from the bedside table and put it on the tray. I don't want to chance carrying it down the steep, poorly lit stairs, so I leave it on the bed but pick up the paper hanky that the cup has been resting on, which is still warm and slightly damp.

Out on the landing I see the oval box that PJ had left there the day before. I don't know why, but I wipe it with the warm, damp tissue, and as if by magic, the dust and grime that had proved so stubborn effortlessly disappear, revealing what is indeed a box for some sort of confectionery. Then a name appears arched around the top of the lid in olde-worlde gold lettering—Les Jacquelines—Jacqueline being PJ's actual name. The coincidence brings me out in goosebumps.

I go downstairs to find her; she's drinking coffee on the terrace, taking advantage of the now warm spring sunshine. I show her the box, and she wells up. This is another of those magic moments Les

Libellules keeps creating. As it was PJ who found this treasure, it is as if the house has given her a sign confirming that they now share a special bond. Indeed if I'd been cleaning the *pigeonnier* with anyone else, this box would probably have been destined to go directly into a bin bag.

Most of the rest of the box is covered by the same olde-worlde text, printed in rose pink. It tells the story of how in 1383, Charles VI of France rewarded Philipe II, Duke of Burgundy, for helping him gain victory over the *Gantois* (inhabitants of Ghent who, from what I can gather, were a revolutionary group against the bourgeoisie). He honoured the town of Dijon with a clock mounted on a bell tower which had an *automate*, a mechanised figure of a man, also known as a *Jacquemart*, who struck the bell with a little hammer on the hour. This was placed on the top of the church of Notre-Dame, where it can still be seen today, and is one of the oldest and most famous examples of a Jacquemart. This made the discovery even more astonishing as PJ's full name is Jacqueline Martin. During the 17th century the people of Dijon added a 'wife' for Jacquemart—Jacqueline—who strikes the half hour, and later two 'children'—Jacquelinet and Jacquelinette—who strike the quarter hours.

Arched around the bottom of the lid, in the same antique gold lettering as on the top, are the words Michelin Dijon. The text also explains that in 1926, Michelin presented the town of Dijon with a sample of these bonbons in homage to 'Jacqueline, the loyal wife of Jacquemart'. Traditionally these almond-shaped sweets have a rose-pink, violet, yellow or brown sugarcane casing. The pink contain praline; the yellow, nougat; the violet, cassis, and the brown, chocolate. You can still buy them in their traditional box, but be warned, they cost €44 for 300 grams.

※　※　※

Panda has expanded his vocabulary and has added *bof* to *oui, oui*. I don't know if this is the right kind of progress as now we have two of them boffing (in the French sense of the word) and pouting and making little 'puh' sounds accompanied by shoulder shrugging when we ask them a question.

'How long will you be?'

'Puh.' Shrug.

'What time do you want to eat?'

'*Bof.*'

'Would you like a cup of tea?'

'Puh, *bof.*'

And so on.

Panda is also drinking tea, albeit the Yorkshire variety, without milk and sugar, and taking a morsel of non-smelly cheese before his dessert. Not only that, he's progressed from a glass of wine with his 'dinner' to participating in one or three glasses of rum or port for an 'extended' apéritif.

'Would you like an apéritif?'

'*Oui, oui!*'

'Rum or port?'

'*Bof.*'

As we only got '*bof*' as an answer when we asked what time Mr V and Panda would be ready to eat, PJ and I are doing the last-minute preparations for a raclette. They're standing with their backs to the fire like naughty schoolboys, their derrières glowing from the heat of the embers, and their faces glowing from the effects of the port.

What I've learnt today: Treasure comes in all forms.

---

1. *Andy Pandy* was a British children's TV series.

THINGS THAT GO BUMP IN THE NIGHT

I've just witnessed the most extraordinary scene. As we have no upstairs toilet, I needed to tiptoe through the living room where I expected to find PJ and Panda sleeping on the sofa bed. So it came as some surprise to see them both crawling around on all fours in their pyjamas at 4 a.m. (Actually, only PJ was wearing pyjamas; Panda was in boxer shorts and a T-shirt.) PJ was brandishing her phone as a torch and Panda holding a heavy, hardbacked book on how to renovate a French country house. House Mouse it seems is really Penthouse Mouse and has installed itself on the rafters. It was this that was attracting Pussy Willow to jump on top of the cupboard, not spiders as I previously thought.

Apparently, PJ had awoken to the sound of scratching and nibbling at the beams, which are, as all other sources of food are now firmly locked away in tins and jars, probably all it has left to eat. There was something not quite adding up with this course of action, as everyone knows, beams are on the ceiling, not the floor. PJ explains that she distinctly heard a thud, well more like a 'plop' really, and is convinced that Penthouse Mouse is now at ground level. While she wasn't entirely happy to have it ferreting around above her, she's positively unhappy at the prospect of sharing a bed with it. Hence she's using the phone as a searchlight, and Panda has the heaviest object he could find to drop on the unfortunate creature should they locate it.

I say the simplest thing would be to put a piece of cheese on the kitchen floor and leave the door ajar as I'm sure it would much prefer to nibble that than PJ's toes, so this is what they do. I continue to the bathroom where the bulb appears to have gone in the light. When I say gone, I don't mean in the figurative sense, as in it no longer works; it literally isn't there. It was there when Mr V and I went to bed, so I ask PJ and Panda if they know what's happened to it, to which they give the same reply: 'It was there when we went to bed.'

The next morning the cheese is still where we left it, and we discover the light bulb, perfectly intact and in working order, in the bath. I don't want to raise alarm, but this is virtually impossible as it's a bayonet-type fitment, and this is the same bulb that no one has touched since July. The ceilings are extremely high, so the fall alone should have shattered the glass, or at least rendered it unusable. The second point is the light isn't even above the bath. Cue the spooky music...

All too soon, it's time to pack up and take Paree Jacques back to Paris to catch the plane to Manchester. Neither she nor Panda had been prepared for the effect that Les Libellules was going to have on them, and they are searching for dates when they can return. Apart from picking up some dodgy French, Panda has been an invaluable help to Mr V, both in terms of practical assistance and advice as he works in the building trade as a painter and decorator and tiler extraordinaire and has also acquired a lot of building knowledge over the years. We all feel more than a little bit richer for this treasured time spent together.

As it was my *Boeuf Bourguignon* that started this metamorphism, here's the recipe for you all to try.

BOEUF BOURGUIGNON

Serves 4

Ingredients

700 g (1.5 lb) of braising steak (chuck steak)
A good glug of olive oil
100 g (3.5 oz) bacon lardons
2 shallots, very finely chopped
A glug of sherry vinegar (I use Maille Vinaigre de Xérès)
2 tbsp cornflour seasoned a little with salt and pepper
500 ml (¾ bottle) red wine (preferably Burgundy)
440 ml (¾ pt) beef stock
25 g (1 oz) chilli chocolate. (Just use 70%+ cocoa solids chocolate if
you don't like chilli, but this doesn't make it spicy, just gives the sauce
a little *je ne sais quoi*.)
1 bay leaf
4 medium carrots, cut into bite-sized chunks
50 g (2 oz) salted butter
12 small pickling onions
A good pinch of brown sugar
200 g (7 oz) small chestnut or button mushrooms
Salt and pepper to season

Method

Cut the meat into medium-sized chunks and toss in the seasoned cornflour.

Heat the olive oil until just starting to sizzle in a heavy-bottomed casserole (preferably le Creuset or similar; alternatively use a slow cooker as I do at Les Libellules) and brown the beef on all sides to seal in the juices, then remove from the pan and set aside. (This is best done in small batches so that it seals quickly; if you put too much meat in the pan at once it will create steam and not brown.)

Reduce the heat and add the bacon lardons to the pan and sauté for 3 minutes until beginning to brown, then add the shallots and cook for a further minute, taking care not to burn.

Return the beef to the pan.

Add the sherry vinegar and allow to evaporate.

Add a good glug of the wine, stirring well to form a paste with the flour.

Add the beef stock, stirring well to avoid lumps developing. If this does happen just continue stirring until they disappear.

Add the remainder of the wine and finally the chocolate, stirring until the chocolate has melted, and is incorporated into the sauce.

Add the bay leaf and reduce the heat as low as possible and gently simmer for at least 5 hours (the longer the better), stirring from time to time.

An hour before serving, sauté the carrots in a third of the butter for 5 minutes then add to the casserole.

Sauté the onions with a third of the butter and a pinch of brown sugar until they are caramelised then add to the casserole.

Immediately before serving, sauté the mushrooms in the remaining butter, add to the casserole and simmer for a further 5 minutes.

Add salt and pepper to taste.

Remove the bay leaf before serving.

I served this with very lightly steamed shredded spring cabbage and mustard mashed potatoes. (After mashing with a little melted butter seasoned with salt and pepper and mustard, I baked it in a hot oven for 10 minutes just to crisp it up to add another texture to the dish.)

A delicious alternative is to top it with a crusty baguette cut into 2 cm (1 in) slices and then some Comté cheese (Cheddar works very well also) and bake in a hot oven until the cheese has melted. Serve immediately.

This is the perfect dinner party dish, as if guests linger over the aperitif, the flavour just gets better, and the mouth-watering aroma while it is cooking fills everyone with anticipation of the gastronomical delights to come.

CULTURE CLUB

*H*aving PJ and Panda to stay not only highlighted cultural differences but also how much I have changed without realising it. When I first got together with Mr V, having never been a typical Francophile (ideally I wanted to marry an Italian man and live in Tuscany), I devoured books of this ilk in an effort to understand from a first-hand account what it was really like to live in France. It soon became clear that language wasn't my only problem. Though separated by the mere 35 kilometres of the English Channel, or *La Manche* as it's called on this side, culturally France and the UK were an ocean apart. I felt like I'd gone through the looking glass. All the codes that I'd previously lived by singled me out as at best a foreigner, or at worst someone who was rude or lacked manners.

The first time Mr V came to stay at my home in Wales, this was glaringly obvious. To the French, food is almost a religion. They have set things to eat at set times. *Le petit déjeuner* (breakfast but translates as small lunch) is anything but *petit*, and I've not met a single French person who would skip this most important meal of the day and grab a coffee and an energy bar (or even worse, an energy drink) on the way to work. Given the chance, Mr V will plough through an entire baguette loaded with jam, followed by croissants, pains au chocolat

186

and pains aux raisins, plus any cake that's on offer. Even if I give him a full English breakfast, he sees that as a prelude to the obligatory carb fest. *Déjeuner* (lunch) isn't to be confused with my idea of a midday snack.

To my horror I discovered that he ate a four-course meal at this time every day consisting of *entrée* (starter), *plat* (main dish), *fromage* (cheese) and dessert. I must point out that these courses are generally smaller and simpler than their English counterparts. The starter is usually vegetable or salad-based, the main a piece of fish or meat served with one or two vegetables, and the dessert is often fruit-based. This takes time to eat and to digest, so most French people take at least an hour for lunch, often longer. In the evening we get to do it all again, only with the added joy of an apéritif beforehand. The apéritif is a most civilised custom, and one that I took to like a duck to water. It provides a valuable pause between the working day and the evening meal to talk and, if you have guests, socialise. This is why French meals are simple, because the hostess would rather be nibbling on some *petits biscuits d'apéritif* (small appetiser biscuits) and downing a *kir* than screaming 'I'll be there in a minute,' from a steamy kitchen.

One important addition I forgot to mention is *le goûter* (literally to taste) which takes place at four o'clock. This is primarily for the children when they come home at this time, to tide them over until dinner, but many adults, Mr V included, continue with this tradition of having something sweet with a drink around four o'clock in the afternoon.

The second point that I discovered was where to place your hands when at the table. I was shocked that Mr V kept his in full view when not eating, when I'd been taught this is impolite and they should rest firmly on your lap out of sight. Not in France, I learnt. While eating out with a French family, the mother severely reprimanded her eight-year-old son for sitting with his hands beneath the table. The child replied in French, 'But Lindy is doing it,' which, to my embarrassment, the mother replied (also in French, not realising that I could understand), 'Lindy doesn't know any better; she's English.' One major lesson learnt the hard way... The story goes that the French keep their hands where they can be seen, or who knows what they could be getting up to under the table—oh là là!

Now we come to what to eat for lunch. Before I realised that this was an actual meal and not just a sandwich, soup and a bread roll, or beans on toast, I presented Mr V with all three (on different occasions). All met with equal horror. To him a sandwich is something you take on long car or train journeys for convenience; it doesn't even make it onto the picnic list. (The French invented the *pique-nique*.) So serving one up on a plate with a little side salad did nothing to disguise the fact that 'this is *not* food'. The soup was happily received as he thought it was the *entrée* and not the main event, until I attempted to tart this up with a crusty roll and a little dish with expertly curled portions of butter. By the look on his face, I knew that I'd offended his Parisian sensibilities.

'Don't they serve bread with soup in France?' I asked.

'Yes…in the country.' He meant this was a bit 'provincial' to say the least.

Wine is also not generally served with soup in France, and my suggestion that I serve a nice crisp Chablis to accompany *soupe de moules* was frowned upon also. Mr V told me that in the country they put a small glass of red wine into soup as we would cream, but don't serve it by the glass.

While we're on the subject of wine, this is something that the French drink with a meal, not while getting ready for a night on the town, or while cooking, or watching a film, or any other of the little guilty pleasures that we in the UK extract from the nectar of the vine. Hence when the meal is over, the bottle goes away. This results in a strategic exercise to finish the bottle while hanging onto a full glass at the end of the meal. This is tricky, as wine isn't drunk with dessert, unless you open a bottle of specific dessert wine or, if you're really pushing the boat out, champagne. This means that you have to make sure you top up during the cheese course.

Frenchmen have a reputation for being romantic, and Mr V certainly lived up to it in the early years. I regularly received bouquets of roses, chocolates, perfume and sometimes tiny boxes containing items of jewellery concealed under a table napkin at a restaurant. One such present was a beautiful necklace, a golden dragonfly with amethyst wings that found its way beneath my pillow after he'd left to return to France. I would find notes and poems tucked between the pages of a book and receive cards and letters and photographs. When we were first courting (I don't think people still use this expression, but it was a definite courtship), Mr V took me to a very fancy restaurant in Paris. On this particular occasion there was no little surprise, just an excellent sole meunière and a rather expensive bottle of Chablis. At the end of the meal there was a good glass and a half left in the bottle. Not wanting to waste such a fine wine, I took the opportunity to quickly fill my glass, and empty it even quicker, while Mr V went to powder his nose. On his return a slightly raised eyebrow signalled that he'd noticed what I'd done. We laugh about this now, but I would never do the same thing in such an establishment again.

Just when I thought I'd cracked it, this evening I served oysters as an *entrée*—with the 'wrong' type of bread: crusty white baguette instead of rye bread with butter.

You live and learn...

MOTHERING SUNDAY

*T*oday is Mother's Day in the UK, but unlike in the past, this morning I haven't woken to the sound of a tea tray rattling its way towards me with a banquet of a cup of half-spilt tea, some underdone soggy toast, a droopy little daffodil in a glass, plus two very proud and excited little girls. No, this morning I'm rudely awakened by Mr V screwing down floorboards in the loft space immediately above my head. Granted, he's been up since 7 a.m. and has been chomping at the bit to get cracking, while my five more minutes, if the church bell clanging in the distance can be believed, have transpired into two more hours. This is what having a real bed means; I'm so happy no longer to be sleeping on an overgrown lilo that I just don't want to get up.

The bells, and Mr V's antics in the attic, aren't the only things beckoning me out of bed. It's a glorious, spring-like morning, with clear blue skies and intense pure light, so after breakfast I decide to attempt to walk to the *boulangerie* in the village where the church bells were ringing to buy bread. Various neighbours have told us that it wasn't possible to walk there as it was too far and the road was too dangerous, hence I've never ventured forth on foot. The road sign says one kilometre, the same distance to the village in the opposite direction which, is easily walkable, but having driven through both by car, the second seemed much further.

I set out in anticipation of what new delights and discoveries I'll encounter. The distance, it turns out, is indeed as the crow flies, as a narrower country lane leaves the main road and snakes its way through the rolling landscape. If I was in any doubt that I was in the heart of rural Burgundy, the aromatic clumps of dung decorating the much patched and pitted path, provide the evidence that this is farming country.

The sounds of nature abound; an exaltation of larks rise in unison from a ploughed field, the flapping of their collective wings sounding like bunting blowing in the breeze. A sparrow hawk swoops like a silent assassin, triggering a frenzy of alarm calls from the treetops. And a stream tumbles down a miniature waterfall, babbling and gurgling as it falls. I pass a few cars, whose occupants are clearly startled by the sight of me tramping along, camera in hand, and I wonder if they put two and two together that I'm the eccentric English woman who has bought 'Leah's house'.

The village is larger than it appears from my bedroom window and is mainly a jumble of stone cottages in various stages of collapse, but obviously still loved and still lived in. Music from a radio drifts from behind broken blue shutters, evoking images from the lyrics of a song 'banjos playing through broken glass'. I head towards the steeple of the church, which stands in a slightly elevated position to my right. This leads me to what I imagine was a latter-day village green bordered by some not-so-dilapidated, and not so picturesque, houses, and my destination, the *boulangerie*.

Wipe any image that you may be conjuring up of one of those pictures that you can buy in popular home furnishing stores of a quaint, provincial patisserie with jolly, red and white awning shading some expectant little tables, and a patron wearing a white apron like Rene from *'Allo 'Allo!*[1] waiting, tray in hand, to take your order. The only thing to distinguish this from all the other nondescript houses is faded red lettering saying Café Boulangerie. There's no clue to indicate that the place is open, or even still in business, until the peace in the square is shattered by several grubby little Citroën vans screeching to a halt, and their equally grubby occupants jumping out and heading towards what look like garage doors at the side of the building. I've obviously arrived at 'rush hour', or maybe they've just been let out of church and are desperate for a coffee or, more likely, a Cognac. I've a feeling that they're not in search of a baguette, so I opt to take what looks like a UPVC back door.

I don't find myself in a traditional French *boulangerie/pâtisserie* with shelves stacked with crusty baguettes, rustic rounds of cottage loaves, and impossible-to-resist cakes and pastries tempting me from a glass-fronted display case. On the contrary, on the counter is one small basket in which sit a couple of crumbly pains au chocolat and croissants, and another containing three forlorn looking baguettes, plus an assortment of cardboard boxes brimming with the type of cheap, rubbishy chocolate and bonbons that attract small children. To my left is a pine bookcase stacked with what look like out-of-date tinned goods, while in the window, taking the place where usually the tempting cakes would be, is a selection of second-hand books and general, tatty bric-à-brac. I'm not sure if I've entered a shop or a jumble sale. Also on the counter is a till, similar to the type that I played with as a child, and a beautifully kept ledger of sales waiting patiently for the next entry, but of the shopkeeper, not a sign.

A clue to her location comes from strains of animated conversation and clattering emitted from the other side of an adjoining door; the café, I presume. I take the plunge and enter not into a café but a bar at which two chubby-cheeked children are perched on high stools, drinking something through a straw. They immediately stop when I walk in and start giggling uncontrollably. I must admit I do find this more than a tad unnerving as it isn't the usual reaction that I elicit. They're not the only ones to fall silent at my entrance; it's like an action replay of my foray into Brico Dépôt.

There are four Formica-topped tables at which groups of men with weather-beaten faces and clothes fresh from the fields, rather than morning mass, are sitting with cigarettes drooping from their mouths (yes, inside), knocking back glasses of what I hazard a guess at as Cognac. All heads turn simultaneously in my direction, displaying expressions ranging from open curiosity and guarded smiles, to a couple of downright leers. A woman, in their bar, on a Sunday morning, not local, and what's more, not French!

A friendly female voice breaks the spell. *'Bonjour, madame. Je peux vous aider?'* (Can I help you?) It's the shopkeeper/barmaid, dressed in a nylon overall of the type my grandmother used to wear for baking, but that they still sell in markets up and down France. I ask for two baguettes, and she scurries from behind the bar and leads me back into the *boulangerie*. On my departure the animated conversation resumes, from which I pick up the words 'English woman' accompanied by some raucous laughter. I make a mental note to return with Mr V, dressed in my best Parisian attire; that will give them something to put in their Gitanes[2] and smoke.

*   *   *

On returning to the hamlet with my hard-earned baguettes tucked beneath my arm, I pass Mr Mouton's field and notice that one of the ewes is lying on her side with her back leg raised in the air, and I realise that she's about to give birth. This thrills me greatly; the ewe, however, seems to be viewing the whole process with disinterest as she calmly nibbles away at the grass. The only sign of the imminent event is two tiny black feet alternately protruding and receding in a 'now you see them, now you don't' manner. After about ten minutes of me subconsciously straining each time the feet appear, the ewe decides to join in the fun and makes little hiccupping motions with her abdomen. Finally, a bit more effort is required, and she arches her neck and lets out a single bleat. And voilà. A new life has entered the world—on Mother's Day!

I feel so privileged to have been able to witness this miracle of nature, which I evidently found more overwhelming than the new mother, who astonishingly continues to graze for what seems to me like minutes, while the newborn lamb lies like a slimy glove puppet on the ground. I'm tempted to climb over the fence and rub the little inanimate animal with straw (as I've seen done by a television vet). Then the ewe finally finds her maternal instincts and at last raises herself and begins to nuzzle and lick the little, lifeless body.

I hold my breath until the lamb lets out a long-awaited 'baaaaa' and struggles to its knees. The mother now pushes it onto its wobbly black legs, and within seconds the newborn is shaking itself and searching for a nipple to suckle. If the mother could have been auditioning for a part in *The Silence of the Lambs*, her offspring is anything but silent. The newcomer is very vocal, sounding like a toy train tooting around a track, not a bit like the lambs I'd heard in the fields close to my home in Wales. Within next to no time, it has fluffed up, found its feet and is springing about like, well, a spring lamb.

This isn't at all like my own experiences in the delivery suite, and I muse over why human mothers seem to be the only ones that suffer such long and painful labours. Maybe the answer lies in the book of Genesis, and we're paying the price for Eve's sins in the Garden of Eden. I give a silent prayer of thanks for the wonder of creation and continue back to Les Libellules, warmed by the late-morning sun and the experience.

The day continues as if spring has arrived at last. There is real warmth in the sun, and we eat our lunch on the terrace for the first time this year, albeit wearing light fleeces. This is such a pleasure after the almost persistent rain and snow of the last three months. We work a little in the garden, finally cutting the spindly rosebush practically back to its roots. I feel a bit guilty doing this, but otherwise the roses will be at the top of one-and-a-half-metre stalks come summer. Bees are buzzing busily between the few flowers hardy enough to survive the snow and frost, and I count four different varieties of butterfly, including an enormous Red Admiral that wouldn't settle long enough for me to photograph. All is a frenzy of activity, including the birds, who are once again back and forth with twigs in their beaks. I for my part have filled the line with washing and am taking great pleasure in watching it flutter in the breeze. The air is filled with birdsong, and I'm beginning to distinguish the different sounds, although I still can't identify all the birds by name.

The fine weather has brought Flaubertine out of hibernation in the barn, and she's lying on the warm paving stones on the patio, cooing and rolling on her back in cat happiness. I've not spoken of Maddy for some time; this isn't to say that she's disappeared from my thoughts; quite the contrary, I think of her all the time. Every time I catch sight of a cat that resembles her, my heart skips a beat. I hope against hope that someone has taken her and given her the home she so much wanted and deserved, but I daren't make enquiries as I fear hearing the worst. Where there's hope, there's still the possibility of life. But I've resigned myself to the fact that she won't suddenly appear with a troupe of kittens as I first hoped. So I'll lay this to rest now, but continue to carry her in my heart.

---

1. A British sitcom set in France during World War II.
2. French brand of cigarettes.

FROM RUSSIA WITH LOVE

*W*e are three days from the start of spring, and it has snowed during the night. The Beast from the East, so called as the extreme weather is coming from Siberia, has struck again. We are in the doldrums here at Les Libellules with nothing much happening. The thing with writing a memoir is that you have absolutely no control over what you're going to write. It isn't like fiction where *you* drive the plot and lead your characters in whatever direction you want. In a novel you can rustle up a storm or bring out the sun to suit yourself, inject humour, horror, sadness and pathos at will, and if it isn't quite working, rip it up and start again. Writing a memoir gives you nowhere to hide; you have to tell it how it is, it's all about finding the remarkable in the sometimes unremarkable.

I think of all the people before me who have kept diaries, never imagining their outcome. Anne Frank springs instantly to mind, writing 'Dear Kitty' to her 'friend and confidant', not aware that she was chronicling one of the darkest periods of history. I'm not professing any such greatness but feel a responsibility to future readers just the same, as what we write today is the history of tomorrow.

The birds are clamouring for fat balls to be hung on the threadbare branches of the feather tree, as the ground is once more too hard and hostile for their little beaks to penetrate. Their nest-building and incessant chirping of a week ago has ceased, as they need all their energy to find food and keep warm. The expectant sheep are tucked snugly away in the barn, so there are no more lambs to report. The shiny green buds that filled the branches with promise are now more like cotton buds, a coating of snow halting any hope of them bursting into leaf.

We need supplies (wine and port) as after the festivities of the weekend with PJ and Panda, our reserves have run a bit dry, and we're expecting our next guests at Easter, so we head for Saulieu. I'm hankering after one of the marzipan figs filled with custard that I described in an earlier section, so we park in the snowy street opposite the *boulangerie* and slip and slide across the road to buy a box of four cakes, two for after lunch and two for after dinner. (Like the birds, we're eating to keep warm.)

When we return to the car, miraculously with the cakes still intact, we notice a very nondescript, dark blue door with a dirty, old sign saying *Antiquités Brocante* (Antiques, Bric-à-Brac). The place looks like it's shut, but we try the door anyway. It creaks open, and we enter into a dark corridor lined with grandfather clocks, all as dusty and dirty as the sign. There's very little natural light, so after the glare of the snow outside it takes a while for our eyes to adjust. The clocks themselves are forming the corridor, leading from which are various alleys, the first having shelves of dolls that look like they come from the Victorian period, and cloth figures of French peasants and trades folk. The next alley has porcelain: fancy clocks and figurines in 18th-century costume, and gorgeous little tea sets whose cups have handles so tiny that they appear to be for a child. There are enormous soup tureens and equally huge oval serving dishes, again embellished with 18th-century-type figures in delicate pink and blue.

Around the next corner I'm in heaven. It is crammed with Art

Nouveau objects: clocks, vases, figurines of elegant ladies with bobbed hair and arms stretched out holding onto the leads of equally elegant dogs. Green-glazed dolphins twist above lapis lazuli waves surrounding a clock face. Glass-topped cases display brooches, hat pins, and buckles and beads. And, there amongst it all, the most gorgeous vase shaped like an iris bulb with two flowers supporting each side. What's more, it is the exact shades of purple and green that I would like in the garden room. I have to have it. Like everything else in the shop, it is filthy dirty and there's a small piece chipped from the top that I figure a touch of the right shade of nail polish should disguise. The man wants €40. He tells us it's genuine, which it does appear to be as it's signed and numbered, and that it would fetch ten times that price if it didn't have the chip, which he himself pointed out to us. Mr V starts to blah blah blah about how we'd just bought a house nearby and would be looking to furnish it when it was finished, and showed particular interest in a kidney-shaped rosewood chest of drawers with a beautiful, pink marble top that I would love for the rose room. The result of which is, the man lets us have the vase for €20, and it has cleaned up a treat. All I need now, like for everything else that I'm accumulating, is the room to put it in.

What I've learnt today: A little blah blah blah goes a long way.

✳   ✳   ✳

Once more it's time to leave, for another three weeks, which as always makes me sad.

When we return it will be Easter, and I wonder if winter will continue to play cat and mouse with spring. It seems that summer was reluctant to give way to autumn, and autumn to winter, but winter is turning out to be more than a match for them all, and I've heard today that they're predicting a white Easter. I don't know what effect this unseasonable weather will have on nature and agriculture. I read in the newspaper that six out of ten gardeners have reported that plants have suffered or died. In this region there are also the vines to consider, but I discovered a couple of local sayings in the *Burgundy Almanac* which translate as 'Snow in January, wheat in the barn' and 'A cold January without snow is bad for the trees and vines'. I don't know if the same is true of snow in March and even April? *On verra* as they say—we shall see. Maybe this year will be an excellent vintage.

PART V
LILAC TIME

APRIL AND MAY 2018

To grace the bush I love—to sing with the birds,
A warble for joy of Lilac-time.
'Warble for Lilac-Time', Walt Whitman

IN SEARCH OF LOST TIME

*J*t's a Wednesday afternoon, and we're driving down to Les Libellules through torrential rain. The spray from lorries that are dangerously overtaking is making visibility very difficult. What's more, as we're planning to stay for six days, we have Pussy Willow with us. She, however, is remarkably contented, with none of the usual scrambling about the car wailing inconsolably or crouching on the parcel shelf growling at the vehicle behind. This is due to Burt Bacharach, or should I say Dionne Warwick singing Burt Bacharach. I found this forgotten music on my Kindle, and it is having a much more calming effect than the Mozart and Bach that Mr V usually plays in the car. She particularly likes it when I join in singing along and is purring. Mr V isn't enjoying the experience quite so much, especially when I do my Cilla Black impersonation and attempt to hit the high notes in 'Anyone Who Had a Heart'.

The date is the 28th of March, so technically we're still in Part Four, but we shall be crossing the border into April on Sunday. The prolonged stay is due to Mr V taking RTT which stands for *Réduction du Temps de Travail*. This is the term given to time accumulated by French employees working more than the statutory 35-hour week, which was introduced in 1981 by the socialist president François

Mitterrand as part of his electoral programme. Monday is the Easter bank holiday, and there's to be the first of many planned train strikes on Tuesday, so Mr V would have no means of getting to work anyway. Just one of the many joys of living in France.

We're passing through fields of green shoots poking through the soil, searching for the evasive sun. The trees are mostly still bare, with the few exceptions brave enough to blossom sheltering amongst the barren branches. The hill of happiness, however, is, for the first time since last summer, cloaked in verdant grass, and the uppermost tips of the tallest deciduous trees have taken leaf. I've never noticed before that buds burst from the top down, but then I'd never noticed a lot of things in nature before moving to the country.

I was an expert at spotting an empty seat through the window of a metro train pulling into the station, and swiftly and smoothly securing it. But the closest I got to the natural world was deadheading the geraniums on the tiny balcony outside our bedroom in Paris, or picking ripe tomatoes from the one outside the kitchen.

We're also passing through a sombre and poignant reminder of recent events. The information panels above the autoroute are bearing the words *Hommage National au Colonel Beltrame*. It's a day of national homage to the brave and selfless *gendarme* (police officer) who gave up his life to save that of a female hostage being held by a terrorist in the Super U supermarket at Trèbes in the southwest of France. Today his body was taken from the Panthéon, the last resting place of the good and the great of the nation, to the forecourt of Les Invalides, where a memorial service with full military honours took place in the presence of the president and many other dignitaries. It isn't the purpose of this memoir to be a chronology of the times, but no matter how much we would like to, we don't live in a bubble, and I, like the rest of the country, and indeed the world, have been profoundly touched by this man's incredible selfless actions.

* * *

The clocks sprang forward last weekend, snatching back the bonus hour and forcing us to decide if we forfeit an hour of sleep or an hour of work; whichever way you look at it, it's *Les Temps perdus* (lost time). Theoretically this should give us an extra hour of daylight in the evening to potter in the garden and do jobs outside. We'd hoped to begin to put the serious renovation plans into action, including making shutters for the downstairs bathroom in preparation for installing the new window in case we hit a problem and are left with a gaping hole in the wall. Also sinking the foundations and preparing a concrete base for the new outbuilding to house the giant fuel tank. Plus, starting to paint the front outside wall, which has been recently rendered but needs to be sealed and painted as it's soaking up all this rain like a sponge. I imagined Mr V making the shutters, and me painting them while Pussy Willow frolicked in the sunshine in the garden, chasing butterflies and no doubt Flaubertine. But the weather forecast once again is for rain all over the holidays, so we'll literally have to take a rain check on all of this. Lost time in every sense.

LAMBS AND LIZARDS

*J*t's Good Friday, and we've woken to blue sky and sunshine, but the weathergirl assures us this is just a temporary blip, and more rain is on its way tomorrow to drown any hopes of a sunny Easter.

I open the shutters and step outside. The air is cold and smells of morning and recent rainfall. The garden that was dry and barren in summer, and green with plant life in autumn, is now a vast tapestry of springtime with pink, yellow and lilac wild primroses. I take my camera outside and Flaubertine is immediately at my heels; or should I say beneath my feet, cooing and yelping in equal measure as I tread on her paws. She jumps on my knee as I stoop to photograph a clump of violets twinkling like tiny jewels amongst a carpet of emerald-green moss. Her needle-like claws pierce my jeans, causing me to yelp also.

Spring it seems is the domain of the birds. Tweets, squeals, whoops, chirrups and caws reverberate through the air; I've never heard such a cacophony of sounds, or perhaps I'd just never listened. The trees have been transformed into mini cities in the sky, each one having at least three nests balancing in its branches. The nests are occupied, presumably by a patient mother guarding her eggs while her mate ferries back and forth with food and twigs to fortify the soon-to-be nursery.

The blue tits that live in the feather tree are becoming more and more tame, and more and more demanding. They sit on the red roof of the birdhouse, and on the green post that supports the washing line, causing a commotion until we tie another fat ball to the tree. They allow me to observe and photograph them from a distance now; I'm fascinated by things that I never gave a second thought to before. I notice that after pecking at the ball, they lift their heads to swallow. It's this constant bobbing about that makes focusing on them to take a clear photograph very difficult. This in turn is forcing me out of my comfort zone of the aperture-led photography that I use for flowers and inanimate objects and into increasing the shutter speed to capture these moving targets.

Another sound has joined that of the birdsong: the faint but distinct bleating of lambs. I abandon the birds and head off down the lane to see if the warm weather has prompted Mr Mouton to let his sheep out of their shelter, and if any more newcomers have joined the early arrival that I had the joy to see being born. There are four additions, newly born and wrinkly, and not yet fitting their skins. They are all busy guzzling greedily from their mothers, still a little unsteady on their foal-like legs. While I'm snapping away, a car pulls up abruptly behind me. I'm expecting to see Mr Mouton jump out, but instead it's Solène, the lady I met at the pre-Christmas drinks in the barn. She fondly kisses me on both cheeks and asks me how the work at the house is going, then stands with me, admiring the lambs before getting back into her car and whizzing off. This touches me; she could have easily just driven past, and I would have been none the wiser. I feel very blessed to have fallen upon such a warm and welcoming community.

* * *

Back at Les Libellules, Mr. V has taken a pickaxe to the concrete on which an old wooden shed stood behind the utility room. He's taking it up in order to lay foundations for a new store for the giant fuel tank, as the present base wouldn't be strong enough to support its weight. There's a veritable jungle underneath the slabs; spiders, beetles, woodlice, millipedes and snails all run for cover (actually the snails just stay put and retreat inside their shells), and a couple of surprising additions: two tiny salamanders each about three centimetres long. We find another rock to put them under close to the *mare*, away from where any digging and building will be taking place. I pause there, and peer profoundly into the murky water, and wonder what life, if any, is lurking beneath the slimy algae. Sporadic little ripples that disturb the surface, indicating some activity, but nothing is visible; I do hope there are frogs.

Although the sunlight is strong, its brightness is deceiving. The air is biting in the shade, and my fingertips turn purple. The sky also turns purple, and within minutes, as often happens, there is a sudden downpour, but not of rain. Huge hailstones begin to batter down, and I feel very guilty for destroying the shelter of all the little creatures. We run inside just as the hail stops and a thunderstorm begins. Twenty minutes later we are back outside in the sunshine, digging and shovelling. This really is like four seasons in one day.

THE SUNDOWNERS

*I*t's Saturday morning, and I know this is just a meteorological blip, but today feels like summer. It awakens my senses and triggers memories of meals on the terrace served with large bowls of fresh cucumber and mint salad, and light fragrant rosé wine cooled by frozen raspberries. Of arm-in-arm, after-dinner walks, and balmy evenings blending into dusks, with music drifting out to a table lit by lanterns and tea-lights. The memories quicken my pulse to the beat of summer, who I sense is waiting in the wings, and if spring doesn't put an end to this eternal winter, she will.

Mr V has gone off again for supplies and left me and Pussy Willow to our own devices. For me this means a blissful day of writing, reading, photography and gardening. Pussy Willow's idea of a blissful day is alternating between lounging beneath my chair on the terrace and marauding around the garden looking for things to chase, catch, torment with her paw and maybe eat. At this moment she's standing on her hind legs like a meerkat, looking over the garden wall. She's spied César, a cocky terrier who thinks he owns the hamlet. Pussy Willow's experience of dogs so far has been confined to Clipper, the golden retriever in the apartment opposite us in Paris.

Clipper is a gentle giant, and he and Pussy Willow are a little bit loved up. She's actually a bit of a tart around him, rolling around with her back legs akimbo. I get the impression that if she rolled on her back in front of César, he would go for her throat. The country and other animals are still a bit of a mystery to Pussy Willow; her ears shoot out on stalks as if she's about to take off every time she hears a cow moo. She prodded a beetle with her paw this morning and promptly ran like the wind when it too rolled onto its back, flaying its legs about in the air. On the other side of the wall César for his part is kicking up the turf with his back legs. He then proceeds to relieve himself all along the entire length, staking his claim.

Pussy Willow looks at me in astonishment as she still asks to go indoors to use the litter tray, not realising that she too could pee al fresco. Mr V says she must learn, but I disagree, as when she's back in Paris she has no choice but to use the tray, so I don't want to confuse her unduly, nor do I want her crying to descend three flights of stairs every time she wants to answer the call of nature. I do so wish that she didn't have to go back to the apartment and could stay here and learn how to be a real cat. I love it when I watch her running through the grass or sitting like a 'totem' cat on a tree stump, guarding her territory.

It's 7:30 p.m. The sun is beginning to sink, and it's getting a bit chilly, but I'm squeezing every drop out of this day, so I put on a fleece and stay until the sky is streaked with red, yellow and pink. I resist the urge to photograph it, preferring to savour the moment and commit it to memory.

The birds have begun their evensong, and the lambs and sheep are bleating and baaing as they are herded into their shelter for the night. Mr V arrives back just as I'm about to go inside.

'Aperitif on the terrace to watch the sun go down?' he asks.

'Why not?'

A sundowner. A perfect way to end the day.

THE BELLS OF EASTER

*I*t's Easter, or should I say *Pâques*, as it's called in France. *La Pâque* translates as the Passover, but without the article *'la'* and the addition of an 's', it becomes Easter. The Passover of course is the Jewish fête to commemorate the Angel of Death passing over the houses of Jewish families in Egypt at the time of Moses, and sparing their firstborn sons. It was this fête that Jesus was commemorating at The Last Supper on the evening before he was arrested.

Easter in France is celebrated in much the same way as it is in the UK, with a few notable differences. As in the UK, lamb is the meat of choice for a traditional family meal; one because it symbolises spring and new life, and two because Jesus is identified as the sacrificial lamb of Jewish tradition. French children also go hunting for eggs on Easter Sunday morning. But it isn't the Easter bunny who brings the eggs, rather the Easter bells.

Something that I hadn't realised while living in Paris is that the church bells in France stop ringing from Good Friday until Easter Sunday morning to commemorate the death and resurrection of Jesus. The story goes that the bells grow two little wings, dress with a ribbon and fly to Rome to be blessed by the pope. Then they fly back with chocolate bells, eggs, chickens, bunnies and, most peculiarly, fish and lobsters, and drop them for children to find. Someone usually shouts, '*Les cloches sont passées*' (the bells have been), and all the children rush out with their baskets. A lot less threatening than a giant rabbit that one of my daughters was terrified of when she was a child. (Incidentally, except for in Alsace, which once belonged to Germany, Good Friday isn't a public holiday.)

I'm not expecting the bells to be dropping any chocolate lobsters at Les Libellules, but I'm hoping Mr V has hidden some Mon Chéri chocolates for me to find...

As it's Easter and one can never have too much chocolate, I'm going to make one of my favourite desserts: *pots au chocolat* (chocolate pots). This is one of the simplest desserts you'll ever make and looks impressive if you serve it, as I do, in tiny coffee cups with a thimbleful of cream on the top (no more as it's very rich).

P.S. The bells have left me a dark chocolate Easter bunny with a smart green and yellow bow around his neck that came from the lovely little patisserie in Saulieu. It has something rattling inside. I crack it open, expecting to find some miniature eggs, or at least miniature bunnies; but no, it is filled with decidedly unattractive milk chocolate fish and lobsters and some mollusc-like creatures. I really must get to the bottom of this.

CHOCOLATE POTS

Serves six to eight

Ingredients

260 ml (½ pt) single cream
150 g (5 oz) good quality plain/dark cooking chocolate, broken into squares
50 g (2 oz) good quality milk cooking chocolate, broken into squares
1 sq of chilli chocolate (optional)
1 tsp brandy
Knob of salted butter
2 egg yolks, very lightly mixed with small hand whisk

Method

Warm the cream very gently in a non-stick saucepan.

Add the chocolate and heat slowly, making sure it has completely melted and that no grainy particles remain. (It should appear smooth and glossy. If you overheat it, it will thicken and become fudgy.)

Add the brandy and the butter and remove from the heat.

Add the egg yolks a little at a time, mixing quickly.

When the mixture is smooth and glossy divide it between your chosen serving dishes.

Leave the dishes to cool completely at room temperature, then chill in the fridge for at least two hours before serving.

Serve in 6-8 small coffee cups or tiny ramekins or *verrines* (small glasses for mini desserts or apéritifs).

The higher the dark chocolate content, the richer and stiffer the dessert. If making this for children I use 50% dark and 50% milk chocolate to give a creamier, mousse-like texture, so adjust quantities to taste. You can also whisk one or both of the egg whites and incorporate this into the mixture at the end to give a lighter mousse effect.

WHITE BEE, WHITE BEE

*J*t's Friday evening, and we're driving through rolling prairies of rapeseed flowers. The contrast of the almost fluorescent yellow against the technicolour blue sky reminds me of a child's painting of the seaside. Even the hill of happiness has succumbed to this riot of colour, the only green remaining being the small copse of trees on the crest. The blossom trees scattered along the route are at last in full bloom with delicate red, white and pink flowers, though the leaves of their larger neighbours remain rolled into shiny green cigars, waiting for a long sunny spell to coax them to unfurl.

Pussy Willow should be with us, but she squeezed herself under one of my kitchen cupboards when she caught sight of her transport box being brought up from the garage. This may be a blessing as we are in the midst of an SNCF (French railways) strike. This is exacerbated by the fact that it's the start of the spring school holidays for zone C, which includes Paris, so there's an even greater mass exodus on the roads as the train is no longer an option. As a result, the GPS is predicting that the usual under-three-hour journey will take four hours forty-five minutes. It's taken us an hour and twenty minutes just to get onto *la Francilienne*, the ring road around Greater

Paris, and the traffic was bumper to bumper until we were virtually into Burgundy.

We arrive as night is drawing in, and the dandelions that have amassed in the garden in our absence have their heads firmly closed. After unpacking the car, Mr V lights the fire, and I defrost some cottage pie that I had in the freezer left over from PJ and Panda's visit. Mr V is exhausted after the stressful drive down. He'd also earlier driven to Paris from Lille where he'd been working, so he goes to bed, leaving me alone with Julian Barnes, or Mr Barnes as my daughter, Kate and I refer to him, as in our opinions, his quality of writing demands that he be addressed as 'Mr'. Kate always buys two copies of his newly published novels so we can read them simultaneously and relish his genius together. This particular book was her Mother's Day present to me, but it came from Germany via the UK, so I'm a bit behind. I put another log on the fire, pour a glass of red wine, tuck my feet up on the sofa, and read by the light of a candle in a Chianti bottle.

* * *

I wake to the sight of the trees opposite the house looking like a million white bees have descended upon them, as minute white flowers have miraculously appeared overnight. They put me in mind of 'White Bee', one of my favourite poems by Paolo Neruda which begins 'White bee, you buzz in my soul'. I wonder if we buzz in Les Libellules' soul when we are gone; does she miss us as I do her? I think of her cold, dark, lonely rooms behind locked shutters, waiting to be filled with warmth and light, the sounds of music and laughter, and the smells of wood fire and cooking. Or does time stand still for her, like my own personal Brigadoon, a magical place that comes alive once every three weeks or so? I constantly check the weather forecast for the region to see what kind of weather my plants will be experiencing, and imagine them flourishing in sunshine and showers, but fret for them if frost is forecast.

One could say that I'm becoming obsessed, or even possessed; I say that I'm connected. I am at one with Les Libellules even when I'm far; it's as though she's spun a tenuous web that binds me to her. I fret also about who will be her guardian when we are gone. I hate the thought of someone who doesn't love and respect her taking custody. I think that the Dutch are the best option. The French, shaking off eons of antiquity, are hell-bent on modernisation, putting in UPVC windows, patio doors and metal electric shutters, and destroying the character of beautiful old houses. If anyone does that to Les Libellules, I think I would add my voice to those of the past and haunt them. I wonder if I'm the first foreign voice that she's heard.

In the field next to the house there are three new lambs to a single mother; in the one opposite there are four newborn calves, and there are two foals in the one behind. We are literally surrounded by life that wasn't in existence the last time we were here. Apart from the 'bees' on the tree opposite, the apple tree also has a hint of blossom, and green, spearheaded tulips have pierced the soil and are standing to attention on the mound of earth surrounding the remains of the spindly rosebush. Best of all my lilac tree has survived both transplantation and winter and has rewarded me with a flock of green leaves on her still-delicate branches. At this moment in time it is more important to me to see her mature to bear flowers than it is to have a kitchen, bathroom or any of the other plans we have for the house.

✳ ✳ ✳

It's midnight, and I've just been in the bathroom cleaning my teeth before going to bed. Mr Barnes is proving to be a distraction, and he's sabotaging not only my to-do list but my writing also, so I've been catching up, hence the late hour. Outside the window is total blackness, as if someone has thrown a blackout curtain across the sky, and neither moon nor starlight can penetrate. There's a world of nocturnal creatures out there. I can hear the eerie 'whooo' of two owls calling to each other from different directions. This doesn't surprise me; what does surprise me, however, is the most beautiful birdsong coming from the direction of the woods behind the house. Being a city dweller, I wasn't aware that birds sing at night, only ever having heard them at dusk and dawn. I climb up onto the deep marble ledge and open the window, feeling the cool, moss-scented night air press against my face, and I listen to the wonderful, melodious sound. Later I learn that there are four common night singers: the robin, blackbird, song thrush and nightingale. I listen to all four on the internet and am thrilled that what I heard was in fact an illustrious nightingale.

BROCANTE À GOGO

We've just been back to the *boulangerie* in the nearby village, and it was even stranger than the time before. Now, there is a shop mannequin in the window, that on first glance I mistook for the owner. There is also an assortment of second-hand clothes (all enormous sizes—hers I think) on a rail outside. The upturned barrel that served as a giant ashtray now has a very friendly ginger and white tomcat lounging on it, along with a huge dish of cat crunchies and a bowl of water. Inside the shop we're greeted by the usual array of miscellaneous items with the addition of a large, high-backed Voltaire chair painted orange with a white seat and back, that are embroidered in pink and orange 1970s-style flowers. It is bizarre, but I sit on it, and it's surprisingly comfortable. I could imagine myself sitting at my writing desk on this ostentatious piece of furniture, maybe not painted orange though.

The Haribo sweets and Chupa Chups lollipops have been meticulously divided into little plastic bags tied with a ribbon. Given that I've only ever see two children in the village, I wonder who the woman expects will buy these. We purchase a baguette, and I spy a book on painting and stencilling old furniture, with a selection of templates in the back. It has an original price of 165 francs on the cover, indicating its age, but she's asking €2 for all books, and this looks practically brand new, and although old, not dated. I pay for it, and she takes that as a cue to usher us outside into a shed where she has lots of old furniture just begging to be painted and stencilled, if only we were at the painting and stencilling stage.

On the way back we read the fatal word *brocante* on a notice attached to a tree. This fills us full of both delight and dread. We have neither the time nor the money to fritter away amongst stalls of bric-à-brac, but we're drawn to these events like metal to a magnet and are powerless to resist.

The stalls are in the indoor, covered market hall, where the Saturday morning open-air market moves to during the winter months. It isn't the usual flea market type of *brocante*, nor is it the professional antique dealers that we see in Paris, rather something in between. Affable collectors man the stalls, and each one has its individual character. There is one selling old picture postcards and letters, another selling sheet music and beautifully illustrated, handwritten menus dating back to the 1890s. When it comes to finally decorating the dining room at Les Libellules, I would be interested in buying one or two, but they aren't cheap.

There's a colourful couple from Dijon with a wonderful array of carpets and tapestries. I resist the tapestry wall hangings as they would be impractical to store in our present interior building site conditions, but I succumb to the beauty of a wool and silk oriental runner for the hall in Paris (totally impractical with a cat I know, but...).

I notice a stall selling antique toys, including a magnificent doll's house, another with white marble busts and statues (again, I'm sorely tempted) and rose marble-topped washstands and bedside tables. There is also a large amount of Art Deco paraphernalia, notably lamps, which Mr V and I have a particular penchant for. I buy a crystal ice bucket with silver tongs that's too small to hold a champagne bottle, so the rosé will be coming out in style, and I eye up an asparagus dish, but the price tag is a bit hefty, and I'm not that desperate, though it is rather lovely...

Seriously, if we'd finished the house, I would be having a field day right now. Apparently this takes place every year, so I'll be back!

ANYTHING YOU CAN BUY, I CAN BUY BETTER

*I*t's Sunday morning, and it is already an unseasonably warm 25 degrees on the terrace where we are taking our breakfast. I feel as if I'm in the opening sequence of *Beauty and the Beast* as the world, his wife and family are passing saying *bonjour*. This is all very nice but a bit puzzling as usually at this time of day we may see the odd dog walker or cyclist, but hordes of people are parking cars on the grass verge opposite the house and heading towards the crossroads. We've clearly missed a vital piece of information as something is obviously going on.

The man who last year promised to show me old photos of the hamlet, whose name we learn is Jacques, stops his bicycle by the wall to talk to Mr V, and I ask him what the attraction is. '*C'est un vide grenier, madame,*' he replies.

What! A car boot sale! How could we possibly have missed the publicity for such a momentous event happening on our doorstep? I abandon my breakfast, grab my bag, and join the throng.

Once again these aren't the items for sale that I'm used to seeing. Here we have farm and garden implements from a bygone era, old ironware and huge, metal cooking pots. There are a lot of the obligatory oil lamps, candelabras and wall sconces, and many things connected with jam and winemaking. Plus, some 18th-century pocket watches whose owners must have hidden them away during the revolution, not a baby's pram or plastic toy in sight.

A makeshift restaurant has also sprung up at the crossroads. This is no hotdog van or caravan selling crêpes, but an actual restaurant with tables and chairs, serving steak and chips, and salmon in a tarragon sauce.

Mr V, who has a talent for finding things, excitedly shows me an enormous radio the size of a large microwave oven with a lot more knobs that looks like something used by the Resistance.

'What are you going to do with that?' I ask.

'It's nice,' he replies sheepishly.

'Yes, but what are you going to *do* with it?'

'It could be useful.'

'Where are you going to put it?'

'*Bof!*'

In retaliation, I buy a brown-leather, satchel-type handbag that he says I don't need. It's brand new, and I get it for €5, which I'm really chuffed with as it looks as if it cost much more. This triggers a tit-for-tat buying spree. Mr V buys yet another two oil lamps and two brass candle sconces. I hit back with a rustic, wicker, three-tier vegetable rack, then he wins the battle by picking up another 100-bottle wine rack for the price of a bottle of wine.

It takes us two trips to carry all our loot back home. On the way, a lady stops me to ask how much I'd paid for the bag. I tell her *cinq* euros. 'Oh là là, *cinquante* (fifty). That's a good price.' I didn't press the point that I'd said *cinq* as she obviously thought that fifty was a fair amount to pay. The bag has a name that means nothing to me as I'm the person least impressed in the world by designer logos, but I have a look on eBay, and there's my bag changing hands at £199—over €200. I win!

When we return to collect the wine and vegetable racks three jolly ladies are carrying a large vat to their car which is parked with a trailer in front of Les Libellules. It's just like one I saw in an old movie with a very young Sophia Loren standing inside, her skirt hitched up to her thighs, trampling on grapes with her bare feet.

'Are you going to dance on the grapes in that?' I ask them jokingly.

'Yes, just symbolically,' they reply. 'Not as a method of crushing them to make wine.'

'I'd love to come to see this and maybe join in,' I tell them.

'We'll let you know when the first grape harvest is going to take place.'

I hope they don't forget as ever since I saw that film as a little girl, this has been a fantasy of mine.

I'm back at the terrace writing when Jacques returns on his bike with a backpack full of baguettes after a trip to the *boulangerie*-cum-bar-cum-jumble sale. I invite him to take a coffee with me, and he says that I'm following in *'une bonne tradition'* (a good tradition).

He begins to tell me of a former occupant, Fernand Lefebvre, who used to sit on this very terrace and strike up friendships with holidaymakers, who were once frequent visitors, out for their evening stroll. As a result, he received a lot of postcards from people, not only from all over France but further afield also, which explains the odd collection of postcards that I've found from Majorca, Marseilles, Nice and Geneva and even New Orleans and Cape Town.

Jacques makes himself comfortable, relishing in the captive audience that he's found in me. I want to pick up my pen and begin taking notes, but that would spoil his flow, so I hold as much as I can in my head. An hour later and we're still on the terrace as more and more stories unfold. Jacques is a mine of information; he's 65 and has lived in the hamlet all his life, so what he doesn't know isn't worth knowing. He's a real local historian and a born storyteller, a living, breathing history book. I realise that I'll now be woven into his stories as much as he'll be in mine.

He goes on to tell me that our little commune has been the scene of not only one but three murders, and grisly ones at that, and was once classed as one of the most criminal communes in France. So now it turns out that we're living in a French version of the *Midsomer Murders* as well as a haven for highwaymen...

What I've learnt today: French car boot sales stop for lunch between 12 and 13:30.

THE PROMISE OF SUMMER

After another spectacular, starry night, we're greeted by a dense morning mist, but this is no damp, clinging, autumnal variety. This is the mist that brings with it the promise of a hot, sultry day. To reinforce this promise of summer, I've just seen my first dragonfly of the year. It has settled on a geranium leaf right in front of me. I daren't breathe in case I disturb it. It is a naiad, a turquoise azure damselfly, but its colours aren't as vivid as those I saw last August; maybe it is still young. I'll have to find out if their colours deepen as they mature. In addition to the dragonfly, tiny white butterflies no bigger than a shirt button are hovering over the *mare*, and a second dragonfly newcomer has just appeared, smaller than an emperor, but still quite large, and a beautiful shade of cornflower blue.

Mr V is planting iris in a shady spot that he's cleared near the water. He's a bit like a dragonfly himself, flitting from job to job. This morning he has begun the rewiring, so we now have holes in the bedroom ceilings and thick black wires that look like the tentacles of a giant squid dangling from them. At the same time, he's in the process of digging the foundations for the fuel store, painting the stonework surrounding the windows, and now, planting iris.

The Three Degrees are back in the field, and they have four calves between them so are not so keen to have me poking my lens in their direction. They position their ample rumps between me and their offspring, eyeing me suspiciously. So I leave them alone and photograph them from a distance.

Everything seems to be moving up a gear and bursting with life. I desperately want to stay to witness all these miraculous changes, but sadly it's time to leave, so we pack up the car, lock up the house and head north. We drive back through fields that have turned deep emerald. Wildflowers have sprung up, lining the roadsides in a stream of yellow, pink, purple and white. It's like someone has spilt the contents of a paint box on the land. The return journey is always a little sad, but this time I fear I'll miss the tulips. I hope that I don't miss the apple blossom.

LOVE IS IN THE AIR

$\mathcal{I}$'ve missed neither the apple blossom nor the tulips. The apple tree is decked out like a bride in a gown of delicate pink and white flowers. The tulips are more like wanton women enticing their lovers, their red petals falling open to reveal a purple heart surrounded by a band of gold. I was expecting them to be uniformly pink or red, so I'm grateful that they stayed long enough to show me their splendour.

The garden, left to run wild for three weeks, is like a meadow of bluebells, buttercups, poppies and clover, and some beautiful, dainty, violet-coloured bells with yellow centres that I've never seen before. The dandelions have gone to seed in our absence, their sturdy yellow flowers transformed into puffballs that bob in the breeze, conjuring up memories of childhood games of 'he loves me, he loves me not', blowing as gently as possible on 'he loves me not' and using all the force we could muster on 'he loves me'.

The Virginia creeper has sprouted green shoots that look like pegs on a washing line, and the trees opposite that were a mass of 'white bee' blossom are now wearing their rather regal coat of burgundy-coloured leaves. The poplars are once again forming a screen of green against the blue sky, and the feather tree is a surprising shade of purple, with clusters of tiny buds, each smaller than a pinhead. I think this tree is the one that reflects the changing of the seasons more than any other.

The herbs and geraniums that I planted are flourishing, as is my little lilac tree. It's evidently lilac time as almost every house in the hamlet has one, two or three trees with purple, white and traditional lilac flowers. I wonder what colour mine will reward me with when she is mature enough.

The air is heady with spring. The scent of lime blossom, apple blossom, lilac and magnolia mingle in an intoxicating perfume that's carried like the dandelion seeds on the breeze. I've never been so aware of the seductive, even sexual, essence of nature, as every plant emits its own enticing aromas and puts on an alluring display of colour, opening its petals and exposing its pistils in order to attract the insects to pollinate them by transferring pollen from their male to female parts.

This exercise in fertilisation isn't confined to plants. Two birds with bright red tail feathers perform a spiralling love dance, encircling each other as they soar and tumble through the air. Two different types of dragonfly have arrived at the *mare*; the naiads have been joined by a small, slim, coral red variety that also appear to be mating in mid-air as they're flying in tandem.

Love is all around on the ground also; even the ants appear to be coupling. I'm enthralled to discover two amorous snails in a prelude to lovemaking. Snails are hermaphrodites, having both male and female organs. During mating they act as neither male nor female, but simultaneously as both. They too perform a love dance during a courtship which can last up to twenty hours. I watch transfixed as both snails raise their heads and press their flat foot soles together. They caress each other tenderly with their tentacles and, most touching of all, they kiss and caress each other with their lips while gently swaying from side to side. It's one of the most tender and erotic sights I've ever seen. I think they could teach a lot of men a thing or two...

As fast as the snail population aims to regenerate itself, Pussy Willow has taken to dispatching them, a habit that I'm discouraging on two counts. One, having been so up close and personal to them, I've developed a fondness for these sensual creatures, and two, they're not agreeing with her delicate, town-cat digestive system. And as she insists on asking to go inside to use the toilet, she isn't exactly the ideal house guest.

Most of the birds have taken to their love nests and are noticeably quieter than three weeks ago except for a late addition—the sound of a distant cuckoo. The birdsong has been replaced by the return of insects humming and buzzing amongst the flowers. The horse-chestnut trees on the lane are in full bloom, and the noise coming from them sounds like a squadron of spitfires droning overhead. I've never heard anything like it. I stand beneath one of the trees and look up to see scores of bees busy amongst the blossom, gathering pollen to take back to their hive. Spring is turning out to be the season that brings the most changes, and for me, the most surprises.

The lambs are no longer gangly legged infants with coats too big for their bodies; they are sturdy and padded out with fat and wool. I'm astonished how much they've grown in three weeks. They no longer cleave to their mothers but are off gambling around their field. Having lost their timidity, but not yet gained caution, they run towards where I'm standing at the fence, and one even lets me pat its head, something the mother objects to loudly.

Back at Les Libellules I hear a sound that I've been longing to hear since we moved here—frogs or toads, I'm not sure which. They're in the *mare*, though when I look there's no sign of them. I think they too have joined the lovefest and are calling to each other, making, as you would expect, a 'rivit rivit' noise which is answered by a throaty, protracted croak. It is highly amusing, and on hearing it, I can't help but laugh out loud with delight.

I call Mr V to come and listen, and he nonchalantly tells me, 'Yes I've already seen one. It's a frog; it's green.' This makes me disproportionately jealous, as I've been peering into the algae-covered water since the first signs of spring, hoping to catch a glimpse of a little frog prince or princess.

Frogs' legs, along with *escargots de Bourgogne*, have now joined Charolais cows and sheep in my list of things that I can no longer eat now that I've viewed them in a whole new light.

But if you're not such a sensitive soul as I, snails are very tasty (not slimy as many people imagine, but can be quite chewy and difficult to digest, so I wouldn't recommend more than six). It is quite a complicated, and not entirely pleasant, process to purge and clean snails before cooking, and I quite frankly didn't have the stomach for it even before I became so attached to them. If preparing live snails, they must be starved, or fed on human-friendly leaves such as lettuce for at least a week. Then you must remove the membrane covering their shell with a sharp knife and put the snails in a basin of cold water with salt and vinegar until all the gunk comes out. Then they must be thoroughly rinsed before cooking (live) in boiling water, something I could never do. Here the supermarkets sell ready-prepared snails, and the freezers are full of parsley butter to stuff them with if you want to try your hand. So, here's my cheat's recipe.

BURGUNDY SNAILS

Serves four as an *entrée*

Ingredients

1 clove garlic, crushed
1 tsp table salt
250 g (8 oz) salted butter
1 dsp shallot, finely minced
1 tbsp fresh flat-leaf parsley, finely chopped
A good twist freshly ground black pepper
1 tbsp dry white wine
6 snails per person (Burgundy if you can get them)
Salt (for stabilising the shells)

Method

Mix the garlic with the salt to form a paste.

Mix the butter, garlic paste, shallot, parsley and pepper and beat until soft, then transfer to an electric mixer and add the wine.

Put a generous amount of the mixture into each snail shell and position them on a shallow baking tray covered in salt to stop them from rolling over and spilling their contents when the butter melts.

Bake at 180-190 C/gas mark 4-5 for around 6 minutes.

Serve with warm crusty baguette to mop up the excess butter.

These are best served in special dishes with indentations for the snail to sit in (they usually hold six) and with special tongs to hold the hot shells and fine, two-pronged forks to winkle them out.

If you don't fancy eating snails then you can use this butter to stuff mussels in their shells. It is also delicious to melt over grilled white fish or steak, or placed beneath the skin of a chicken before roasting. (You can substitute tarragon for the parsley, and lemon juice can either be added, or replace the white wine for some variations.)

STONE THE CROWS!

I spoke too soon about the birds becoming quieter. We've had a mass invasion of crows. They're roosting in the highest branches of the tallest trees, giving a literal meaning to the nautical expression 'the crow's nest'. The peace and tranquillity is well and truly shattered; they're the most vocal animals I've ever heard. They don't give up for an instant; they're cawing from the moment I wake up until the moment I go to bed. I don't know if this is a regular occurrence as we weren't here this time last year, but their noise is incessant. They drown out all other birdsong, and even the frogs can't make themselves heard above the racket. The sound is neither melodic nor amusing, and they are having a greater effect on the other birds than just drowning out their song.

There is a noticeable lack of swallows around Les Libellules, though they are in abundance further into the hamlet. The magpies, who are usually full of bravado, are unusually subdued. Periodically Mr V stands beneath their trees and claps his hands loudly, and they all go quiet, but five minutes' later, they're off again. It may sound trivial, but they are really spoiling my enjoyment when I sit outside in the evening. I can't even hear my music filtering out from the utility room unless it's at full blast.

Judging by the constant traffic in the treetops, I presume that there are eggs or chicks in the nests. I imagine the commotion is one bird signalling to their partner to bring food, or them all signalling to each other to warn of danger, but from what I can deduct, it would take 'spider cat' to scale those heights. I hope they all go back to wherever they came from as soon as the chicks are strong enough to leave the nests. I know, they were probably here long before me, and they have as much right as I (probably more) to live their lives how they think fit. But at this moment I would seriously love one of those machines that makes loud noises to scare birds around airports; either that or invest in an eagle or a gun.

This afternoon, however, the crows are eerily silent. There's a storm coming. I detect this with all my senses, more than I've ever experienced before. I feel it in the conflicting currents of intense hot and cold air in different parts of the garden, as keenly as you can feel currents of warm and cool water when you're bathing in the sea. I see it. Purple-grey clouds are rolling in from the north, pushing a freshening wind before them that is sending leaves and blossom like confetti through the air. I hear it, not only in the approaching rumbles of thunder, but the lambs are issuing warning cries, and the frogs have reached a crescendo. I smell it also; the air has a damp, organic aroma, like mushrooms in a forest.

We jump to action stations, me gathering up my laptop and notebooks, and winding down the parasol to take indoors, Mr V turning off all the electrical equipment that he's switched on outside and shutting the upstairs windows and door. We bring the garden table inside as I've not yet got around to weatherproofing it, close the shutters and wait. And wait and wait, and nothing happens. Then moments later the wind changes direction, and the storm rumbles off to the west.

✻ ✻ ✻

I've learnt to read other signs of an approaching change in the weather. I'm writing at the table on the terrace, and I can hear the leaves in the very tops of the tall trees behind the house stirring in a wind that hasn't yet reached the ground. The sky is still deep blue and the sun hot and intense, but the upmost branches of the poplar screen are now gently swaying like seaweed caressed by the tide. I gather up my books and camera and move all but one of the chairs indoors. When I return, the feather tree is dancing in a breeze that is now also blowing the washing on the line, and has heralded forth some fluffy, white clouds, many of which have suspiciously dark centres. The clouds burst, releasing their precious cargo of much-needed rain, then a moment later they disappear, and steam rises from the ground as the sun reclaims her throne.

* * *

I must stop to tell you that I'm very excited to have just seen my first frog in the *mare*, an enormous, lime-green specimen with yellow spots on its back. I heard him as I was cutting back the Virginia creeper that has gone from being non-existent to taking over the path in the space of less than a week. When I looked into the water, I saw frothy bubbles on the algae-covered surface. Then, two bulging yellow eyes appeared, followed by a sturdy muscular body and finally, two impressive thighs that looked like they'd be more at home on a small chicken. I thought, given his size, that this was a toad, but Mr V assures me that it is a frog, because he is green. I've waited hour after hour gazing into the murky *mare*, being feasted upon by midges and mosquitoes in the hope of catching a glimpse of a member of the frog chorus, without success. Mr V, however, has them hopping out of the water every time he happens to pass. So this is really a noteworthy occasion.

What I later learn: In these parts, toads are smaller than frogs. You live and learn.

ECOLOGY FOR ART'S SAKE

*T*he neighbour who smelt of strong spirits at the Advent get-together has arrived in a slightly inebriated state. He has brought two border strimmers, one for him and one for Mr V, to cut back the wild, waist-high grass. The pair set to work like two assassins, indiscriminately annihilating some of the beautiful wildflowers that I was photographing this morning. I rush outside to protest, physically planting myself in front of a clump of bluebells and the delicate violet flowers with a yellow centre that aren't yet fully open. To my horror Fifi (this apparently is what he's known as locally) has cut the cluster of flowers protecting my tantric-sex snail lovers. I have visions of them decapitated in the throes of ecstasy, but they seem to be oblivious, locked in their slimy embrace. I cover them up with grass and order the maverick gardeners to leave well alone. They're attacking every plant in sight that isn't a rose, telling me they are *mauvaises herbes* (weeds). I yell at them to stop and say they are wildflowers, not weeds, and are essential to the bees and butterflies.

Fifi says, 'Oh, you are an ecologist,' more as an accusation than a question, so I don't think he means it as a compliment. To which I reply, 'Yes,' and quickly fetch my camera and show him the beautiful photos that I had taken earlier. He then calls me an 'artist', which I feel he approves of slightly more than me being an ecologist, and seeing the method behind my madness, leaves my plants alone. Mr V meanwhile has got trigger-happy, and I see him dangerously close to Lila, my tiny lilac tree. I shout to no avail as he can't hear me above the noise, so I throw myself into his path, protecting her with outstretched hands, risking an ankle-lashing from his wildly rotating, orange cable.

The whole episode has been traumatic for me, not to mention the plants. Lila hasn't escaped the whip of Mr V's strimmer. She has a wound in her bark about ten centimetres from the ground, and four or five lesser cuts elsewhere. This has distressed me greatly, as not only am I learning about the life of trees and how they can, in a sense, feel pain, but also because of the huge personal significance of once again having a garden and a lilac tree. I'm no horticulturalist, as you've probably guessed, but I instinctively cover the wound with some soft moss and loosely secure it with a fine gauze bandage tied with a blade of grass. I stroke the branch that is injured and speak gently to her. Mr V thinks I'm mad, and he's right. I'm mad at him and won't let him forget this for a long time.

His actions are even more incomprehensible given that he usually has a real love and respect for nature and has grown blue cedar and oak trees from seeds. I'm deeply disappointed in him.

RIGHT SAID FRED

*M*y friend Christelle has come to stay for the weekend. We are astral twins, and it's our birthdays on Thursday. We kick off the celebrations with champagne and oysters on the terrace for an apero. Flaubertine is doing her best to get herself adopted, and Chris is tempted, but as she works every day and is often away at the weekend, it's neither practical nor fair to have a cat. Still, Flaubertine is enjoying the attention.

Chris and I are visiting Lac de Chamboux, which is actually three lakes separated by a road and a bridge. Chamboux is the most recently created of the six major man-made lakes in the Morvan and serves a reservoir for drinking water. Having said that, it has a great outdoors feel and has been likened to a Canadian lake, though on a much smaller scale. The circumference of all three is ten kilometres, but we opt to walk seven around the largest and smallest sections as although it's still early May, the temperature is in the high 20s.

The lakeside is surprisingly void of people. We pass a few couples and families picnicking on the handful of small sandy coves, and solitary fishermen sitting patiently on the odd jetty, plus the occasional dog walker coming in the opposite direction, but by and large we're alone with nature.

Pine forests fringe the north side, providing cool and fragrant shade. The forest trails are close enough to the lake to allow glimpses of the placid, blue surface, shimmering with glints of sunshine. Here and there the trees give way to tall, poker-headed reeds that reach to our shoulders, dipping their toes in the shallows. Ancient oak and sycamore trees border the south side where the trail passes closer to the water's edge, and the sandy coves become small beaches, which again are oddly deserted; it's like we've stumbled upon our personal paradise. As we leave the larger lake the terrain becomes wilder surrounding the smallest of the three. Huge, mossy boulders block our way, driving us further away from the water into a dense pine forest.

When we finally emerge once again at the lakeside, it is more a series of large ponds teaming with wildlife. There are tiny white and yellow butterflies; enormous, prehistoric-looking lizards adorned with Aztec patterns in green, yellow, white and black; herons standing motionless on one leg, scouring the water for the sight of a fish, and a plethora of insects. I wonder if this area is natural as it has none of the structure of the other two parts. Willow trees bend so low that they're almost horizontal, their finger-like branches brushing the surface of the water, and clumps of spiky, green water grasses protrude like giant stepping stones. There are parts here where the path becomes so narrow and overgrown that we have to beat back brambles to pass, and the ground is muddy and marshy.

Chris compliments me on our choice of location to buy the house and says that we must have researched the area well. In actuality I had no idea that all this was on our doorstep; I simply fell in love with a tower...

✳ ✳ ✳

Back at Les Libellules, Mr V needs to move the remaining, weighty paving slabs from behind the house to make way for the foundations of the building to store the fuel tank. He is intending to use them to extend the patio at the front. Fifi is bringing 'the boys' to help as Mr V is giving himself a hernia trying to move them on his own. Chris and I did offer our assistance, but we could hardly raise them from the ground let alone carry them around to the front of the house (they are too big and too heavy for the wheelbarrow), plus before moving the slabs, the concrete which is holding them in place needs to be broken up; backbreaking work in itself.

I'm expecting 'the boys' to be a couple of strapping youths similar to the one that brought the roof ladders. However, when they arrive it is in the form of Fifi himself and Jacques. Jacques again resembles a Canadian septuagenarian wearing his custom lumberjack shirt and baseball cap bearing the logo of the New York Yankees and blue shorts meeting his wellington boots. Fifi by contrast looks like an ageing roadie in tight jeans and Rolling Stones T-shirt. Between the three of them they have an accumulative age of 180, so this should be interesting.

Fifi wielding a sledgehammer is a sight to behold, his sinewy arms slamming it into the concrete like a teenager showing off at a test-your-strength machine at the funfair, but despite his best efforts the slabs aren't budging. Jacques produces a crowbar and says it's better to prise rather than smash them out. In the end it's a joint smashing and prising effort that finally dislodges the slabs.

Chris and I are in the bedroom listening to the pantomime below as the three stooges now discuss how they're going to lay the paving stones from the back into a new patio at the front; it puts me in mind of the song 'Right Said Fred[1]'. You don't need an extensive command of French to get the gist of the procedures.

'*Oui, oui, oui, c'est bon; ça va aller.*' (Yeah, yeah, yeah, that's good; that'll work.)

'*Non, non, ça ne marche pas.*' (No, no, that's no good.)

'*Si, si.*' (Yes, yes.)

'*Non, non. Putain!*' (I won't translate that one for you.)

'*Vas y, vas y; ça va aller.*' (Go on, go on; that'll work.)

'*Allez, allez.*' (Go on, go on.)

'*VOILA!*' (Told you so!)

'*Ça y est. Bon.*' (That's it. Good)

I breathe a sigh of relief. All the slabs are finally placed into the *bon position* at the front.

Customary beers follow on the terrace, but as it's almost our birthdays, Christelle and I have a nice glass of chilled *crémant de Bourgogne,* the local bubbly. Cheers boys!

---

1. A comic 1960s song about three men working as labourers trying to move furniture without success.

IT'S MY BIRTHDAY, AND I'LL WEAR
WHAT I WANT TO

*T*omorrow is my birthday. Actually it's the day after tomorrow, but we'll be celebrating it tomorrow with an eagerly anticipated trip to Beaune via Autun. I'm finally going to see beyond the aisles of a furniture store or DIY depot. We had wanted to do this on my actual birthday, but the bank holiday to mark the Ascension of Jesus has fallen on the same day this year, and there wasn't a hotel room to be had in Beaune. As this also happens to be a Thursday, everyone is taking Friday off as well. This is what is termed as *Faire le pont,* literally to make the bridge, and it is a very popular pastime in France. Due to numerous bank holidays in May falling on either a Tuesday or Thursday this year, a lot of bridges have been made. One week was left with only a solitary Wednesday in the middle, so that became a bridge too, wiping out the entire five working days.

The weather is forecast to be changeable, so I've packed for hot and dry, cool and dry, warm and wet, and cold and wet. I've hedged my bets and painted my toenails for the first time this year in the hope that they won't be hidden under boots, but now boots might be the best option. The light in the bedroom isn't great, and my eyesight isn't good in poor light. I chose what I thought was a rosy-beige shade of polish that has turned out to be bright, bubblegum pink. It's called 'Miami'. (Do people get paid to come up with these names?) I would have called it 'Bazooka' as it's the same shade as the vile gum of the same name that we used to have clinging to our faces when we were ten.

To make matters worse I went outside wearing flip-flops while it was still tacky to ask Mr V's opinion, and Flaubertine came bounding over and did her usual routine of rubbing her head on my feet. So now my toes are bright pink with ginger cat fur stuck to them. So much for trying to glam up a bit.

Mr V looked horrified when he saw the colour but uncharacteristically tactfully said, 'Darling, it's your birthday. You can wear whatever colour you want on your toes.' Which made it worse to think that he thought I deliberately chose this.

For all her bounding up to me, Flaubertine isn't in such good condition. I can see in her for the first time that same air that Maddy had: a sort of resentful acceptance; she has lost some of her spirit. I do what I can to help her, but I swear I'm never getting attached to another farm cat.

* * *

We've woken to pristine blue skies, not a thunder cloud in sight. We take a meandering route off the main road through villages with picturesque *pigeonniers,* and beautifully restored houses with conservatories and swimming pools; this is obviously the affluent end of the department. The road passes through gently rolling hills crowned with poplars that put me in mind of one of my favourite poems by William Cowper, 'The Poplar Field', with its opening lines: 'The poplars are fell'd, farewell to the shade/And the whispering sound of the cool colonnade'; beautiful but sad words. Here, however, the cool colonnades are sheltering not white, but light tan-coloured cows from the sun. The hills give way to flat fields of yellow rapeseed flowers, which in turn give way to the inevitable industrial parks that surround almost every town.

Autun comes as a surprise. It is bigger than I imagined, with a Mediterranean air. There's a rather grand town hall and a traditional marketplace fringed by cafés whose tables and chairs tumble out beneath the shade of the bordering plane trees. At one end of this square, is a striking war memorial, with a statue of an angel supporting a naked man, that commemorates the 1914-1918 war on one side, and on the other, there are the inscriptions of the names of 138 soldiers from the 2nd Dragoon Regiment who died in September 1944 during the liberation of the town. The opposite end of the square, is dominated by the imposing, solid structure of a church and the majestic *Lycée Bonaparte* a college dating back to the early 18th century.

The market itself is small but bustling with stalls selling fruit and vegetables, and colourful rustic baskets to carry them home in. There are plants and flowers and bunches of fragrant herbs, pungent cheeses and strings of *saucisson* (dried cured sausage). Plus household items that were once sold in old-fashioned chandler's shops such as metal mop buckets, watering cans, petrol cans, oil lamps and enamel basins like the one my grandmother used to make rice pudding in.

The streets of the medieval quarter lead directly off the square and wind their way towards the 12th-century cathedral of St Lazare. We zigzag up the steep cobbles, pausing at the numerous antique shops, dotted amongst which, are shops selling hunting gear displaying an alarming array of knives and rifles. There are also charming, artisan boutiques selling handmade soaps and gifts, and magical toy shops with windows crammed full of nostalgic wooden toys that make me wish I had someone to buy for. We're fatefully drawn into one of the antique shops and end up spending almost an hour talking with Willem, the Dutch owner, who has a fine collection of very reasonably priced furniture in excellent condition, and as in Saulieu, lots of Art Deco lamps and ornaments.

My eye is caught by a large, 18th-century *armoire*, a cupboard-cum-wardrobe, in rose-tinted dove-grey wood, with a large, bevelled, mirrored central panel. Willem assures me that he'll dismantle it and store it until we're ready for him to deliver it. I'm so tempted as it's perfect for the rose room, but I think Willem is thinking more in terms of a timescale of six months, when in reality we may not be ready to receive it for six years. Still, I must give this some serious thought, as the price is a mere fraction of what we would pay in Paris.

We come away with yet another oil lamp with a porcelain base, which weighs a ton that we now have to lug up the hill in the heat as Willem is closing for lunch.

As we approach the cathedral, we pass an unexpected amount of pizza restaurants; not fast food venues, but authentic Italian establishments with traditional, wood-fired pizzas. If we didn't have a meal booked in a fancy restaurant in Beaune this evening I would be feasting on a margherita at this very moment. I'm particularly attracted by a charming little restaurant with half a dozen tables decked out in green-gingham cloths on a small balcony which is shaded by a wooden canopy. A profusion of pink and red geraniums tumble from the balcony railings, almost reaching the pavement.

There's a pleasantly plump Italian lady in a black dress and floral apron fanning herself at the open door. She smiles and nods as she catches my eye. The heavenly smell of garlic and wood smoke drifts past her enticingly, almost drawing me inside. Alas we've said that we'll eat frugally this lunchtime to save ourselves for the anticipated gastronomic delights in store at dinner, so we continue up past the Rolin Museum, which looks more like a medieval castle than a museum. I don't have a clue who Rolin is, or why he merits a museum, but make a mental note of him to look up on Google later.

The cathedral itself is stunning. It is a many-towered, Gothic masterpiece with a high, pointy steeple and striking, sculptured stone arches surrounding the heavy, panelled doors, with a photo opportunity at every angle. The interior is obscured under scaffolding as restoration work is being carried out, so we can't appreciate it at its best. Still, it's nice to escape from the sun for ten minutes.

We continue to seek out some shade and see a crêperie opposite the side entrance to the cathedral; this is even more unusual than a pizzeria, as crêpes are traditionally from the Brittany region of

France, and the French are very much the sticklers for eating regionally.

Shunning the tables outside we go down some stone steps with a rope bannister fastened by metal loops to the wall, like the entrance to a dungeon, and emerge into a high-vaulted cellar with narrow windows cut into the metre-thick stone walls just above ground level. What little light manages to seep through the slender panes, is blocked by Roman-style busts and statues, and huge vases of peonies on the deep sloping window ledges. The room is lit instead by the soft glow of candlelight-effect bulbs in exotic, fringed lamps on each of the unusually well-spaced-out tables, and strategically concealed spotlights illuminating the statues. The effect is delightful, and thankfully the room is refreshingly cool.

There's a gorgeous old till sitting on a wooden counter behind which are racks of wine glasses and coffee cups. This time the scene does actually look like a set from 'Allo 'Allo!, and Renée wouldn't look at all out of place, but instead we're greeted by a waitress who offers us the choice of three tables. We choose one, but it's decidedly wobbly, so we move to another, which is equally so. She doesn't offer us a solution, so we hang on to complimentary kirs Bourgignons, of crème de cassis and white Burgundy wine, which come served in brandy glasses, as no matter how gently we put them down, the table registers five on the Richter scale. The waitress is somewhere between 60 and 70 and reed thin. Unlike the ample Italian lady, she obviously doesn't indulge in the restaurant's delicacies. She is like a relic from the 1960s with platinum-blonde, backcombed hair, and metallic blue eye shadow reaching from her mascara-laden lids to her alarmingly arched, pencilled-in brows. She's at odds with the homely olde-worlde decor and would look more at home at blousy Chez Louisette at the flea market in Paris.

I don't know if it's my accent or if she's just stone deaf, but she doesn't appear to understand a word I'm saying, so I resort to pointing at the menu. Mr V follows suit. We each choose a simple savoury crêpe, not wanting to over-indulge. It's delicious, but thicker and chewier, more like an English pancake, rather than wafer thin and crisp as a traditional Breton crêpe. Maybe this is why the French eat regionally; they simply can't do justice to another region's food.

After I manage to tear Mr V away from the dessert menu, we step out from the dimly lit interior into the eye-watering brightness and promptly retrieve our sunglasses from the tops of our heads. Our intention now is to find the Roman remains, though Mr V is challenging the wisdom of traipsing around an amphitheatre with no shade, and is opting for a siesta in the car before heading off to Beaune. We see on the tourist map that one of the sites—Porte St-André—is almost en route to where the car is parked, so we decide to visit there and play the rest by ear, as we don't want to arrive frazzled for my un-birthday meal. After all, the Roman remains have been here for over 2,000 years, so another couple of months won't make much difference.

The tourist map isn't exactly accurate (as tourist maps tend not to be), and somewhere along the line we've taken a wrong turn, and we are on the opposite side of the map to where the Porte St-André is, and are now taking the long way around to get back to the car. We come across some stairs leading to an underpass of some sort, and I deduce if we go down we'll come up near the marketplace and cut out a sizable chunk of our detour. We find ourselves in a beautiful, Art Deco arcade of shops, which are sadly all empty. There are elegant, mirrored, Grecian columns with globe lamps on gilt stands, and panels with mock Egyptian designs and hieroglyphics that were very popular during this epoch. We emerge in the new town area of the city, where the Art Deco influences continue to be seen everywhere, from the unmistakable lines of 1920s architecture, to beautiful shop fronts with exquisite, inlaid panels. But you have to keep your eyes peeled, as the shops appear in the most incongruous places such as a little back street butcher's shop and a hairdressers tucked in amongst more nondescript, modern shopfronts.

We're heading for Beaune. The heat was becoming intense, so we have left the Roman sites for another day. We've stopped for tea at a picnic area halfway along the route, and Mr V is taking his siesta while I'm writing beneath the shade of a lime tree. The sky in the direction of Autun is a deep indigo, and I think the threatened storm is hot on our heels. I'd like to get to the hotel and unpack the car before it catches us up, so I wake him, and we take to the road once more.

This is wine country; the names of vineyards roll off Mr V's tongue as we pass—Meursault, Volnay, Pommard, Saint-Romain— names I'd only ever seen printed on fancy labels on expensive bottles. The vines are still only knee-high to the *vignerons* (winegrowers) who are bent double tending them like a scene from the painting 'The Gleaners'. Tall, narrow tractors that appear to be on stilts and look like something from an apocalyptic *Mad Max* movie drive towards us on the road. Mr V explains that they're specially designed to straddle the vines and not damage them. The vines stretch as far as the eye can see and will surely be a sight in autumn. I make Mr V promise to bring me back here.

✳   ✳   ✳

We're still ahead of the storm when we check into our elegant, Belle-Époque style hotel. We have a meal booked for 7:30, but as we didn't stay to visit the Roman remains at Autun, we have a couple of hours to spare so head off to the Hospices de Beaune or Hôtel-Dieu.

Beaune is surrounded by medieval ramparts punctuated by towers and bastions and an elaborate arched gateway—the Porte St Nicolas —which are all illuminated at various times throughout the year as part of the spectacular *chemins de lumières* (trail of light), which also takes in all the major architectural sites. The town has a relaxed, casually chic almost Italian air, with shady, winding streets opening onto surprise little squares surrounded by cafés, with guitarists and saxophonists playing relaxed, casually chic jazz. The storm-laden sky has caught up with us, and hovers menacingly above and behind the Romanesque Notre-Dame Cathedral, making it stand out like a cardboard cut-out of a giant wedding cake against a deep plum background.

L'Hôtel-Dieu has none of the charm of the cathedral and looks very nondescript from the street: a flat, grey, stone facade with an imposing, grey, slate roof and tiny windows. The view from the other side however, is breathtaking. The cobbled courtyard is flanked on three sides by the same imposing roof, but here it is made of intricate yellow, red, green and black polychrome tiles. There's a covered balcony held up by stone, Grecian-style columns encompassing the first floor, and turrets with tall, pointed roofs at the corners. Diamond patterned leaded windows look down onto the courtyard and a charming wishing well. The whole effect is like something from a fairy-tale book. Thankfully, the rain has kept off long enough for me to get some wonderful photos of the magnificent roof.

Now I discover who Rolin was—chancellor to Philip the Good, the Duke of Burgundy. It was he and his wife, Guigone de Salins, who founded l'Hôtel-Dieu in 1443. It opened its doors as a free hospital and refuge for the poor, which was unique at this time. Initially designed to take care of 60 patients in 30 beds (2 to a bed), the hospice was expanded on the instruction of Louis XIV, who thought it unseemly to have men and women in the same room, so the St Nicolas' room was built to house female patients.

Not only was the concept of a free hospital for the poor unique, Rolin had some pretty unique architectural ideas also. He designed the building to be aesthetically beautiful on the inside and out, using the distinctive polychrome tiles that the region is famous for on the magnificent roof. The reason that the view from the inner courtyard is so much more beautiful than the view from the street is so that it was the patients who benefited from the beauty and not the passers-by, as he believed that the environment played a part in their wellbeing and recovery.

He also founded a training school for local women of good repute to nurse the patients and assist in the pharmacy, where all the medicines were prepared, and founded the religious order *Les Soeurs Hospitalières de Beaune* (Sisters of Beaune Hospital), who cared for patients as recently as the 1970s. As a former nurse, I absolutely love it here, I find all the porcelain jars lining the shelves in the pharmacy containing herbs and spices, and roots and seeds of plants fascinating.

Rolin also had revolutionary ideas on standards of cleanliness, and the provision of fresh food from the hospice's well-equipped kitchens and water from the well. But the water was used solely for washing and cooking purposes; the patients drank only wine as he believed that water was bad for the health. He also believed that cold food was bad for the health; that included fruit, which was only eaten warm after being cooked in wine; he obviously was my type of guy.

Wine continues to play a big part in the life of the new Hôpital de Beaune, which is still based on the same values that Nicolas Rolin started more than five centuries ago.

Funds for the hospital come directly from profits made from visits to l'Hôtel-Dieu and from the proceeds of the annual wine auction that takes place on the third weekend in November and is organised by no other than Christie's. I'm hankering after going to visit during the three days of festivities, but with so much to do still in the house, this will have to wait for at least another couple of years. Shame my birthday isn't in November.

⁂

The restaurant lives up to its reputation. We have an intimate little table by the window with a spectacular view of both the cathedral and the storm which arrives just as we're going inside. I hope it blows over before we leave as I'm wearing inappropriate shoes: strappy, beige-suede wedge heels with diamante studs on the straps. They set off my furry bubblegum toes a treat.

I order asparagus with a freshly made lemon mayonnaise for *entrée*. Then fillet of sea bream on a bed of courgette salsa verde for my main course, followed by *Crémeux de Bourgogne à la moutarde à l'ancienne* (a cheese with traditional mustard) and *Bleu de Bresse* (a local blue cheese), two creamy regional cheeses, ending the meal with a crisp shelled crème brûlée laced with Madagascan vanilla. All washed down with, of course, a silky Chablis.

The rain miraculously stops, and the ground dries enough for us to enjoy a stroll by the river before going back to our hotel. A perfect end to a perfect day. Happy birthday indeed.

HOW TO MAKE A DRUNKEN SLUG

I've woken to the most astonishing sight, though why I should be astonished I don't know, as I've been observing nature close at hand for nine months now. The tiny, purple buds on the feather tree haven't burst into green leaves but a show stopping display of minute blossoms, like an array of powder-pink caterpillars clinging to its branches. The sky above is baby blue, and the field behind startling yellow with rapeseed flowers. The effect is like waking in a scene from a picture-book image of spring.

The small, blue and yellow birds that are feasting on the flowers on the feather tree are causing such a racket that it's they who have woken me. I open the window and kneel on the floor, looking out over the garden and beyond. I still can't quite believe that this is real. It's as if I'm in one of those films where the characters step into a cartoon world filled with colour and birdsong. I feel like bursting into song myself, and would do if it weren't for Jacques passing on his bicycle at that very moment and pausing to speak with Mr V who's already in the garden.

It's still not yet seven in the morning, but Mr V has been out since the crack of dawn with a bucket, inspecting his slug traps. No we're not going to introduce a new delicacy to the palates of our friends and family; rather he's going to take them on a little sojourn down the lane to Mr Mouton's field. They've been feasting on his tomato plants and devoured all but two of the twelve lettuces that he planted, so he isn't happy. They've also been munching on my mint. Jacques said that we must buy a liquid soap known as *savon noir*, and mix it with water to spray around the base of the plants. But Mr V read somewhere that they're attracted to the smell of beer, and you can make a trap by cutting a plastic bottle in half and putting some beer in the bottom, then turning the top half upside down and inserting it into the bottle. You then lie it on its side, close to the lettuce and tomatoes. The idea is that the slugs will crawl into the wide opening and slither through the bottle top into the chamber containing the beer, where they're trapped but happy. So last night he set his traps and arranged them amongst the plants, including one in my pot of mint.

I'm eager to see how many (if any) slugs we've trapped so pull on a pair of jeans and T-shirt and rush downstairs. We have seven. I think this is pretty good, but Mr V was hoping for more. We fill the bucket with a further fourteen that are loitering around the lettuces and take them down to join the sheep.

* * *

My new office is the garden table on the terrace with a parasol providing shade for the computer, but it's becoming increasingly difficult to write outside, as I'm becoming somewhat of a local attraction. Not only does Jacques keep on popping up on his bike, but every five minutes an old Citroën passes with an ancient admirer at its wheel. I'm beginning to have a collection. They all toot and wave and I have to wave back. Most of the time I don't have a clue who I'm waving at; there's only one of me and seemingly multitudes of them. Most dreaded is when they stop and get out of their car, and I have to put down my pen and apprehend them at the fence, otherwise they'll be through the gate. And that will lead to sitting down, which inevitably leads to coffee or Pastis, and by the time I settle down again I've lost my train of thought.

It isn't only my admirers who disturb me. There are a number of holidaymakers in the hamlet who are attracted more by Les Libellules than me, but I have to greet them nevertheless. They often ask permission to take a photo of the house; she is extremely photogenic. But then the usual blah blah blah begins, so I'm contemplating moving back indoors behind the safety of the window.

The Three Degrees and their entourage also pass regularly, usually on Sunday mornings, all off for a jolly outing to a nearby field. I'm not sure why the farmer does this as the field they're in is plenty big enough for them to roam around and eat fresh grass. But there they go in a trailer, like stately ladies in an open-top bus. I shout 'bonjour' to them as they pass with their heads lolling over the rails looking at me with curiosity; then they moo back.

This morning, however, there's an obstruction further down the road, and they stop right opposite where I'm sitting. A little like babies who are fine when their pram is rolling and begin crying as soon as it stops, they all become agitated, and to my horror one of them knocks open the gate at the back of the trailer, and makes a bid for freedom running up the lane at quite an impressive speed. The drop is too high for the calves to tackle, and they're mooing furiously. A second cow tries to make her escape, but by now the farmer has jumped down from his tractor and firmly closed the gate, pushing her back. This still leaves one cow running wild and free through the hamlet.

The little excursion comes to an abrupt end with the six other cows being deposited back in their field. The farmer then turns his tractor around and heads off after the renegade, who appears to have run out of steam and is eating grass about 150 metres away. The farmer slips a rope around its neck and leads it back to the field at a leisurely pace, like a scene from a Thomas Hardy novel. Drama over, I get back to my writing.

P.S. A gaggle of holidaymakers have just 'bonjoured' past as I'm sitting like a stereotypical eccentric lady writer in a black, floppy hat, scribbling away furiously about a frog and a runaway cow.

Alas, once more it's almost time to pack up and go. It's always sad to leave after an extended stay. When we return it will be June, but without a doubt, May has been my favourite month.

PART VI
BONFIRES AND BUTTERFLIES

JUNE AND JULY 2018

Where the bee sucks, there suck I:
In a cowslip's bell I lie;
There I couch when owls do cry.
Ariel's song from *The Tempest*, William Shakespeare

PHOTOGRAPHING DRAGONFLIES

*I*t's the first of June, three weeks off the longest day. The time is a quarter to nine in the morning, and we're driving through a landscape viewed through the mellow filter of the low, early morning sun. My heart rises as we approach the hill of happiness, which is now dun brown and striped with freshly ploughed fallows. The pale blue sky has strands of high cloud like spun sugar stretched across it, and the sun casts the long shadows of trees and hedgerows over the honeyed fields. A distant *pigeonnier* rises red-roofed from the cluster of a village, and the spun-sugar clouds gather in clumps of pale-pink cotton candy.

It's been three weeks since we were last at Les Libellules. When we arrive, the lawn is no longer yellow. The buttercups have had their moment of glory, and now it's the turn of the clover, their trefoil leaves giving rise to an abundance of deep mauve and ivory lollipop flowers that have attracted a multitude of white butterflies. The fresh scent of lilac and lime blossom has been replaced by the heady aroma of the ancient roses, that have formed a fortress of fragrance and foliage around the terrace. Unlike the neat, velvety, often scentless modern varieties, these untamed beauties fling open their tightly rolled, pastel-pink buds into unruly, flat flowers, enticingly displaying their sunflower-shaped yellow centres. Their scent is a mingling of rose and lemon sherbet and like fine wine, you can taste it on your tongue when you inhale deeply.

The crows have gone. I think I may have had a guilty hand in their premature departure by wishing them away so fervently, as their tree has been struck by lightning in the once again unprecedented storms that battered the east of France in our absence, with the Côte-d'Or just catching the tail end. The charred and broken branches are lying like a barricade, cutting off the *mare*. This means we've had to shelve our plans to go to Dijon for more essential supplies, and Mr V has now taken up the role of a saw- and axe-wielding lumberjack. Every cloud (or in this case lightning strike) has a silver lining, and apart from the obvious absence of the crows, the fallen tree has provided us with an excellent supply of firewood.

Once the wood is safely stacked, Mr V continues to hack away at brambles and weeds to clear a space to create what will eventually be a woodland garden. He's on a roll, and I think relishing an excuse to work in the garden instead of the house. I'm summoned to decide where I'd like the iris bulbs planting and the bluebells transplanting, as where they are now is in an awkward position directly below the washing line, and every time I hang out a sheet or duvet cover, their bells are scattered on the ground. I select a position against the rustic, hazel fence separating our land from our Dutch neighbours'. I would eventually like to put a stone bench here, and a secret fountain hidden amongst the trees, where you can sit in the shade and look towards the *mare*, listening to the soothing, cooling sound of cascading water.

The gardening bug is infectious, and it bites me also. I put down my pen, pick up a pair of secateurs and begin trimming back the wayward tendrils of Virginia creeper that are invading the path. The vine is alive with dragonflies. I'm captivated by the beauty of two varieties that I've not previously seen, both around five cms long, with svelte bodies and wings like delicate black lace. The first is a red-bodied nymph, which as the name suggests, has a fiery-red body. The second is a startling colour of deep, sky blue and is an azure damselfly. They flit from vine to vine, occasionally coming to rest on a freshly unfurled leaf.

The secateurs now lie on the table beside the pen, and I'm standing camera in hand like a Greek statue, hardly daring to breathe as I wait for one of them to rest long enough for me to focus my lens and finally get a shot that isn't blurred. I wait for what seems like an eternity with the sun beating down on my bare shoulders and a host of airborne insects using my arms as landing pads. Finally, my patience is rewarded, and a red nymph settles to sun itself just long enough for me to capture it. Then magically a damselfly lands fleetingly in almost the same spot so I can quickly snap that also. Seen close up and stationary, they're not uniformly red or blue as they appear in flight, but have fine black markings as if they've been etched with a pen and ink, the evenly spaced stripes on their tails giving the appearance of bamboo. Then, a solitary beautiful broad-bodied chaser the size and shape of a small Perfecto cigar lands less than a metre away, the tip of its tail looking like it's been dipped in electric-blue paint. It appears to stare straight at me and pose as I take three stunning photos, then it spreads its beautiful filigree wings and flies off over the *mare*.

In this world of instant gratification, patience is a lost virtue that the creatures of the garden, be it dragonflies, butterflies, birds or bees, are teaching me to regain. I observe nature with the curiosity and fascination of an infant who has discovered their hands and am learning as much about myself as I am the mating habits of snails.

But although much longed-for, without the constant cawing of the crows, the silence is quite eerie. This is amplified by the fact that neither Fifi nor Jacques has passed by, and my extra chair and coffee cup remain empty. Even odder is the absence of Flaubertine cooing for food and attention.

NOT QUITE THE TOUR DE FRANCE

*I*t's Sunday morning, and there's still no sign of Flaubertine. It is almost 48 hours since we arrived on Friday, and I fear the worst. Nature is a duel-edged sword, and life in the country is both beautiful and cruel. For the farm cats, freedom and hardship walk hand in glove.

When we were last here, Flaubertine was drinking dirty water from our storage butt, and I was half afraid to look inside in case she'd fallen in and drowned. My friend Christelle was torn between leaving her and taking her back to Paris, but Flaubertine has a wild element and is used to wandering wherever, whenever she pleases. To confine her to a one-bedroom apartment with no balcony would be equally as cruel, like putting a tiger in a zoo for its own protection. Still, I've actually cried this morning, with tears smudging the ink as I write, so I decide to busy myself in the garden again, transplanting the thyme into a bigger pot and potting cuttings taken from a neighbour's rosemary and lavender bushes. I haven't got a clue whether it's a good time to do this or not, and I don't have the internet to check, but the last sprigs of rosemary that I unceremoniously stuck in some soil in a pot seem to be flourishing.

The garden has gone wild in our absence. There are long grasses that reach to my shoulder, their feathery heads looking too heavy for their slender stems. The wildflowers that have rooted themselves around the walls are in such abundance that they're making it impossible to open the shutters to the garden room and kitchen. There are peonies with blooms the size of cricket balls in puce, powder pink and milky white, tumbling onto paths and almost obscuring my lilac tree. So, I set about cutting back all the out-of-control bushes and wildflowers, and tidying up the others. I pull out the grasses by hand as we don't have a strimmer of our own, and they're far too long for the lawnmower.

I pause, fascinated by a small troupe of ants attempting to move the wizened body of a lizard. They continually reposition themselves, pushing from one side then the other, and then from the back, but all to no avail. Then, another group arrives. After some inter-ant communication, they form a horseshoe around the back and sides, and off they go again. They succeed in moving the lizard, but no great distance, until a virtual army arrives and surrounds the entire body, animating it so it appears to be moving of its own accord to the gap between the wall and the ground where they obviously have a nest. Who could fail to be impressed by such a display of determination, cooperation and teamwork? If only we humans could be more like ants and put our collective strengths, knowledge and resources together, what a world we could inhabit.

Mr V has raked over two small rectangles of stony earth, intending to make beds to plant more salad crops, but as he's losing the war with the slugs, and only one valiant, little lettuce remains, he's abandoned this plan. I commandeer these beds to attempt to sow some meadow herbs. I have a box that simply tells me to 'rake and shake' then water, so I'm relying on promised rain over the next two weeks to do this for me, otherwise the seeds will make an excellent, all-day buffet for the birds. I think that the latter is the most likely scenario as I fear that I'm too late in the year to be sowing them, and they were too long in the box in damp conditions, so I'm not holding out much hope, but all will be revealed in two weeks when we return.

My birthday present of an *Atlas of Birds of Burgundy* is proving more useful than I anticipated. I've so far been able to identify the birds of prey on *La Route des Aigles* as a common buzzard and a smaller hawk-like creature, that's taken up residence under the eaves of our Dutch neighbours' roof, as a hobby falcon. I've also spotted magpies, swallows, sparrows, robins, larks, blackbirds, woodpeckers, jackdaws, hoopoes, blue tits and of course the dreaded crows. And, to my delight, nightingales. There are many other small and medium-sized birds in an array of colours that I need to look in the book to identify, many of which I've never seen in the UK.

⚹ ⚹ ⚹

The peace and tranquillity of the morning is abruptly shattered. A red and white Mini with hazard lights flashing is fast approaching down the dusty lane usually reserved for farm vehicles and tractors. A loudspeaker is perched on the top, and it's blaring out an incomprehensible announcement that appears to be a warning of some kind for people to get off the road. It reminds me of being in Greece at the time of some local elections when these little vehicles regularly patrolled the streets, albeit it at a more leisurely pace, encouraging people to go and vote for whoever's face was plastered to the side of the car. This all felt completely normal there, but here it feels decidedly out of place.

Seconds later the reason becomes apparent as a group of eight or nine cyclists speeds past, kitted out in tight florescent Lycra and wrap-around sunglasses. A minute or so later another similarly sized band of bicycles passes in a blur of red, blue and yellow, followed by an emergency first aid vehicle; impressive, but a bit excessive, as although they were travelling at a fair pace, they hardly constituted the Tour de France.

I settle down to write again, only to be disturbed by yet another advance warning vehicle. I detect the word *moto* amongst the muffled sounds, and sure enough a squadron of motorbikes follows, not the high-handlebar variety ridden by bikers out for a weekend rally, but gleaming machines with equally gleaming riders who look like they're living their male menopausal dreams. Next the bread lady passes in her little van, going in the opposite direction to the far end of the lane. I get my purse and wait at the gate for her to turn around and return.

What follows next takes me by total surprise. Around 100 bikes swing into view and come hurtling through the tiny hamlet at breakneck speed. The bread lady makes a hasty manoeuvre onto the grass verge outside one of the cottages as they swish past. I'm standing rooted at the gate. They pass so close that I can feel their rush of air on my face and hear the whoosh and whir of their wheels.

Then they're gone, and life resumes its usual leisurely pace. The bread lady trundles up and greets me at her counter at the back of the van saying, 'That was impressionable, yes?' The smell of the bread drifting from her shelves is heavenly, and I come away armed with two long, fat, crusty baguettes, that I rush inside with to cut off a triangular end and spread it with salty butter. There is nothing in the world like sinking your teeth into a chunk of freshly baked French bread, breaking through the crisp, crunchy crust to the light, fluffy centre that melts away with the butter, leaving you craving more. Sinful, I know, but too tempting to resist.

What I've learnt today: How many ants does it take to move a lizard? As many as it takes to make it move.

ARRIVALS AND DEPARTURES

*W*e've arrived back from Paris with Pussy Willow who became very excited in the car as we entered the hamlet. The good news, if you can call it that, is that Flaubertine was there to greet us almost immediately. The not-so-good news is that she is painfully thin. Now that it's summer, we'll be here more regularly, and for longer periods, so I can feed her up. There's still no sign of either Fifi or Jacques though. I hope I haven't frightened them off now that they've discovered I'm writing a book as, like everyone else except for PJ and Panda, their real identities have been protected.

The garden once again reminds me that it is nature, not I who is the master. The resilience of the plant life is astounding. The ornamental rosebush that I cut down almost to the ground has risen like a phoenix and is now up to my waist. The new leaves at its top are deep red, turning reddish green and finally, fully green. As a complete garden novice, I find this incredible as only weeks ago this plant was just a collection of dry wooden stumps.

The wildflowers have run riot again. This, however, has attracted an abundance of butterflies, which must be seasonal also as I've only seen half a dozen of the white variety that were flourishing a fortnight ago. Now, there are scores of a gorgeous orange species, with yellow and black stripes on the upper edge of their wings and cornflower blue crescents on the lower. These are proving to be even more difficult to photograph than the dragonflies, but standing still waiting for one to settle at a good angle has taught me that they are not just aimlessly flitting from flower to flower. Once landed, they draw their wings together and use them like bellows to rotate a full 360 degrees before taking off to the next. The trick is to snap them the instant they land.

This morning the orange, black and yellow butterflies have been joined by some gorgeous, citrus lemon ones, and others with silvery opaque wings through which I can see the muted colours of the flowers they land upon.

I was going to cut back some of the more wayward plants but am now going to leave them as I would much rather sit here surrounded by these beautiful creatures than by a neatly manicured garden.

I have, however, suffered for my art the last weekend; my arms, shoulders and chest are a mass of small insect bites, but the photos are well worth it.

*   *   *

Not only have the crows taken flight, but Penthouse Mouse has bitten the cheese, literally. Yesterday I discovered that he'd not only munched his way through an entire three-strip packet of Chinese noodles and two sachets of tomato ketchup, but he'd also demolished a fair part of the cupboard wall, leaving a typical Tom and Jerry-style mousehole that enabled him to make a quick exit if I or Pussy Willow interrupted him. Mr V said something had to be done and produced two nasty mousetraps loaded with smelly French cheese. Usually, I would have absolutely forbidden this, but he was right, it was all very well feasting on my noodles and couscous, but once he went into the demolition business, he signed his death warrant. I know that people say this is the quickest and cleanest way to dispatch mice, as I've heard countless tales of them dying slow deaths in 'humane' traps, but I still feel like judge, jury and executioner.

As one pest departs, another arrives in this kaleidoscope of birds, butterflies and beasties. The latest kids on the block are minute ants, not much bigger than a speck of grit, that lurk in the grass and jump onto my feet and ankles, clinging to them like the tiny metal particles in one of those magnetic picture boards I had when I was a child. When they bite, you certainly know about it, as it feels like red hot needles are piercing your skin. So much so that I've now taken to wearing my wellies when I'm hanging out the washing.

The absence of the crows has seen the return of the swallows, but while they're putting paid to the biting beasts of the air, the ants at ground level appear to have no predators.

* * *

The swallows aren't the only things to have returned. We've received our first 'offering' of the season. Fifi has called with a crisp, curly lettuce heavy with soil that he's just plucked from his garden. I think he's trying to get back into my good books after the Lila incident, but it's going to take more than a lettuce to placate me.

We've also received an invitation to *la Fête des Voisins*, a lovely annual tradition that takes place all over France where *voisins* (neighbours) get together for a sort of street party. Once more we are in the land where bureaucracy rules. I have a form to fill in to give our name and how many of us will be attending, and to specify if we'll be bringing a starter, a salad, a main course, cheese, tart or other type of dessert, plus the obligatory bottle of wine and one baguette for every two people. We've also been asked to bring our own *couvert*, which usually means cutlery, but I think this might also mean plates and glasses. I'm looking forward to this with anticipation of it being as entertaining as the fête at Advent.

I now need to decide what to make. It can't be anything too ambitious as we'll be driving down from Paris and will only arrive about 30 minutes before the fête is due to start, plus anything made in advance would have to be able to travel well. As I'm English, and the English have a very undeserved reputation for not being able to cook, there's more than my reputation at stake. The 'gince' pies went down well at Christmas, so I need to at least equal them.

I'm also not sure what to wear as most of the women frequently go around in cropped trousers and T-shirts, except Valerie from the farm behind, who I've seen floating about in a maxi dress. Looking through my limited wardrobe down here, I finally decide on a flattering, figure-hugging, 'fit and flare' sundress in pale turquoise with petrol blue, Indian-inspired patterns. Turquoise and blue are Mr V's favourite colours, and as I have blonde hair and green eyes, these colours suit me well. Plus, the dress is cool, easy to wear and not too dressy.

We're driving back from Paris in the early evening to avoid the heat of the day. The countryside has melted into a tangerine haze as the sun sinks low in the west. I have the window open and my pen in my hand to write in my notebook.

We pass the little café whose defiant chairs and tables sat empty in the snow, and sadly they're still empty now in the evening glow. One day I'm going to stop here and sit at one of those tables, but not with Mr V. He won't stop the car to sit at a café so close to home.

We leave the country roads and villages and continue on the almost deserted autoroute, which still has an oasis shimmer of heat hovering on its surface. The sun sinks lower behind the gentle swell of a hill, and the sky turns soft peach. The fields take on the green/grey hue of lavender as the sun bleeds into the earth, and I lose the light to write by.

LA FÊTE DES VOISINS

*I*t's the day after the summer solstice, the evening of *la Fête des Voisins*. The common land between Les Libellules, our Dutch neighbours and the farm behind has been transformed into a village green. In the centre is a large marquee with panelled, plastic windows, through which I can see tables and chairs set out in a horseshoe, with a long trestle table at the near end expectantly awaiting the arrival of the food. There are already ice buckets containing bottles of rosé for the apéritif on a makeshift bar outside the tent, and bottles of red and white wine and corkscrews on the tables inside.

For my contribution, I've made a grated carrot salad and my crowd-pleasing pear and chocolate frangipane tart. I head off into the garden to pick some fresh mint to make a strawberry and mint salad also. I can see people coming down the lane, carrying tarts and quiches, and platters of cooked meats and cheeses and, of course, bottles of wine and baguettes. Everyone is milling around outside the tent where the kisses are flying from cheek to cheek, and the rosé is flowing from bottle to plastic picnic glass, as is the rum punch and the Pastis.

Marie-Claire (the owner of César) pours Fifi almost a glassful of

Pastis topped up with two fingers of water as opposed to the ones that I mix for Mr V that have the same ingredients in opposite measures. She flicks up an eyebrow in my direction for me to watch his reaction as he takes a gulp of what looks like concentrated grapefruit juice; there is none. Another flick of an eyebrow passes between us. I for one would be unceremoniously spitting it out now. For such a small man, he has quite a capacity for alcohol.

Marie-Claire is of Guadeloupian origin, and she's made the most delicious patties of spicy salted cod and vegetables. I devour them almost single-handedly as the French eye them suspiciously and ask me are they spicy, to which I reply, 'Oh yes, *very*,' so they make a beeline for the nice safe goat's cheese and olive savoury cake and the *saucisson*. There are also moreish, miniature cheese sandwiches that have been dipped in a batter of sorts and deep-fried. They taste like a cross between Greek fried cheese and *croque monsieur* minus the ham —crunchy on the outside and chewy and gooey in the middle—but alas I don't quite have the monopoly on these.

We've been summoned to the table by Solène, who has a surprisingly powerful set of lungs for such a seemingly frail lady of advanced years. Mr V and I have put our plates and cutlery in a space between two sets of four, so we don't have a clue who we'll be sitting next to. I think that this is part of the plan. Unless you're familiar with someone's flatware, then everyone is jumbled up together, encouraging you to mix with new people. Of course, to us the vast majority of people are new, but it stops us gravitating towards those who already feel like old friends.

I've been talking outside with a couple from the opposite end of the hamlet who also have a house in La Rochelle where they spend the winter months as the weather is milder by the coast. The wife, Mireille, is a former psychiatric nurse. On hearing that I'm a former nurse also, she introduces me to two others: Agathe, who worked at St Louis in Paris where I teach, and another lady, Fabienne, who lived and worked in the Congo, not only as a nurse, but also as a veterinary surgeon, describing herself as a Jack or Jill of all trades. She tells us harrowing stories of how she had to escape the war there in 1997.

This little place is such a melting pot, and far from being a sleepy backwater, it is teeming with characters and stories.

Our immediate neighbours for dinner arrive: a couple that we've never seen before with their son and his girlfriend. The young couple don't drink, and the husband has to be up for work early in the morning, so that leaves three of us to enjoy the excellent Côte de Nuits wine. We all go and help ourselves to the buffet, after which an enormous tray appears with twelve different cheeses from the region, each bearing a little flag with their name: Epoisses, Langres, Bleu de Bresse and Comté being the only ones I'm familiar with. The tray is passed around along with the baguettes. Everyone rips off a chunk of bread with their hands and passes it on like a baton. As tradition, the cheese is passed around twice, then it's time for dessert. In addition to my chocolate and pear masterpiece, there's a rectangular cherry lattice, a deep custard tart, my strawberry and mint salad, small glasses of strawberry mousse and something which is a cross between a chocolate mousse and a brownie. The conversation ceases for the first time during the evening, as everyone gets down to the serious business of eating 'the most important part of the meal'; that is according to Mr V anyway.

Valerie from the farm, who has organised the event, switches off the music that has been playing in the background and announces that Jean-Pierre is going to treat us to a turn on his accordion. Jean-Pierre, who looks like Bjorn from ABBA, perches on a stool and whips out his, in my opinion, rather small accordion. But I'm used to seeing ones the size of bathroom cabinets blocking the doors in the Paris Metro. I'm expecting to hear 'Padam, Padam' or some other Parisian, café-style tune, but he strikes up what sounds to me like Breton Celtic music. My neighbour at the table, who hails from Dijon, tells me that it's a local folk song, which it seems is also a local folk dance, as no sooner has Jean-Pierre finished his first bar than almost everyone is on their feet, young and old alike, ranging from around two years old to what must be at least eighty-two.

Young are dancing with old, young with young, old with old. Men are dancing with women, women with women, men with men. The best sight of all is that the two young 'dudes' of the hamlet, both aged around nineteen and usually seen strutting about in shades and gigantic headphones, are linking arms and swirling around with the rest of them. None of the self-conscious clowning that I would expect from this age group; this is serious stuff. Some of the footwork is fancy enough to be seen on *Riverdance*. I'm impressed with the agility of everyone, or maybe they're just well-oiled with wine. Fifi, having consumed a rocket-fuel-strength apero, is spinning like a top, and his footwork is more than a tad fancier than most.

I feel a gentle pat on my knee and look down to see Alicia, aged four, looking up at me with big, brown eyes and asking, *'Voulez-vous dancer avec moi, madame?'* (Would you like to dance with me, madam?) How can I refuse? I don't know the steps, but at least Alicia isn't going to be as fast and furious as the rest, so I should be able to keep up, plus, it takes me out of circulation in case another dervish decides to mark my dance card. Then the dreaded thing happens. Marie-Claire taps me on the shoulder, whips Alicia up into her arms and pushes her wiry *gendarme* husband into mine. Suddenly I'm on the waltzers, the room passes in a blur as my feet can no longer keep up and are getting dragged around with my body. I've never been more grateful than when we collide like two satellites spinning out of orbit with Fifi and his partner, who I have to say, looks as relieved as me. We exaggerate our injuries and hobble convincingly back to our chairs.

The dancers are now kicking up more dust from the terracotta earth than the Calgary Stampede. Mr V, who is sitting opposite me, is obscured by a red haze, my throat feels as if I've just smoked twenty Gitanes, and my legs look as if I'm wearing rust-coloured fake tan. I hastily cover my wine glass with a napkin as clouds of grit are settling on the surface. The partygoers are all in full swing, and there's even an elderly gentleman on two sticks attempting to hobble around.

Then someone breaks away from the throng and begins to weave their way between the tables, grabbing people and pushing them behind to do the conga. I'm swept up once more and am thrilled that one of the young dudes in a tight, white T-shirt with even tighter abs pushes in front of me. Off we go into the cooling night air, past Les

Libellules to the end of the lane. We conga around the cross of the war memorial and back towards the marquee. Mr Mutton, who has just had a hip replacement, is now in the lead dictating the pace, which has become decidedly slower at the front than at the back, so people keep crashing into one another from behind and causing the entire line to become a giant concertina.

The whole event seems as if we're at a wedding or a family get-together. When you enter the hamlet there's a sign saying 'Commune' of the village where the town hall is situated. If *commune* translates into community, then this is a commune in every sense of the word.

It is half past midnight, and people are beginning to gather their dishes and start the cheek-kissing ritual again as they drift back to their beds. Mr V has been up since half past five this morning, done a full day's work and driven three hours to get here, so we follow suit, leaving the handful of hardcore dancers and drinkers. Back in Les Libellules we drift off to sleep to the sound of The Beatles coming from the tent aptly singing 'Yesterday'.

THE BREAKFAST CLUB

I am woken at 7:30 in the morning by a combination of the sun piercing through a gap in the curtains and voices outside. I drag myself bleary-eyed from the comfort of my bed to see where the noise is coming from. The hamlet is like a ghost town, with everyone nursing their hangovers behind closed shutters. Everyone, that is, except for Fifi who is bright-eyed and bushy-tailed standing at the gate having a loud, jovial conversation with Mr V, who, being used to getting up at 5:30 every morning, considers 7am a *grasse matinée* (a lie-in).

They've now moved into the living room, which poses me with a problem. The inside stairs open directly into there, and I'm only wearing a little bit of flimsy silk that passes for a nightie, bought for my honeymoon. The only thing for it is to go down the outside stairs and sneak in through the back door to get washed and decently dressed.

My plan hasn't worked. As I reach the back door, they are coming out. Mr V looks aghast and says, 'Oh, are you up?' Fifi, looking like I've made his morning, pushes past Mr V to kiss me and asks if I've slept well. I try to take it all in my stride, and smile and say, 'Yes, very well, thank you,' which is a lie. Mr V has been lying on his back like a beached whale, snoring half the night, and their conversation beneath my bedroom window had scuppered the only chance I had of getting a decent couple of hours in. I scurry off to the bathroom, conscious of just how short and clingy and totally out of place in the country this nightdress is. It is ivory silk with muted pink and mauve flowers and a strappy, criss-cross back that plunges almost to my waist; the front is dangerously low also.

I disappear into the bathroom and re-emerge in a pink floral shirt and black crop pants. Fifi looks decidedly disappointed. I offer him a coffee and set the table on the terrace for breakfast. There's a knock on the door; it's still not 8 a.m., and I haven't seen or heard as much as a tractor passing in the distance, while Les Libellules is a hub of activity. Jacques has come to join the breakfast club, to which I seem to have been nominated cook and waitress.

We are on a very short visit this weekend as Mr V has to go away to work on Sunday, so we have a lot of things to do before we leave immediately after an early lunch (which I'd envisaged more as brunch after an extended lie-in). I have a pile of ironing that's still here from our last visit and I wanted to empty the Penthouse Mouse cupboard and give it a thorough clean. But it's now 10 o'clock, we're on our second pot of coffee, and Jacques is in full flow, telling me all about *la Fête de la Saint-Jean,* that I'll tell you all about later. There's a bit of schoolboy rivalry going on for my attention as Fifi keeps contradicting Jacques and doesn't seem a fan of *la Fête de la Saint-Jean* at all but told us we had to go at least once just to see.

Mr Mouton is the first of the other neighbours to drive past to tend his little flock. I get the impression that there's a considerable amount of rivalry between him and Fifi also; he looks quite dejected to see us all sitting conspiratorially around the table. I begin to clear away the breakfast things, saying I must get on, and they make moves to leave but only get as far as the gate. Mr V has given up on his plans for the morning entirely; we'll never get the house started, let alone finished at this rate. Finally, they go and I begin to reset the table for lunch.

Mr Mouton is on his way back from feeding his sheep and slows his car down to a snail's pace, smiling and waving as he sees the coast is clear. I smile and wave back, which he takes as an invitation to park his car and approach the garden gate.

The opening gambit is, 'How are you?' which is a bit less personal than Fifi's, 'Have you slept well?' I tell him, 'I'm very well, thank you,' and the next thing you know the pre-programmed offer of a coffee is out of my mouth before I can stop it. One more cup and I shall be spinning with caffeine as much as Fifi was with Pastis last night, and we'll be stopping at every picnic area along the route back to Paris for a comfort break.

Mr Mouton isn't as entertaining as Jacques and proceeds to go into detail about his hip operation. As I worked on an orthopaedic ward in the past, it's like teaching your grandmother to suck eggs. I let him ramble on and hope that Mr V won't materialise as he's of a squeamish disposition, and the sight of Mr Mouton's scar when he pulls down the side of his elastic waist shorts to show me would make him decidedly queasy. I think Mr Mouton is holding out for an apéritif as it's nearer that time than coffee time. But I tell him that we're leaving in the next hour, so he thanks me for the coffee and shuffles off.

At last, I'm able to whip up a tomato and feta cheese omelette and toss some salad in a bowl, and we sit down to eat a hasty lunch. We've just begun on some rather delicious Bleu de Bresse cheese that was left over from last night, when Pappy Cardigan and Noëlle arrive bearing two dozen eggs. They hesitate at the gate when they see us at the table (it was only 11:45 after all), but I rush to greet them and tell them it isn't a problem as we've almost finished eating anyway. As you know, I like Noëlle very much. She gathers me to her ample bosom, almost creating another omelette with the eggs that I'm now clutching, and I wish we didn't have to go. I so want to hear her stories about her chickens, ducks and the donkey. Another coffee and another half hour delay and they leave us, saying they'll come for a longer visit next Saturday afternoon, which I'll look forward to immensely.

* * *

As I'm clearing the table once again, and we're finally about to leave, a car full of strangers stops by the fence, and the driver asks me if today is *la Fête de la Saint-Jean*. I tell him no, that it's next Saturday. But, like him and his expectant passengers, you'll have to wait until the next chapter before I tell you about that, as I don't want to spoil the surprise.

While you're waiting, here's my show-stopping tart recipe.

PEAR AND CHOCOLATE FRANGIPANE TART

Serves 8 generous portions

Ingredients

Pastry

200 g (7 oz) plain flour
80 g (3 oz) Trex or 100 g (3.5 oz) margarine (Trex has a higher water content so 20% less is needed)
1 egg yolk
2 tbsp ice-cold water
Pinch of salt

Filling

200 g (7 oz) cooking chocolate. I use 100 g dark and 100 g milk; I find all milk too sickly and all dark too rich and difficult to work with.
6 medium pears, cored and sliced into 6, or a large tin of pear halves in light syrup, drained (saving the syrup) and cut into 3. I prefer the tinned variety for this recipe.
1 medium egg
100 g (3.5 oz) castor sugar
50 g (2 oz) plain flour
3 tbsp crème fraîche

Method

Pastry

Wash your hands and rinse in cold water (cool hands are essential to make good pastry).

Sieve the flour with the salt into a large, preferably pottery, mixing bowl.

Chop the Trex (or equivalent) into the flour with a cold knife, then quickly work the mixture into a breadcrumb texture, using the tips of your fingers only and lifting the mix from the bowl as you work it to incorporate as much air as possible.

Cut the egg yolk into the mixture, again using a cold knife.

Add the water (direct from the fridge) little by little so not to make the pastry to wet, and mix with a cold knife.

Quickly draw the mixture into a ball, wrap in cling film and put in the fridge to rest for at least 30 minutes.

Remove from fridge for 5 minutes before rolling out to fit a 30 cm (12 in) flan/quiche dish.

Put back in fridge until ready to fill.

The three main factors for making a good pastry are:

1. The speed of making it—pastry doesn't like to be overhandled.
2. The temperature—the cooler the room, your hands, the surface, and the water, the better.
3. The amount of moisture—the drier the pastry, the lighter

and crumblier (short) it is. Even if it's more difficult to work with and you may need to patch it, it's worth it for the result. The wetter it is, the more you'll break your teeth!

Filling

Line a tart dish with the pastry.

Melt the chocolate in a basin over a pan of simmering water, stirring occasionally and taking care not to get any water inside the basin or the chocolate will turn fudgy.

Spread the melted chocolate quickly and evenly over the base of the tart and arrange the pears on top.

Beat the egg and sugar together with a wooden spoon until light and fluffy.

Add the flour and crème fraîche a little at a time (alternating) and mix well.

If the mixture is too stiff, loosen it with a little of the saved pear juice, or fresh fruit juice.

Pour the mixture over the top of the pears and chocolate.

Bake in a preheated oven at 200 C/gas mark 6 for around 35 minutes, until the top is just firm, checking to take care that it doesn't overbrown.

This dish must be served warm to be appreciated at its best, as if it's too hot, then the chocolate will be too runny, and if too cold, the chocolate will be too set.

Serve with a little dollop of crème fraîche on the side.

GOODNESS GRACIOUS, GREAT BOARS
ON FIRE

*L*a *Fête de la Saint-Jean* was traditionally a religious ceremony to celebrate the birth of Saint John the Baptist but is now a great fête with music, dancing, feasting, fireworks and, the most important element, bonfires. This tradition hasn't been kept alive all over France. In fact, I'd never heard of it in Paris. But it is still alive and kicking in the Pyrenees region, and very much so in our little commune.

The fête in its present incarnation began in 2008, when the then Dutch neighbour from the house behind (not he who puts out the bins in his underwear), stood around the meagre bonfire built on the top of the hill with twenty or thirty others, ate a hotdog, drank a beer and returned home.

The next day he called on Jacques and asked him what he thought of the fête.

'It's incredible,' said Jacques.

'Yes, but I think it could be better,' replied our Dutchman, who for the purposes of the tale I will call Dik. 'What's the most important animal in these parts?' Dik continued.

'Well, it has to be the Charolais cow.'

'Right. Charolais cow it is then.'

Jacques had no idea what Dik was planning, but the next day he returned with a model of a cow made from lolly ice sticks. Jacques was impressed; it was perfectly proportioned, but he was still none the wiser. I must explain that Dik is an artist, and, Jacques informs me, a Buddhist, as if this excused Dik's strange behaviour. He planned to build a much larger cow to the same scale as the miniature model.

'Incredible,' Jacques said once more. 'What are you going to make it out of?'

And this is where it all gets interesting, or bonkers, or both. Dik told Jacques that he was going to make it out of pallets, and he was going to start collecting them immediately from various places and put out an appeal for everyone in the five communes to do the same.

Jacques thought that this could potentially mean a lot of pallets, but Jacques at this stage had no idea of just *how* bonkers Dik's plan was.

The cow was going to be about three metres high, not including the horns, and four metres long, not including the tail. He was going to build it on the land where the marquee was last weekend, and he had hired a professional cameraman to come and film its progress at regular stages. The finished piece had to be lifted by a crane and loaded onto an enormous cattle truck, which was then pulled by a tractor to the top of the hill, where at nightfall it was ceremoniously set on fire. As the news got around, this attracted rather more than twenty or thirty locals with a bottle of Stella Artois and a frankfurter in a bun. More than 100 people turned up. There was music and a makeshift dance floor, and people brought food, much as we did for *la Fête des Voisins*.

No sooner than the embers had begun to cool than Dik was at Jacques' door again with another model, this time of a wild boar (hunting, as you've read, is very popular in this area).

For the next year this was to be made to the same proportions as the cow, but with the addition of a cordless drill being attached to the tail on the inside, and the carcass being filled with fireworks. Dik climbed inside from the underneath and set the drill in motion, which in turn sent the tail spinning around. He then lit a fuse wire that ignited the fireworks which came shooting out of the tail as it spun. That year there were between 200 and 300 spectators and, of course, a hog roast.

Just when Jacques thought that Dik had reached his peak came his wackiest idea yet: a giant cockerel, astoundingly almost six metres high by six metres long. Not only was this ambitious in terms of sheer size but also in terms of complexity. In comparison to the fairly uniform physique of a cow or boar, a cockerel has feet with claws on which it has to balance, plus an enormous set of tail feathers and intricate cockscomb. This time Dik had not only hired a regular cameraman, but also a helicopter and an aerial cameraman to film his pièce de résistance going up in flames from above.

The word had by this time spread far and wide, and there were an estimated 1,000 people on the hillside that evening, along with a live band, dancing, trestle tables and an organised meal.

Sadly, this was Dik's last masterpiece, as some vague, not discussed, family issues called him back to the land of the tulip, but the tradition has continued. Last year the local men built a giant tractor, again from pallets, with huge wooden wheels and pulled it on ropes to the top of the hill where it was filled with straw and ritually burnt. There was also a proper firework display, and the local fire brigade supervised the whole event. Numbers were over 2,000, which if they rose any higher would be challenging to manage in terms of logistics and safety, so this year it's ticket only. You have to register on the town hall website, with priority being given to locals. The entry price is €10, which includes the meal, and any proceeds go to the firemen to help pay for their annual summer ball.

The event takes place next Saturday evening, so I'm very excited to see what transpires.

ANT INVASION

*O*ur priorities have changed. When we arrived previously, the first thing we used to do was empty the car and put things away in their prospective places. I would then begin to cook while Mr V opened the shutters or lit the fire, depending on the time and the season. Now we both go straight to the garden—me to inspect my herbs and geraniums and of course Lila, Mr V to his tomatoes and seedlings. We fret over their condition in this intense, hot, dry spell (though Jacques has been watering the tomatoes without us having asked him to).

Summer has already begun to bleach the colour out of spring. The feather tree looks like a sepia version of itself, the dusty blossom having fallen to the ground like ash, and only spindly, green needles remain. The apple tree is bare of blossom and her parched leaves are curling inwards. Mr V sets about filling two large watering cans from which I fill my smaller lighter one and give everything a much-needed drink. The *mare* is at risk of drying up, and I fear for the frogs as much as the plants. It is so dry this year that as we drove down, the farmers were already harvesting their corn and making bales of hay, and it isn't yet July. The grass, like the corn, is pale yellow and dried to a crisp. I can now see the merit of having a swimming pool. Jacques said that it may be too hot and dry to risk lighting the bonfire on Saturday. Each week for the past four it has promised rain, but it never materialises. This really has been a flaming June.

✳   ✳   ✳

This evening Flaubertine was in the kitchen even before me. She's still as thin as a rake, but I'm heartened to see the return of some of her former spirit. She looks like she may have been in a fight as there's a wound on her neck, but nothing anywhere near as bad as what Maddy had sustained. I still miss Maddy and feel sad when I think of her. I give Flaubertine a large dish of Pussy Willow's best cat food and a bowl of milk mixed with water. Her hunger satisfied, she installs herself on the terrace where she sees me setting the table for dinner. We eat outside under her watchful eye: fish and potatoes fried in garlic, served with a bowl of green salad. Fish and chips Les Libellules style.

✳   ✳   ✳

As we went directly to the garden, we hadn't been into the living room this evening. What greets us when we put on the light is like something from a Hitchcock film. The room is a mass of huge, flying ants. They are swirling around the light in the same direction, like a bizarre, insect carousel. They're also scaling the windows and chimney breast and are all over the sofa and coffee table, making themselves at home on my cushions and books. Everywhere I look there are hundreds of them. They are landing on my arms and in my hair. I feel my skin itching and crawling even where they have not. In short, it's horrific. Mr V and I each grab a spray gun of Bloq' Insectes and proceed to saturate the room. The floor is now a slimy mass of insect repellent and dead ants. Lampshades, curtains, cushions, throws and even books are soaked as I am like a latter-day Annie Oakley with my gun of toxic chemicals.

Far from enjoying an after-dinner drink on the terrace listening to the frogs and cicadas, I have a shower and go to bed, using the outside stairs to avoid setting foot in the ironically named 'living room,' which is now full of dead and dying ants.

This morning we're crunching on a carpet of tiny corpses. I take off all the throws and cushion covers and shake them violently before putting them in the washing machine. I do the same with the curtains. Next, I remove everything from the table and shelves and begin vacuuming these before tackling the floor. The entire exercise takes me the best part of three hours.

I'm now showered and taking a well-earned rest on my clean sofa in the living room, which is smelling pleasantly of lavender-scented floor cleaner. My peace is disturbed by a rustling noise coming from the built-in cupboard where Mr V now keeps his electrical tools. I immediately think that Penthouse Mouse Two has taken up residence on the opposite side of the room. I get up and press my ear to the cupboard door; there's no mistaking that the noise is coming from inside, but it's more crackling than rustling. I tentatively open the door and see hundreds more flying ants swarming all over two of the shelves, which look as if they've been smeared with black treacle, the sight of which makes me feel physically sick.

I begin to lose heart, and I can honestly say that during all the challenges and setbacks of the last ten months, I've never once looked back until this moment. I just want to get on a plane, sit by a pool with a book and not be faced with emptying a large, packed-to-the-hilt cupboard in 33 degrees' heat and risk sending more of these invaders flying around the room that I've just spent the last three hours of my life cleaning.

I wearily drag the hoover from under the stairs and suck up so many ants that it overheats and seizes up completely, leaving me to brush the remainder into a dustpan and spray them immediately. Next, I gingerly lift boxes of tools to brush up those scurrying for cover underneath, then deposit the tools into a large cardboard box on the patio.

Finally, the cupboard is clear, but I can still hear a crackling sound. The wallpaper next to the cupboard is undulating. In places it has been pushed about five centimetres from the wall, and a gap between the joins has opened up. I call Mr V, who comes with an industrial vacuum cleaner and slides the long, thin nozzle into the gap before removing the wallpaper and revealing a hole in the wall, which obviously leads to the nest. I spray Bloq' Insectes down the hole, and he goes to mix some cement to seal it up. Shower number two is now urgently called for. Oh for that swimming pool…

CHERRY RIPE, CHERRY RIPE, RIPE CHERRY RIPE

*T*he saving grace of the morning comes in the form of Jacques, who arrives to tell me that his cherries are ripe and need picking today or tomorrow, or the birds will have them. They are sour cherries, not the sweet, deep crimson ones that I'm used to buying in the market. These beauties are bright, lipstick red, just as juicy but slightly firmer and a lot tarter, better suited to preserving in alcohol than making jam.

Mr V and I go with Jacques to pick a basketful. While I am there, I'm introduced to Poulette, Jacques' pet hen. He's had her since she was a chick. She was the smallest of the brood that he'd bought along with a rooster in order to have fresh eggs. The rooster was rather taken with poor little Poulette and chased her around the farmyard every morning to have his wicked way. So Jacques separated her for her own safety, and she became so tame that she sits on the sofa as would a dog or a cat, comes when he calls her name, allows you to pick her up and stroke her, and coos with pleasure very much like Flaubertine. She also loves cherries and will take them from your hand. Speaking of Flaubertine, I fear that she's pregnant as I noticed this morning that she has enlarged teats, and this could explain why she wasn't herself last time. All will be revealed, but I hope she doesn't come calling with six hungry little mouths in tow. Maybe I could persuade Jacques to take one or two.

After we've filled our basket, Jacques asks me if I would like to see his box tree moth larvae that are eating his hedges. I have to say that this is the first time anyone has ever proposed this to me. He thinks I might like to photograph them, so I follow him into his impressive vegetable garden, which is laid out with neat rows of leeks, carrots, cabbages, beetroot and green beans. His box hedging most certainly has been eaten by these rather beautiful, bright-green caterpillars, which are wreaking havoc to hedges in 51 departments in France. Jacques holds back the branches while I position lens inside the plant and capture some great close-up shots. Mr V returns to Les Libellules with the cherries, and I go on a guided tour of Jacques' wonderful, rambling old house.

The house used to be a hotel and has what was a public toilet that from the outside looks like a stone-age dwelling; from the inside, however, it's like something from a Victorian curiosity peepshow. There are strategically placed little spy holes that you can look out of when you're seated (not the inverse I must add), giving views over the hamlet, the courtyard and the hillside. Some of these are concealed behind a plaque or picture; others are positioned so that you can only see through them from a certain angle. It is ingenious and amusing; some plaques and pictures are red herrings with nothing but wall behind them. We play a game with me having five guesses to find the five hidden peepholes. I delight Jacques by getting only three of them, allowing him to reveal the remaining two. There's also a sort of church altar inside the toilet if anyone feels the need to pray while in there.

Apparently in the days when the house was a hotel, quite a lot of famous French dignitaries stayed there, but the only one I'd heard of was Abbé Pierre, a French priest who was born not too far away in Lyon and was part of the Resistance during the war. He later founded the Emmaus movement to help the homeless and refugees.

Next, we visit the restored bread oven, which like the toilet, was also a public domain at one time, where women from the village would come to bake their bread each morning. We end the tour inside the house drinking a shot of Jacques' 50% proof prune liqueur and eating juicy mirabelles preserved in alcohol. Before I leave, Jacques gives me his mother's recipe for preserved cherries, and Mr V and I have begun the process. So, here's what to do if you want to try it at home.

PRESERVED CHERRIES

Ingredients

1 kg (2 lb) cherries
Eau de vie (50% alcohol)
Several tbsp cane sugar syrup

Method

Fill a 1-litre preserve jar with cherries.

Top up with *eau de vie* or similar high percentage alcohol.

Stir well (I used a chopstick).

Seal and leave in a cool place out of direct sunlight for 1 month.

Open and remove 1 tbsp of the alcohol liquid.

Add 1 tbsp of cane sugar syrup.

Taste and continue to take out liquid and replace with syrup 1 tbsp at a time until the desired balance of sweetness and alcohol is achieved.

Reseal and store for at least 1 month. Sealed, the cherries will stay good for about 10 years. They are delicious poured over vanilla or coconut ice cream or mixed with natural Greek yogurt.

MOULIN 'FEU' ROUGE

*T*he hour of *la Fête de la Saint-Jean* has arrived; Cinderella has finally put away her vacuum cleaner, mop bucket and insect spray, and is ready to don her ballgown and glass slippers. Actually, silky harem pants and espadrilles as I don't want my feet and legs to be savaged by any creepy-crawlies or low-flying ants. We take the car up through the village and into the hills behind, which give rise to spectacular views over the low plains of the Tuscanesque countryside. The evening haze softens the landscape into a patchwork of dusty yellow and muted green. The road is little more than a dirt track; clouds of arid earth hang in the air, stirred up from the car in front. We come to an abrupt halt as people are parking along the roadside, so we join the end of the line and continue on foot.

A simple plank of wood, roughly fashioned into the shape of an arrow, with the words *Feu de la Saint-Jean* (Saint-John's bonfire) daubed on it in green paint, points the way. Two marquees are set out with long trestle tables and the sort of benches that we used to wobble along, balancing bean bags on our heads, at school.

In an open-sided tent opposite, trays are being prepared for the meal; everything that I hate on a plate, as it turns out. There's a fatty terrine wrapped in equally fatty ham, a cold, insipid potato salad and thick pieces of steak that have spent ten seconds each side on the grill to give them the deceptive appearance of being cooked. I'm not of the 'well-done' brigade and like my meat pink, even a little bloody in the middle, but this is truly Shylock's pound of flesh. I pretty much like all cheese except for goat's cheese, that I can't stand the smell of, and Camembert, which doesn't like me. The latter is the only choice. All topped off with a sludgy, grey chocolate mousse. I eat the bread and drink the wine, both of which are excellent.

To be fair they are just a group of locals catering en masse, and the French were all happily wolfing it down, Mr V happily wolfing down mine as well.

Two strapping firemen are doubling as disc jockeys next to a makeshift dance floor made from uneven chipboard balancing on low scaffolding, that springs up and down when you walk on it, so it will be like a bouncy castle once people start dancing. French singer Christophe Maé is hogging the turntable, which is fine by me, his raspy vocals oozing out '*J'ai Laissé*' the French equivalent of The Beatles 'Let it Be'. At the edge of the dance floor are barricades cordoning off the bonfire and a life-size wooden model of a windmill, with an equally life-size scarecrow propped up in the doorway. Surely they're not going to set fire to such a masterpiece?

'*C'est dommage de le brûler*' a woman says to me, and I have to agree, it *is* a shame to burn it, but then that's the whole point of the occasion.

The music pauses, and there's an announcement that the fire will be lit in fifteen minutes. I cross the dance floor and install myself on an elevated bank on the far side, as being small I need a good vantage point to get some hopefully spectacular photos. People begin to crowd near to the barricade. I see Mr V head and shoulders above the rest, somehow right at the front, camera at the ready. Years of fighting for a seat on the Paris Metro have obviously prepared us well for working a crowd.

Christophe Maé fades away, and an expectant silence fills the air. I hear the haunting strains of what I'm informed is a hurdy-gurdy, an instrument that features heavily in the local folk music of the Morvan region. It's like a sound coming from deep in the past to bind us to these ancient traditions. The hairs prickle on my neck, and I come out in goosebumps on my arms. Even the children have fallen silent. The atmosphere is charged with expectation, then, the silence is pierced by the first whoosh of a firework. The spell is broken, and a collective cheer goes up as the hurdy-gurdy man picks up the pace, and the lament becomes a jig which sets the stage hopping. I sincerely hope the scaffolding is bolted properly together.

The fireworks continue to explode in a mass of green, red and gold. Then the wooden sails of the windmill begin to spin around, slowly at first then faster and faster like a giant Catherine wheel with fireworks shooting out in all directions. Finally, they put a torch to the bonfire, and the flames light up the windmill from behind, illuminating the window and door, the figure in the doorway is transformed into an eerie silhouette, the effect of which is very dramatic. Then, the entire structure goes up in flames, and a rousing dance tune replaces the hurdy-gurdy. The crowd backs away from the barriers, as unlike in the UK where bonfire night is in November and you need warming up, here the temperature is already in the high twenties, so the added heat from the fire is intolerable.

The dance floor is put to the test and seems to be holding up. I'm caught up in the joy and celebration of the moment and let go to some 1980s post-punk, courtesy of Indochine's 'l'Aventurier'. This is my kind of music. I may have failed miserably at the folk dancing last week, but I can still do the pogo like a seventeen-year-old.

I've been asked for both my strawberry and mint salad and grated carrot recipes, so I'd better include them both now before I get carried away writing about the final fête: the 14th of July, Bastille Day.

STRAWBERRY SALAD WITH FRESH MINT

Ingredients

500 g (1 lb) punnet strawberries. (I favour Gariguette as they have a deep-red flesh and soft, dense texture. They are naturally sweet and have a wonderful intense aroma, but I'm not sure if these are available everywhere unless you grow your own.)
8-10 mint leaves, freshly picked, refreshed and finely chopped
1 dsp sugar (I use a small sachet of vanilla sugar)
1 tbsp fruit vinegar (I use Olivier & Co Vinaigre de Pommes in France, but Belberry Lime Vinegar, available in UK, is excellent. Just shop around and see what you can find then experiment, or make your own.)
1 tsp fresh lime juice
1 dsp rosé wine (slightly sparkling is great)

Method

Remove the stalks and finely slice strawberries lengthways. (Gariguettes are perfect as they have an elongated shape.)

Put a layer of strawberries into a pretty crystal or glass serving bowl.

Add a little mint.

Sprinkle very lightly with sugar then fruit vinegar.

Continue until all the strawberries and mint have been used.

Add lime juice and rosé wine.

Cover with cling film and chill in fridge for at least 30 minutes or until ready to serve.

I don't think this dish really needs any accompaniment; cream is certainly too heavy and will overpower the other flavours.

I sometimes serve a lime or, if I have time to make it, rosé sorbet on the side.

GRATED CARROT SALAD

Ingredients

1 tbsp light olive oil (I use Oliviers & Co Olive Oil with Mandarin)
1 dsp orange juice
1 dsp apple cider vinegar
4-5 medium carrots, grated (not too finely)
Handful of raisins
Handful of pine nuts, lightly toasted and cooled

Method

Mix olive oil, orange juice and apple cider vinegar in a large salad bowl.

Toss the carrots in the mixture.

Add raisins and pine nuts.

Cover and refrigerate for around 30 minutes to allow the carrots to soak up the dressing.

This will keep for two days in the fridge and is great to take on picnics or to serve with pizza as an alternative to traditional coleslaw.

GLOWWORMS IN THE GRASS

*I*t's the 12th of July. We've arrived for a weekend of celebration as the 14th is Bastille Day, the National Day of France. The day when in 1789 the Bastille Prison in Paris was stormed by an angry mob and all seven prisoners inside were freed. The unfortunate governor became the first victim of what unfolded as a bloody revolution in which the king and queen, along with thousands of lesser nobles, lost their heads. Ten years of terror followed, after which the Republic rose triumphant, symbolised by a bare-breasted Liberty leading the people, brandishing the *tricolour* (French flag), as in Delacroix's painting which hangs in the Louvre.

Bastille Day, is a national holiday, with military parades and firework displays all over the country. Everywhere, that is, except for our commune.

I was expecting a hog roast, dancing and fireworks only to be disappointed. I discover that our peculiar little community decided that as news of the revolution didn't reach this remote corner of the country until three or four days after the notorious events in far-flung Paris, they don't celebrate with the rest of the nation, but on the first Sunday after the 14th. (I've yet to discover what happens when the 14th falls on a Sunday. I must consult the oracle who is Jacques.)

This year Sunday happens to be the 15th. This is a blow to me as we must leave after lunch, but it also poses a double dilemma for the rest of the inhabitants of the commune. The 15th is World Cup Final day, and France is in the final for the first time since 2006 (the year that Mr V and I met). They haven't won since 1998, so a lot of hope and expectation hangs in the air along with the *tricolours* that are hanging from almost every house.

✳ ✳ ✳

I'm in the garden with Pussy Willow, listening to the crickets who are as incessant as the crows, but I prefer their chirruping to the constant cawing. The evening is otherwise silent except for a faint mewing coming from the direction of the dense bushes in the corner beneath the feather tree. Mewing! On closer inspection I see six shy eyes peering at me from the foliage, pale-sapphire buttons shining from three tiny grey and white faces. Flaubertine has had her kittens, and she's chosen our garden as their nursery. I realise that this is the reason she disappeared for a weekend, and why she's become so thin, with three hungry mouths to feed. I put Pussy Willow inside and return to the table with a glass of wine and my camera to do what I'm best at: drinking wine and waiting.

One by one the kittens emerge, timid at first, then when they see their mother approach me without fear, they begin to frolic in the cool, not quite night air, leaping vertically like fluffy springboks. I watch them rearing up on their hind legs and tumbling on the grass in mock battles, their tiny back paws lashing out at their siblings. Every now and then they return to their mother for a brief suckle, which I feel is more for comfort than nourishment. Flaubertine for her part is happy to abandon them to their play and come and sit on the terrace with me, glad, I sense, of a little adult company. The kitties are climbing the feather tree. Playing a furry game of snakes and ladders with them scrambling up, then sliding down, the branches.

Mr V comes out to water the tomatoes. He calls excitedly to me to come and look at the grass. It is spangled with tiny, green lights like emeralds sparkling in the moonlight. I feel, not for the first time, that I've stepped into a magical kingdom with jewel-encrusted grass. It's as if I'm standing on the Milky Way with stars at my feet. They are of course glowworms. This is the first time in my life that I've seen them, and I'm enthralled. I try to photograph them, but they just look like fluorescent splodges on a jet-black background, so I'm relying on my writing to show you what I saw. Who needs fireworks when nature puts on such a spectacular display?

WHO WEARS SHORT SHORTS?

J'm reading an account of another couple who bought a ruin in France, and I've realised that the lack of DIY disaster stories singles me out. You may be forgiven for thinking that not much happens here except for me scribbling in notebooks or standing for hours on end waiting for a butterfly to open its wings, and Mr V pottering in the garden or chin wagging with his entourage on the terrace.

As we're not going to a party tomorrow, we plan on taking out the old, decrepit window in the bathroom and replacing it with a shiny, new, double-glazed one. No more turning blue in the shower or sitting in the flight path of a gale-force wind while on the toilet for me.

Plans are also underway to build the store for the giant fuel tank, and Jacques and Fifi are bringing the builder, known by everyone as Marcel the maçon, around after seven this evening to price up the job. Marcel sounds more like a Parisian hairdresser than a builder, but 'the boys' assure me 'he's the best'. Note the time of the rendezvous coincides with apero time, so I've pre-empted a late dinner and bought a frozen pizza.

✳ ⁂ ✳

Fifi is the first to arrive, wearing a pair of shorts that are bordering on indecent, looking like a geriatric Bjorn Bjorg in a 1970s tennis tournament. Jacques is next in his usual long shorts, check shirt, baseball cap and boots. Marcel rolls up in an astonishingly clean white van, which has me thinking he isn't really a builder but as I suspected a hairdresser from Paris. But his appearance as he emerges from his pristine van puts all thoughts of 'pinky curls' and 'Marcel waves' totally out of my mind. He is larger than life, rippling muscles straining to be liberated from his tight, again sparkling white, T-shirt; his impressive height made more impressive by his hard hat and serious builder's boots. His presence seems to occupy every inch of the space that he is in, even in the garden. He has a deep, rich voice that sounds like calypso, and he would look more at home shaking cocktails in Montego Bay than shovelling cement.

There are a lot of *'ouais, ouais, ouais'* (yeah, yeah, yeah, pronounced way, way, way) coming from around the back of the house, and none of the 'Right Said Fred' carry-on that we had when 'the boys' were discussing how to move the paving stones. It seems for the first time that something is going to begin to happen as Marcel is giving Mr V explicit instructions of what materials to buy and says he'll be here with his cement mixer to begin work the last Monday of the month.

Marcel joins Mr V, Fifi, Jacques and me on the terrace for Pastis. Mr Mouton, not wanting to be done out of a potential apero, trundles down on his sit-and-ride lawnmower that he's now using as his main mode of transport, as getting in and out of his car after his hip replacement is still giving him jip. Marcel munches his way through an entire jar of cornichons and all our nuts and pretzels, but I discover that he's also a tiler, so I pour him another glass of Pastis.

We're all relaxed and winding down when Flaubertine lets out a howl the like of which I've never heard before. One of the kitties, who I've named Belle (I know, after all I've written about not getting attached to another cat...) has gone behind one of the paving slabs that Mr V and 'the boys' salvaged from the back. She (far too pretty to be a he) has somehow fallen down a small gap between the drain cover and the wall. The drain has water in it, albeit not a lot due to the prolonged dry spell, but enough to drown a small kitten.

I'm hysterical, and Marcel looks a bit scared at my extreme reaction. People around here drown kittens deliberately, so for one to drown accidently is seen as a bonus. Mr V and I rush for our work gloves and move the heavy paving stone. I can't bear to look as Mr V removes the drain cover, and there, shaking, fur sleeked down with mud, but alive, is Belle. Mr V scoops up the quivering, little body and gently carries her to Flaubertine, who, in a unique display of motherliness, licks her furiously until she's clean and fluffy once more.

HEAT AND DUST

The window is out. For something that's been threatening to fall out every time we opened it, it was reluctant to leave and required a hefty hammer to help it on its way. Not surprisingly a fair bit of wall went with it, so now Mr V is making a wooden frame the size of the new one, then will cement that in place and patch up the wall. As it's the 14th July there are impressive military parades on TV, so he's alternating between working in the bathroom and watching on the sofa with a trowel in his hand.

It's scorching outside. I'm smothered in suntan lotion, and smell like I'm on holiday, I once again, fantasise about a swimming pool. I'm grateful for the 40-centimetre-thick walls and narrow windows as Les Libellules is a cool haven to escape from the punishing heat. The garden is dry and the grass shrunk back to the barren, stony ground that greeted us last August. What plants remain are shrivelled, dusty and faded, except for the ruby-red roses who seem to adore the heat.

The *mare* is now one-third hard, dried-up-river-bed mud; the remaining two thirds have only about a tenth of the depth that they had in spring. My amorous frogs have hopped off. I can hear them faintly in the distance where they've obviously found a more convivial place to conduct their affairs. Once we've drained and cleaned the *mare* at the end of October, we're going to try to increase the number of pipes that supply it with rainwater from the gutters, and fit all the gutters with collection tanks to protect the *mare* and the wildlife it harbours. There are noticeably fewer dragonflies also, though I've spotted a solitary emperor today. The swallows, however, are back in force with their showy, aerial displays now that the crows have gone elsewhere, and last night I saw my first pipistrelle, so I still have plenty of allies keeping the mosquitoes in check.

Pussy Willow is too hot and lying under my chair. She won't let me out of her sight, I think, as she's never seen one before, she's a little wary of the kitties. The kitties for their part are exploring and expanding their world and are beginning to venture beyond the garden where they seem to be drawn to another drain. Flaubertine is doing nothing to keep them in check. She isn't going to win any mother of the year awards and gets quite snappy with them if they want to play when she's taking a nap. I suppose she's doing her best, given her egotistical nature and the fact that she's little more than a kitten herself.

I've now named all three: Belle, Napoleon and Penelope (pronounced the French way— Pen-ee-lope, as in hope). She is the least boisterous and the least pretty of the three. Napoleon is constantly goading his siblings and mother into a play fight, jumping on their heads and tails; hence he receives more reprimands than the others. Belle loves to play with the long-stemmed valerian, jumping up and hitting their flowers with her paws and trying to catch them as they spring back. This reminds me of a garden game I used to play as a child, hitting a ball on a piece of elastic that was attached to a post.

Drains seem to be the big attraction, and not just with the kitties. Pussy Willow found herself lodged inside a large pipe that feeds water from the gutters of the outbuildings into the *mare*, which is usually submerged. Mr V once more found himself in the role of cat rescuer, easing her out like a breech-birth baby. We've now covered the opening with a wide-gauge grille. There's always something we haven't foreseen. Living here certainly keeps us on our toes.

What I've learnt today: Cats have a dangerous fascination with drains.

THE GIFT OF RAIN

*I*t's the last weekend in July, and we've arrived to the most joyous sound: thunder. A storm is gathering, and this time I hope it's for real and isn't going to pass us by or pour down for ten minutes only to have the sun come out immediately after. After over two months of no rain, give or take a few spits and spots, the ground is parched. The Virginia creeper that enclosed us in our private world last year has withered on the fence before it had the chance to grow, and now its sparse, crisp, brown leaves shrivel in the sun. The *mare* is stone dry, like a basin of cracked clay filled with straw. It can no longer support life, which saddens me as there's nowhere for my beloved dragonflies to feed, and I've only seen a handful compared to the multitudes last summer. The butterflies also have gone, along with almost all of the flowers. The geraniums are hanging on forlornly by the skin of their teeth; only the mint and thyme have flourished.

The grass is, in places, scorched to a black/brown cinder as if someone has taken a blowtorch to it, but not everywhere. In a repetition of what happened on the last evenings that we were here, when the garden magically lit up with green glowworms, I catch sight of something sparkling on the ground like a discarded diamond ring, reflecting a myriad of colours as oil in water. I stoop to see what it is.

It's a tiny flower which looks very much like a clover, but its petals are flattened into what resembles a yoga chakra, sparkling brilliantly in the sun.

I call Mr V, who is discussing the state of the *mare* with Jacques, to come and see. Jacques has the answer immediately. I haven't discovered magic crystal flowers at the bottom of my garden, though that would be nice, wouldn't it? The reality is far less romantic, but the result equally beautiful. It seems that what is causing the phenomenon is snail mucous. Yes, you did hear that right. Snails have crawled across the flowers, leaving their silvery trail in their wake, transforming the garden once more into a jewelled carpet.

The air is heavy, and the sky thick with cloud. It's frustrating that the storm will arrive tonight of all nights as there is going to be a blood moon, and now it won't be visible, but this is a small price to pay for the gift of rain.

Alas the rain wasn't worth missing the moon for. It barely dampened the crust of the top soil. It did however refresh our first crop of tomatoes. Large, bulbous beauties weighing down their stems, four of which are deep red and ready for picking, the others in varying shades of yellow and green. Their scent after the rain is *piquant*. I use a French word, as I can't find an English alternative to describe the fresh, peppery aroma that's prickling my nose. Pussy Willow smells it too and backs away from them. Their taste, when I bite into one, is sweet and succulent, their skins much thinner than any variety I've ever grown in a greenhouse.

The kitties no longer seem to be living in the garden, but Flaubertine has brought them over to play in the feather tree; they are up and down it like monkeys on a pole. They're tamer than before, which isn't entirely a good thing as Poly (Napoleon has been downgraded) has just been cornered by a snarling Pussy Willow in the garden room. Mr V has reprimanded Willow, but I think it's important that she establishes that this is her territory, as they won't be kitties forever. Flaubertine isn't keen on them muscling in and coming inside either. This I feel isn't due to a sudden surge of maternal protectiveness, rather she too knows that they won't be kitties forever and sees them as future rivals for food and affection.

The kitties are already ramming their heads into the bowl of food that I give Flaubertine three times a day, so I've now given them a bowl with two compartments, but Penny (aka Penelope) isn't getting her fair share. I wait until the others are preoccupied and sneak her a little plate of her own. Poly and Belle have both licked my hand to take a little food I had on my fingers, and all three have been playing with a flower that I dangled above their heads. I run my fingers like a spider along the wall where Belle has just finished eating, and she approaches tentatively then plucks up the courage to tap my hand and run away. I'm amazed that she does this so gently with her claws retracted, as I expected to receive my first kitty scratches.

※　→　※

It is dark, and I'm alone on the terrace with Pussy Willow. All is quiet except for the crickets and the faint snorting/sniffling of pigs. Pigs? There are no pigs near here. Pussy Willow has heard it too, and her ears shoot up as if she's about to take off. The bushes in front of the terrace are being disturbed by something larger than a cricket. A dark shape, too big and slow to be a mouse or a water rat, trundles out of the bushes and shuffles across the path, heading towards the *mare*. I think it must be one of the moles that are redesigning the landscape of what will be the vegetable patch, so I get up to investigate. Snuffling and grunting like a piglet beneath the hedge is an enormous hedgehog. I understand now why they have such a strange name, as it really does sound like a hog. Then five others appear in assorted sizes ranging from what I consider standard hedgehog size (but I'm no expert) to tiny ones that you could fit into the palm of your hand, though I wouldn't recommend it. When they sense me approaching they hiss like angry snakes and roll into tight, spiky sea anemones.

I warn Pussy Willow off any further exploration, but her pussycat curiosity gets the better of her, and she rushes indoors with a sting in her paw and a startled expression on her face. I remain outside writing, and I'm joined by a very friendly cricket who leaps onto my page and makes no attempt to leave, even when I gently stroke his wings. At the very beginning of this journal, I set out to chart the changes in myself. I never for an instant imagined I would be caressing a cricket like it was the most natural thing in the world, but life is full of surprises. Thirteen years ago I never imagined I'd be married to a Frenchman, living in Paris and with a beautiful old house in the Burgundy countryside, but c'est la vie.

What I've learnt today: I've just read in my French gardening magazine that hedgehogs can swim, and they're impressive walkers, often covering up to four kilometres in a single night. Given the speed these lot are moving around the garden I find this hard to believe.

THE GARDEN AT MIDNIGHT

*O*ur first year at Les Libellules is almost at an end. We've come full circle. Boxes of courgettes and tomatoes have once again begun to arrive, brought by people who last year were neighbours, and have now become friends.

It's almost midnight, and I'm in the garden on the last evening in July. I'm reading by the light of an oil lamp. Although we have the outdoor lamp, this gives a softer light that matches better my reflective mood. I have a glass of wine and a book, *The Cottingley Secret* —a magical story for a magical place. I'm going to leave you here with the sounds of crickets, cicadas and hedgehogs; the glow of the lamp, and the twinkling of the stars. The perfect place to say *au revoir*, or maybe *à bientôt*—see you soon.

EXTRACT FROM BOOK TWO:
BLACKBERRIES AND BUTTERFLIES

SECOND SUMMER

I left you in the garden at midnight, so this is where you can find me at 8:30 in the morning on the 1st of August; the start of our second year at Les Libellules. For me this is merely the turn of a page on the calendar, but for you it may have been a year or more since we last met.

The air is still refreshingly cool and the ground laden with dew. I'm pruning the masses of rosebushes that surround the walled terrace before the sun rises any higher. This time last year I didn't know a thing about gardening, and if truth be known, my knowledge is still pretty primitive, but I'm learning from the garden itself. What was once a complete mystery is slowly revealing its secrets to me like rose petals opening one by one.

During the day, the air reverberates with the sounds of heat: the humming, buzzing and droning of insects, the dominant species being wasps, hornets and undernourished houseflies. The music of the night is hedgehogs shuffling in the bushes, crickets chirping in the grass,

313

and owls, who I love to hear almost as much as I did the frogs, whoo-whooing in the trees.

The hot, dry summer has stopped many plants from flourishing, notably the Virginia creeper that last year covered practically everything with its rampant foliage. The bonus of this stunted growth in the garden is that I can now see more easily where parts of plants have died and where weeds are choking others. I've discovered blackberry bushes that were completely obscured from view, though their berries are small and shrivelled where they are in direct sunlight. Every morning I take a walk before breakfast, inspecting all the plants for any signs of change; this way I'm getting to know them. I cut back anything that looks dead or diseased to a point where it is green and healthy. I deadhead roses to encourage a second batch of flowers and prune the wildflowers that have gone to seed to avoid them running riot next spring.

Beneath a clump of these wildflowers that I've just cut down to ground level I've uncovered a group of snails sheltering from the heat. I can't leave them exposed, so I place them beneath a nearby rosebush. Again, I marvel at the fact that I spend a good half an hour rehousing snails; how much I've changed. Not only am I enjoying working in the garden, I'm finding it quite addictive and get a great sense of satisfaction when I see things beginning to take shape.

I realise now that what I considered full summer before I moved here is in fact the beginning of autumn. Granted, everything has come early this year due to the lack of rain, but I think the signs, although more subtle, were there last year, but I failed to see them.

This year is exceptional though, and the temperature here is constantly hovering around 36 degrees. In Spain and Greece temperatures have reached 48; it's officially the hottest summer on record in Europe. The poplars and horse chestnut trees are already turning yellow, gold and brown, and their leaves are fluttering to the ground like tiny symbols, lining the lane with a deep, crisp frieze. The conkers are larger than golf balls and also look ready to fall. When I compare recent photos with those that I took at the same time last year, the difference in the colours of the landscape is remarkable. Last year's photos were lush, and I wrote about the myriad shades of green; this year all has a dusty, Tuscan appearance, with different shades of muted yellow. The cattle in the fields are having to eat hay that generally would be saved for winter, so I don't know what farmers will feed them with when winter arrives.

The heavy rain at the beginning of the year produced a bumper crop of apples, but the tree is also losing its leaves a good eight weeks earlier than last year, and our grapes that were sweet and succulent a year ago are clinging to the vine like shrivelled raisins. We are planning a trip to Dijon next week, so it will be interesting to see how the vineyards are faring. Hopefully these aren't the signs of things to come. Only time will tell.

What I've learnt today: A group of snails is called an escargatoire. I ask myself what other gems of knowledge I will uncover along with the snails as our second year at Les Libellules unfolds...

GLOSSARY—CONVERSION FROM METRIC TO US CUPS

Flour: 125 g = 1 cup
Sugar: 200 g = 1 cup
Butter: 225 g =1cup (1 stick = 138 g)
Liquid: 250 ml = 1 cup

MESSAGE FROM THE AUTHOR

If you enjoyed reading this book as much as I enjoyed writing it, I would love to read your review on Amazon.

To see photos of my life at Les Libellules, you can follow me on Instagram at:
www.instagram.com/la.belle.vie.in.burgundy

Or come and join me and other memoir authors and readers in the We Love Memoirs Facebook group, the friendliest group on Facebook. www.facebook.com/groups/welovememoirs

ACKNOWLEDGEMENTS

An author writes a story, but it takes a team to make a book. I couldn't have achieved this without the advice and support of the terrific team at Ant Press, particularly Jacky Donovan, my editor, whose patience and professionalism have guided me with encouragement and humour, and Victoria Twead for her attention to detail.

Thanks also to Beth Haslam for letting me bend her ear and keeping me sane, Karen Conrad for her invaluable honest opinions and advice, and the talented Mel Beswick who took my original photos and captured the essence of my story in her enchanting illustrations.

Also thanks to my beta readers: Judith Benson, Pat Ellis, Julie Haigh, Rebecca Hislop, Susan Jackson and Sue Raymond for your encouraging feedback, and Pam Hughes, who avidly read chapter by chapter as I wrote and spurred me on with her eagerness to read more.

I am eternally grateful for the constant love and inspiration from my daughters, Kate and Natasia. Thank you, Kate, for meticulously proofreading the manuscript.

Lastly, thanks to my husband, the enigmatic Mr V, for making my dreams come true and his unerring belief in me, renovating Les Libellules almost single-handedly while I was scribbling away.

Lindy

Printed in Great Britain
by Amazon

77009639R00196